THE WIFE'S VICTORY;

AND OTHER NOUVELLETTES.

BY

MRS. EMMA D. E. N. SOUTHWORTH.

BROTHERTON HALL.

"Mrs. Southworth is the finest authoress in the country. Her style is forcible and bold. There is an exciting interest throughout all her compositions, which renders them the most popular novels in the English language."—*New York Mirror.*
"Mrs. Southworth is the best American writer of the age."—*Phila. Merchant.*
"She has no superior; and there is a chasteness and purity in all that she writes which commends her to the approbation of every thoughtful mind."—*Baltimore Republican.*
"She is a woman of brilliant genius."—*Olive Branch.*
"She is the best fiction writer in the country."—*Buffalo Express.*
"She is the most original and talented of living female writers."—*Public Ledger.*

Philadelphia:
T. B PETERSON AND BROTHERS,
806 CHESTNUT STREET.

MRS. E. D. E. N. SOUTHWORTH'S COMPLETE WORKS,

EACH WORK IS COMPLETE IN ONE LARGE DUODECIMO VOLUME.

SELF-RAISED; or, FROM THE DEPTHS. Sequel to Ishmael.
ISHMAEL; or, IN THE DEPTHS. (Being Self-Made.)
THE MOTHER-IN-LAW; or, MARRIED IN HASTE.
THE PHANTOM WEDDING; or, Fall of House of Hint.
THE MISSING BRIDE; or, MIRIAM, THE AVENGER.
A BEAUTIFUL FIEND; or, THROUGH THE FIRE.
VICTOR'S TRIUMPH. A Sequel to "A Beautiful Fiend."
THE FATAL MARRIAGE; or, Orville Deville.
FAIR PLAY; or, BRITOMARTE, the MAN HATER.
HOW HE WON HER. A Sequel to "Fair Play."
THE CHANGED BRIDES; or, Winning Her Way.
THE BRIDE'S FATE. Sequel to "The Changed Brides."
CRUEL AS THE GRAVE; or, Hallow-Eve Mystery.
TRIED FOR HER LIFE. A Sequel to "Cruel as the Grave."
THE CHRISTMAS GUEST; or, The Crime and the Curse
THE LADY OF THE ISLE; or, The Island Princess.
THE LOST HEIR OF LINLITHGOW; or, The Brothers.
A NOBLE LORD. Sequel to "The Lost Heir of Linlithgow."
THE FAMILY DOOM; or, the SIN OF A COUNTESS
THE MAIDEN WIDOW. Sequel to "The Family Doom."
THE GIPSY'S PROPHECY; or, The Bride of an Evening.
THE FORTUNE SEEKER; or, Astrea, the Bridal Day.
THE THREE BEAUTIES; or, Shannondale.
ALLWORTH ABBEY; or, Eudora.
FALLEN PRIDE; or, THE MOUNTAIN GIRL'S LOVE.
INDIA; or, THE PEARL OF PEARL RIVER.
VIVIA; or, THE SECRET OF POWER.
THE WIDOW'S SON; or, Left Alone.
THE DISCARDED DAUGHTER; or, The Children of the Isle
BRIDE OF LLEWELLYN. Sequel to "The Widow's Son."
THE BRIDAL EVE; or, Rose Elmer.
THE PRINCE OF DARKNESS; or, Hickory Hall.

THE DESERTED WIFE.	*HAUNTED HOMESTEAD.*
THE LOST HEIRESS.	*THE SPECTRE LOVER.*
THE WIFE'S VICTORY.	*THE FATAL SECRET.*
THE CURSE OF CLIFTON.	*THE TWO SISTERS.*
THE ARTIST'S LOVE.	*LOVE'S LABOR WON.*
MYSTERY OF DARK HOLLOW.	*RETRIBUTION.*

Above Books are Bound in Morocco Cloth. Price $1.50 Each.

Printing Statement:

Due to the very old age and scarcity of this book,
many of the pages may be hard to read due to the
blurring of the original text, possible missing pages,
missing text, dark backgrounds and other issues
beyond our control.

Because this is such an important and rare work, we
believe it is best to reproduce this book regardless of
its original condition.

Thank you for your understanding.

TO

MISS CHARLOTTE LECOMPTE NEVITTE,

OF MISSISSIPPI,

This Volume is affectionately inscribed,

BY HER SISTER,

THE AUTHOR.

CONTENTS.

PREFACE.

THE author does not know how, better to introduce this book to her friends than by telling them its short history.

The nouvellettes that form the collection were written—each to illustrate that distinct principle of Christian ethics or social philosophy, indicated by the text of Scripture selected as its motto.

That they were the very first productions of the author's pen—composed in the midst of sickness, privation, toil, and great sorrow—is her apology for their numerous imperfections. That they were, nevertheless, warmly welcomed, and extensively copied by the literary and Christian journals, and that their publication in book form has been called for, is her excuse for now collecting and presenting them in this manner

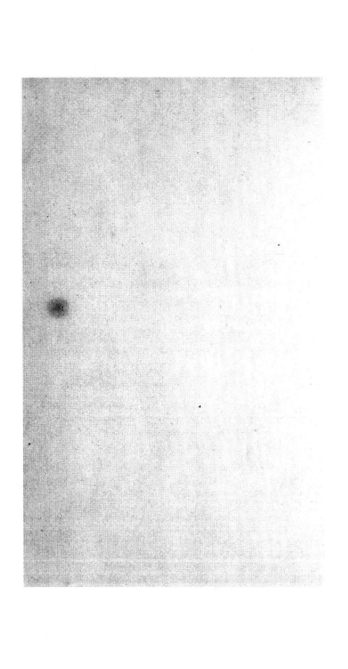

THE WIFE'S VICTORY.

———

The husband is head of the wife, even as Christ is head of the Church; Therefore, as the Church is subject to Christ, so let the wives be to their own husbands in everything.—EPHESIANS, v. 23, 24.

Such duty as the subject owes the prince,
Even such a woman oweth to her husband.—SHAKSPEARE.

What thou bid'st
Unargued I obey; so God ordains.
God is thy law; thou mine.—MILTON.

"I WOULD not have him, though he owned all the mines of Golconda," said bright Kate Gleason to her sister, Mrs. Lindal

"And why not, pray?" said gentle Mary Lindal.

"Oh! because he has got such a horrible temper."

"How do you know that?"

"By a great many signs; by the shape of his head and the colour of his hair, the glance of his eye, the curl of his nose, and the set of his mouth——"

"Oh! stop, stop, stop; of whom are you speaking? That incomparable man, in philanthropy a Howard, in wisdom a Newton, in patriotism a Washington, in——"

"Temper a Bluebeard."

"Kate! I will not hear another word of this. You are speaking of—of—" and Mary Lindal blushed

(31)

"Out with it! of Grenville Dormer Leslie, your future husband. But I give you fair warning, Mary, that though you may feel a vocation to become Mrs. Bluebeard, I am not particularly inspired to play 'Anne! sister Anne!' and run the risk of catching my death of cold by standing on a windy tower, to 'see if anybody is coming,' when he is about to slay you for your disobedience."

"But perhaps I shall not *be* disobedient," said Mary.

"Perhaps you shall not *be* disobedient," repeated Kate, with a withering sneer. "Well, for my part, when *I* am married, if ever my husband ventures to lay a command on *me*, I shall make a point of breaking it, at whatever cost of convenience, by way of asserting my independence."

"Not if you love, Kate."

"Either way, either way. Now, I like Lem Dunn very well; and if neither of us change our minds, we may be married when he returns from sea; but fancy Lem Dunn playing husband *a la Grand Turque*, and daring to say, 'you shall' and 'you shall not!' really, if I were in a good humour I should laugh in his face, and if in a bad one, I should be apt to box his ears."

"I must believe you are jesting, Catherine."

"Then I will be as serious as His Eminence Archbishop Leslie himself, and say that I really cannot see why we women should be called upon to 'honour and obey' so implicitly, unless we could be first convinced of their superior excellence by whom such honour and obedience are claimed."

"We are not. We *should* be first convinced of men's superiority, before we give them that 'right Divine' to control our actions and destinies, which by all Christian and human law is the just prerogative of a husband, whether or not he be mentally or morally superior to his wife."

"Pooh! nonsense! fiddlestick! with your Divine prerogative and the rest of it. If a woman marries a fool, I suppose she is bound to obey him!"

"When a woman marries a man whom she feels she cannot respect, she places herself in a false position, from which nothing can extricate her; and, however repugnant, however galling they may become, the same duties of submission and obedience are incumbent upon her, in all cases where they do not clash with the laws of God. A woman, in such a case, is an object of deep commiseration, although, having brought the evil upon herself, by a desecration of all her most holy instincts, she suffers but a just and most fitting expiation of her fault. I could not love, and would not give myself away to a man on whose wisdom I could not rely as on God's, to whose will I could not submit as to God's."

"Idolater! Would you set up an earthly God, and fall down and worship him?"

"'Wives, submit yourselves to your husbands *as to the Lord!'* There is Scripture for the idolatry, if you choose to call it so."

"Pshaw! If you were not talking foolishly, you would be talking wickedly. 'Satan can quote Scripture for his purpose.'"

"So he can. I am now quite convinced of that fact. But do not let us trifle with such holy and beautiful mysteries, dear Kate. There is another text of Scripture to the same purpose——"

"Oh, yes! There are hundreds; pray don't recite them."

"Just this one, Kate, I love it so much. 'The head of the woman is man; the head of the man is Christ; and the head of Christ is God.' Is it not a lovely chain, a beautiful climax, from weakness to Omnipotence; like Jacob's ladder from earth to heaven?"

"Sweet Providence! You have put my brains in a complete whirl, with heaven and earth, and chains and ladders, and heads and husbands; but out of the chaos one fact and feeling stands very distinctly. If Lem Dunn expects any such subordination from me, he will find himself very much mistaken; but he is not so presuming, poor Lem Dunn "

"I think *you* will find yourself mistaken in your estimate of his character and expectations."

"Well, perhaps so; in that case, I shall only have a little more trouble in breaking him in. But suppose now, only for argument, that you are deceived in Leslie; suppose his temper to be violent?"

"I will take care not to arouse it."

"His will unbending?"

"I shall not waste my strength nor risk my peace by seeking to bend it."

"His nature selfish?"

"Methinks, as I love and esteem him more highly than myself, I should only unite with him in his self-worship."

"His heart and mind unprincipled and depraved?"

"Impossible! impossible!" exclaimed Mary indignantly. "I will not for a single instant suppose such a thing, even for argument's sake. I have seen my error in permitting you to go on so long. Leslie has none of the bad qualities you have named. He is every way worthy of the highest esteem."

"And if he were not so?"

"If I were his wife, my duties would not be less incumbent upon me—would not be less scrupulously performed. But I shall not find myself in the degrading position of a wife who cannot reverence her husband, in giving myself to Leslie. I obey a Divine instinct that will not mislead me; in loving him, I shall offer the best worship, and in obeying him the most acceptable service to the Deity."

Mary and Catherine Gleason had lost their parents during their infancy, and had become the charge of their grandfather old Captain Gleason, a retired merchant. At the time Captain Gleason received his granddaughters into his house, he was mourning the loss of his younger son, who was supposed to have perished at sea, on his passage home from Europe. The snip in which he was to have taken passage had never been heard of since her setting sail from Liverpool, and was now believed to have been wrecked. Years flew by, and no clue was obtained to the fate of the lost ship or the lost son.

Mary Gleason, at the age of sixteen, had, in obedience to her grandfather, given her hand to Mr. Lindal, a wealthy merchant, some twenty years her senior. In the second year of her marriage, she became the mother of a lovely little girl. Soon after the birth of the little Sylvia, the failure and death of Mr. Lindal left Mary again dependent on the bounty of her grandfather, who received her and her child with the deepest sympathy and affection. Little Sylvia soon became the especial pet and plaything of the whole household.

Although Mary Lindal had faithfully discharged her duties as a wife, she had never loved her husband, except as a friend. Her whole affections centered upon her child, the little Sylvia. She was her constant companion, in doors and out doors, in parlour, chamber, and street, by day; and at night she slept encircled in her arms, pressed to her bosom. At the age of four years, Sylvia had been attacked with a violent and contagious fever. No words can describe the anguish of the mother, as she watched, day after day, and night after night, for weeks, beside the bed of the little sufferer; no pen can portray the joy when, at last, her darling was pronounced out of danger.

Mrs. Lindal was very beautiful, graceful, and accomplished, and a co-heiress with her sister Catherine; consequently, she was much followed and flattered. Notwithstanding her numerous admirers, and some very eligible offers, the seventh year of her widowhood had passed away, and she was still unmarried. In the mean time, Catherine Gleason had grown up to womanhood, more radiantly beautiful than her sister had ever been.

At length, in the twenty-fifth year of her age, Mrs. Lindal became acquainted with Mr. Leslie, the subject of the conversation with which this sketch opens. Mr. Leslie was a man of great personal attractions, pure morals, and distinguished talents. Mary Lindal ever listened to his brilliant conversation with delighted attention. Convinced by his clear-sighted views and able exposition of truth, she had insensibly acquired a habit of shaping her opinions by his own. There was one circumstance about their acquaintance that peculiarly attracted Mary. It was this: He *never* flattered her, never by any chance paid her a compliment, excepting this—the most, the only acceptable one, of constantly seeking her society.

I think it was that agreeable giber, Rochefoucault, who somewhere asserted that any woman may be safely flattered on any subject, from the profundity of her understanding to the exquisite taste of her fan. Without venturing to differ from such authority, I will simply assert that Mary Lindal was an exception to this rule.

*   *   *   *   *   *   *   *

At the end of a twelvemonth's acquaintance, Grenville Dormer Leslie and Mary Lindal were married, and took possession of a handsome house, in a fashionable quarter of the city.

An event occurred soon after their marriage, that greatly pained the affectionate heart of Mary. This was the death of her grandfather. The old gentleman had made a will, leaving his property equally divided between the sisters, Mary and Catherine. This property, however, as is frequently the case, was not half so large as had been reported, and his granddaughters inherited only about twenty thousand dollars apiece. A few moments before his death, while holding little Sylvia's hand within his own, Captain Gleason turned his dim eyes on Leslie, and said, "I have been thinking of this poor child, Leslie; if time were allowed me, I would alter my will, giving her mother's share of the property to her at her mother's death, or perhaps at her own marriage. You are wealthy,

Leslie, and your children, if you shall have any, will be handsomely provided for, while poor Sylvia——"

"Shall fare as one of my own," said Leslie.

"I believe you, and I thank you; now call Mary."

Leslie summoned his wife.

"Mary," said the dying man, as she came up to the bedside,
'I leave you a certain sum; I wish you and Leslie to consider
it as intrusted to your care for the future use of Sylvia. *You
will, of course, have the use of it for—for many years to
come.*" The old man spoke with difficulty. Turning his fast-
failing eyes once more on Mr. and Mrs. Leslie, he added, "I
have been so strangely thoughtless of this poor child's future—
but now promise to do as I ask you." Mary promised, through
her tears, while Leslie assured him that his wishes should
be scrupulously fulfilled.

The old man soon after breathed his last.

*   *   *   *   *   *   *   *

Six months after the death of Captain Gleason, Mrs. Leslie
and Catherine Gleason, who was an inmate of her house, were
sitting together in the parlour, engaged in needlework, and
talking of the expected return of Lieutenant Lemuel Dunn,
the affianced husband of Catherine, whose marriage was to take
place upon the promotion of the lieutenant to a captaincy.
There was a ring at the hall door, and a few minutes after—

"Mr. Gleason" was announced.

Both ladies rose to receive him, looking strangely at each
other, and at him.

"I suppose it is impossible, ladies, that you should remember or recognise a relative who left his native country while
you were yet in the nursery. I am Henry Willis Gleason, at
your service."

Mrs. Leslie and Miss Gleason stood speechless with surprise
and incredulity for an instant, but, quickly recovering their
self-possession, greeted their new-found relative with the warm-
est affection.

"But my father! girls, my dear old father. Where is he?
How is he?" The ladies wept. At last, Catherine found
words to say—

"It is six months since grandfather went to Heaven."

"Oh! that he had lived to see this day!" exclaimed Mary.
"Oh! that he could have lived to be blessed in your return."

"He believed me dead?" questioned Gleason.

"Yes," said Mary, "for the last ten years he has believed
you dead."

The reason for his protracted absence and apparent death
was now demanded and explained. It was a long story, in
substance the following: Ten years before, he had left his native shores, to make a voyage to Europe and a tour of the Con-
tinent. After having travelled over the greater part of Europe,
he visited the city of St. Petersburg and the court of Russia,
where, after a residence of some months, he was so unfortunate
as to give offence in some unknown manner to the Emperor,
for which he was banished to Siberia for a term of ten years;
and these ten years had actually been passed among the everlasting snows of Asiatic Russia. Upon his return to St. Petersburg, after receiving his discharge, he met with some travelling countrymen of his own, who furnished him with money
and everything requisite for his comfortable return home.
Gleason had but just concluded his narrative, when Leslie entered, who, on being introduced to him, expressed the most
sincere satisfaction at his unexpected return.

*   *   *   *   *   *   *   *   *   *

"Mary," said Mr. Leslie, entering his wife's room, on the
morning succeeding that of Gleason's arrival, "Mary, I wish
to hold a few moments' counsel with you."

Mrs. Leslie, who, with a flushed check and kindling eye,
was gazing upon an exquisite picture upon the easel before her,
while the brush was half raised in her hand to give another
touch to the piece, did not immediately hear the entrance of

remark of her husband, and she started with surprise and pain, as an impatient voice exclaimed at her side—

"I wish, madam, you would not consume so much time over that paltry daubing, nor become so engrossed in it as to be utterly unconscious of all that is going on around you."

Mary instantly laid down her brush (and it was years before she again resumed it), and turned with a gentle and cheerful smile to listen to what her husband had to say.

" At the time that Captain Gleason made his will, he supposed his son to be deceased, did he not ?"

" Yes; from the loss of the ship, and as Uncle Henry did not return or write."

" And, if he had known that his son was living, he would, of course, have left him the bulk of his property ?"

" Doubtless."

" Then you must see, as I do, that the property should and must be restored to him, as the rightful heir."

" The whole of it ?"

" Of course, the whole of it."

" Catherine will not agree to it."

" Catherine may do as she pleases with that which she may choose to consider is *justly* as well as legally her own, but the portion left to us must be given to the proper inheritor."

" The portion left to *Sylvia*, you mean," amended the mother, gently.

" I mean nothing of the kind," said Leslie, with cold gravity.

" Surely you remember your promise," said Mary.

" Surely, madam, I remember the promise given to a dying father, who little thought when he exacted it that he had a living son, or that the promise ever would be urged as an excuse for keeping that son out of his just inheritance. I am pained to see, madam, that your feelings as a mother somewhat obscure your sense of justice. I shall be glad to obtain your

2

cheerful co-operation in this matter, but if that is impossible I must act without it."

Mary, who saw that she had been wrong, and that a cloud had gathered upon the brow of her irritable lord, hastened to dissipate it by saying, "Yes, my motherly love *has* made me wish to be unjust; forgive me, and do whatever seems to you to be right; my dear husband, I will subscribe to all."

"Thank you, dear Mary; and now I will confess to you that the giving up of that money will be as great a sacrifice on *my* part as it is on *yours* in behalf of your daughter; for just at this time my business is greatly embarrassed, and the use of twenty thousand dollars for a year or so would be of incalculable benefit to me. But the sacrifice must be made, notwithstanding."

"Yes, it must be made. You are right, as you always are." But the child's interest was sacrificed, not so much to the mother's sense of justice as to her wifely duty—to her husband's will.

"Mary Leslie!" said Catherine, bursting into her sister's bedroom, with a heated and angry brow, "I hope you have not really consented to sign away all that property you had in trust for little Sylvia?"

"Yes," said Mary, quietly.

"And why? why? why have you made your child a beggar?"

"My husband thought it right to give up the property, and I obey his wishes."

"Spaniel!" exclaimed Catherine, with a withering sneer, and flung out of the room.

The necessary arrangements were soon made, and Gleason put in possession of one-half the wealth of his deceased father. Mary Leslie saw that her child's only chance of independence was cut off for ever; but she was a loyal Christian and a loving wife, and she reposed trustingly under the shadow of the good-ness of God, and in the righteousness of the husband to whom he had given her. And even though it did sometimes painfully cross her mind, that Leslie might have been a little more gentle with her, in a controversy in which her maternal feelings were so deeply involved, she considered that his somewhat overbearing temper was the sole defect in an otherwise excellent character, and she prayed for patience and strength to "overcome evil with good." She remembered with pride and pleasure the purity and strength of principle that had forced him to alienate a sum which, however finally disposed of, would just now have so materially assisted him in his business. With Kate, however, she had much ado to keep her temper; and she looked forward, with secret joy, to the time when "Lem Dunn's" promotion should deliver her from the trial. Kate often indulged in a recreation which she herself denominated "speaking her mind," and which was anything but an amusement to Mrs. Leslie; so that Mary could not always refrain from repaying her in kind; for, in her love for Kate, there was not, of course, that feminine instinct of submission that characterized her love for her husband. With Mary, love was religion; and her love to God and to her husband always acted upon and augmented each other. Mary Leslie could not, therefore, be unhappy; on the contrary, her daily sacrifice of obedience would have been a source of the greatest heart happiness, but that her husband, from real or seeming insensibility, never noticed the offering, by commending the votary.

But the greatest trial and the greatest triumph of the wife were now at hand.

Twelve months succeeding the events recorded above, Mrs. Leslie sat in her parlour. It was eight o'clock in the evening, the snow was falling fast without, within everything wore an air of the greatest possible comfort. A coal fire was glowing in the grate, a snow-white cloth was laid for tea. Mrs. Leslie reclined upon a lounging chair, near the fire; her face was somewhat paler and thinner than when we noticed her last, but scarcely less attractive. Her large, tender eyes wore an expression of holy and meditative love that was very beautiful. Her work (an embroidered slip) had fallen from her hands upon the carpet. Sylvia sat on a low stool at her feet, dressing a doll. Catherine reclined upon a distant sofa, absorbed in a novel (her constant occupation, when not visiting, dressing or disputing).

"Who are you making this for, mamma?" inquired Sylvia, taking up the little dress.

"*For whom.* You should try to speak correctly, darling," said her mother, coaxingly.

"Well, then, *for whom,* mamma, are you working this little frock?" persisted Sylvia.

"First find out what rule of grammar you have just now transgressed, and then perhaps I may tell you, darling."

"Why can't you tell the child? For my part I don't see the use of mystifying children," exclaimed Kate, throwing aside her book, and coming to the fire.

The front door was now heard to open, and in another instant Mr. Leslie entered.

Going up to Mary, with more tenderness than we have ever yet seen him display, he took her hand, and pressing a kiss upon her brow, said—

"How are you, this evening, sweet wife? Nay, sit still I will ring for tea, or Sylvia, do *you* do so. Why, Sylvia, an affectionate daughter should be ever on the watch to save her mother trouble."

Sylvia sprang to obey. Tea was soon brought in, and they gathered around the table.

"I bring you good tidings, Catherine. Lieutenant Dunn has received his promotion."

"Then I congratulate the lieutenants. There is one fool the less among their number," said Catherine, piqued, perhaps, that "Lem Dunn" had not hastened to her with the news himself.

"Capt. Dunn is now on duty, but will pay his respects to you to-morrow," said Leslie, divining her cause of dissatisfaction.

After the tea service was removed, the conversation became rather constrained. Catherine took up her everlasting novel, Mary resumed her seat and her needlework. Sylvia, bent on following up the hint of her step-father, began to arrange her mother's work-box, while Leslie walked up and down the floor, after the manner of a man who *has done*, or is *about* to do, something disagreeable. At last he took a seat, drew a letter from his pocket, examined the superscription, turned it over, glanced at Catherine, who had closed the book, and was now looking at him with quiet impudence, and finally replaced the letter in his pocket. He evidently had something to say, but was withheld by the presence of Catherine. I am really mortified to be obliged to record such a weakness on the part of the stately Mr. Leslie, but truth must come, and Mr. Leslie really stood in a little awe of Catherine. He had no sort of influence over her. She would do and say just exactly what she pleased, however disagreeable it might be, and he could not prevent her; nor could he decently turn her out of the house, nor would he descend to quarrel with her. Consequently, Mr. Leslie was ever on his guard to avoid any chance of controversy with Miss Gleason.

Fortunately, Mary, with her usual tact, saw the impatience of Leslie to unburden his mind, and, making an excuse to Catherine, retired early to her own room. Leslie followed her almost immediately.

Catherine's beautiful lips were disfigured by a mocking smile, as her glance followed Leslie from the room.

"Come, Sylvia, honey, let us go up stairs to bed The Bashaw is meditating some new atrocity. I know it by his looks. He is afraid to let *me* know it, though."

"Ma'am?" said Sylvia, raising her large eyes to the face of her aunt.

"Yes; and I should not wonder if it was against *you* again, too. Perhaps he wants to black your face, and crisp your hair, and sell you for a negro."

"Who—no—of whom are you speaking, Aunt Catherine?"

"Of His Infallibility the Grand Seignior, your step-father."

"Then, please do not speak of him in that way, Aunt Catherine, and call him bad names."

"Why not, miss?"

"Because mamma would not like it."

"Oh! your mamma is as great a ——. But what are you staring me in the face in that manner for? Don't you know it is very rude? Come along up stairs, child."

And they left the room.

*　*　*　*　*　*　*　*　*

"Something has disturbed you, Leslie," said Mary, after waiting for a few moments in vain for Leslie to open the conversation. "May I inquire, without indiscretion, what it is?"

"Certainly, Mary. I have not now, nor have I ever had, any concealments from you. I have never, from a false sentiment of tenderness, withheld from you any cause I might have for anxiety. I have several vexing cases just now. In one of them, you have an especial, perhaps you may think, an exclusive interest."

Leslie then drew the letter from his pocket, and added—

"This letter is from Madame D'Arblay, of New Orleans, now in this city, at the Astor House."

"From whom?"

"Madame D'Arblay, the mother of the late Mr. Lindal, and the grandmother of your daughter, Sylvia."

"Oh! yes; I recollect now having heard that the mother of Mr. Lindal married the second time a Frenchman by the name of D'Arblay, and removed to New Orleans; but that was many years ago."

"Yes. And now she writes that she has been left, by the

recent death of Mr. D'Arblay, entirely alone, the sole mistress of a large fortune, without a relative on earth, except her grandchild, our daughter, Sylvia."

"Well?" questioned Mary, pale with a presentiment of what was coming.

"Madame D'Arblay makes us the very handsome proposal to make Sylvia her heiress, on condition that we allow her to return with her grandmother to New Orleans, and reside permanently beneath her roof."

"But I cannot part with Sylvia," said Mrs. Leslie.

"Do not decide hastily, Mary; you must consider in this matter your child's interests, not your own feelings," said Leslie, tenderly but gravely.

"I cannot! I cannot part with her. Indeed, indeed, I cannot," cried Mary, trembling.

"But this is childish, Mary."

"It would break Sylvia's heart to leave me."

"Not at all. By no means. Grief is very short-lived with children of her age."

"Yes! yes!" exclaimed Mary, passionately, "and affection, too! and impressions, too! She will soon forget her mother. She will only be consoled for her separation from, by ceasing to love, her mother!"

"You have not a mother's *disinterestedness*, Mary, or you would be willing to make any sacrifice of your own feelings to secure for your child the immense advantages offered by her grandmother."

"You did not seem to consider wealth such an immense advantage twelve months ago," said Mary, bitterly.

"Mrs. Leslie forgets herself, and forgets what is due to me," said Leslie, rising and walking towards the door, adding, as he was about to leave the room, "I will leave you, Mary, by reflection and solitude, to recover your lost recollection."

Mary sprang to his side, and, seizing his hand, exclaimed, as she burst into tears—

"Forgive me! forgive me! It is the first time; it shall be the last. But my heart is *so* wrung, *so* tortured; you do not know—you could not understand, unless you were a parent. But tell me, then, how you have decided; for that you *have* decided I know, and that your decision is immovable I know; therefore, tell me at once; it will save us a world of useless argument, controversy, and vexation. How have you decided?"

"That Sylvia shall return with her grandmother," said Leslie, gently but firmly.

Mary let fall the hand of her husband, and, growing very faint, sunk back on her chair.

"These are the reasons that have influenced my decision," said Leslie, resuming his seat by her side: "We have deprived Sylvia, justly and righteously, it is true, but we *have* deprived her, of the reversion of a sum that would have made her independent. At the period of that transaction, I believed that I should be able to secure for Sylvia every advantage which that money would have given, and, finally, to have given her a portion of equal amount. I will now admit, that the temporary possession of that sum led me into a speculation which failed by the sudden withdrawal of it. I have never recovered that failure, and I am now on the very brink of insolvency. Nothing but the strictest economy and the most careful financial diplomacy will save me. I have therefore great doubts of ever being able to carry out my plans for Sylvia; consequently, it becomes my duty, my painful duty, to determine that our daughter be given up to her grandmother."

"I did intend to say no more," murmured Mary, in a quivering voice, "yet——"

"Well?"

"Madame D'Arblay, is she a proper person, at her advanced age, to bring up a girl?"

"Read her letter," said Leslie, handing it. "You will find no infirmity there; and for the rest, you have doubtless

heard enough of her piety and intelligence to feel secure that
the moral and intellectual welfare of your daughter will be
safe, while her vast wealth will insure her all the more worldly
advantages of which she is now deprived."

"But is it not very sickly at New Orleans?"

"You have not yet read Madame D'Arblay's letter through,
or you would see that she spends her summers at her villa on
the Gulf, which, she says, is remarkably healthy in its loca-
tion."

"When shall we have an interview with Madame D'Arblay?"

"I was thinking to-morrow, about twelve o'clock, you had
better make her a call."

"And do you know—do you know how long she will stay
in the city? I mean, how long shall I yet have dear Sylvia
with me?" And the mother burst into tears.

"I do not know, of course, as I have not yet seen Madame
D'Arblay. But we will talk no more at present, Mary; you
must compose yourself. I will leave you for that purpose for
a few moments. On my return, let me find you quiet."
And Leslie descended the stairs.

Mary threw herself on her knees, and prayed long and
earnestly, then arose calmly, and retired to rest.

"See here, Mr. Leslie," exclaimed Kate Gleason, as she
entered the breakfast parlour the next morning, "What have
you been saying to Mary? She is up in her chamber in tears
and Sylvia is sobbing by her side. I can't get anything out
of her, but I know you are at the bottom of it. Now, what
is it all about?"

"I have no explanations to make you, Miss Gleason," replied Leslie, taking his hat, and leaving the room to evade a
quarrel.

"I'll make Lem Dunn call you out for that, sir!" cried
Kate, as he went out.

Kate looked the very idea of a beautiful scold, as she stood
there, her bosom heaving, her cheeks glowing, eyes sparkling.

lips curling and quivering, and the tangled masses of jet-black ringlets falling in tear-sprinkled disorder about her face and neck.

"Captain Dunn!" announced a servant, throwing open the door, and Captain Dunn entered.

"Ah! I'm glad you've come! I'm *very* glad you've come. You're come in *excellent* times. Go after that man! Go after him! He's—he's"——Kate was out of breath.

"What man, dear Kate? What is the matter?" inquired Captain Dunn, in surprise.

"That Leslie!"

"Leslie! Why, what has he done?"

"He has abused his wife, and insulted me; that is, he has made her weep, and treated me with contempt."

"Tell me all about it, Kate—tell me all about it; and if he has been wanting in proper respect to my little betrothed—I'll—I'll annihilate him," said Captain Dunn, laughing; for he had known Leslie too long and too well to imagine that there could be any real cause of complaint. Unfortunately, Catherine could tell him but little about it, and that little was not very much to her credit.

"He's a terrible fellow, Kate," laughed Captain Dunn, as she concluded her account, "a very terrible fellow, indeed. Upon second thought, I should rather not fight him. He would shoot at me—he might hit me—in which case, I might be mortally wounded, and the service would lose"——

"A coward! an arrant coward! a poltroon, who will one day bring disgrace upon the flag, if he is not hung before that day comes!" exclaimed Kate, as she flounced out of the room, in a great passion, passing Leslie, who was about to re-enter.

Captain Dunn was laughing heartily.

"You laugh now, my dear Dunn," said Leslie, smiling, "but will you laugh a year hence?"

"Yes! oh, yes! that is, I hope to do so."

"Have you no misgivings concerning your future peace?"
asked Leslie, seriously.

"For my *peace?* I don't know; for my *happiness*, not one.
Kate's temper amuses me beyond measure."

"Yet, I heard some ugly names called, as I came in."

"Yes! yes! Oh! I've no doubt Kate will have given me
twenty beatings before this time next year."

"You will weary of it."

"Well, when the blows grow unpleasant, I have only to
catch the little shrew in my arms, and hold her very tight,
until she becomes quiet and good," said Dunn, laughing.

"Ah! and then—do you know what she will do?"

"No. What?"

"Try to frighten you to death, by going into a hysteric fit,
or worse—falling into a swoon."

"Ha! ha! ha! Is that Mrs. Leslie's method!"

"No! Bless dear Mary! Don't jest with her name, Dunn."

"I'll be hanged if I don't, just as much as I please. What!
Haven't you been jesting with Kate's? 'It's a bad rule that
won't work both ways.'"

Mrs. Leslie entered at this moment, equipped for a drive,
and Leslie excused himself, and attended his wife to her carriage.

Mrs. Leslie drove to the Astor House, and was shown into
the private parlour of Madame D'Arblay. Madame d'Arblay
was at this time in her sixty-fifth year. Her tall, graceful,
and majestic figure and stately carriage would have rather re-
pulsed the gentle Mary, had not her face been so sweetly pre-
possessing. Her countenance wore an expression of holy calm,
of heavenly goodness, very beautiful to look upon. Mary was
at once reassured by her countenance and demeanor. They
conversed a long time, the subject being a recapitulation of
and enlargement upon the plan proposed in her letter. She
made many inquiries, however, about Sylvia, and expressed a
great desire to see her. At Mary's earnest entreaty, Madame

d'Arblay consented to leave her apartments at Astor's, and take up her abode for the period of her visit at Mrs. Leslie's.

The next hour, Madame D'Arblay was comfortably ensconced in Mary's large easy chair, by the parlour fireside. Sylvia who had fallen in love with her at first sight, was nestling at her feet. Mrs. Leslie sat with her back to the light, to shade as much as possible her tear-stained face. Kate was sulking in her own room, and " would not be entreated" to come down and be sociable. There was so much in the pious and intelligent conversation of Madame D'Arblay to set the fears of Mary at rest on the subject of the welfare of her child, that when the dinner hour arrived, and Leslie, Captain Dunn, "Uncle Gleason," and Kate, had joined them, Mary had actually become cheerful.

The month of Madame D'Arblay's visit drew to a close. Mary, after a severe struggle with herself, and much prayer, had grown composed, and tranquilly prepared Sylvia for her journey. Leslie was unusually attentive and tender towards her; Madame D'Arblay mentally condemned the seeming indifference of Mrs. Leslie to the departure of her child, but she quietly ascribed it to the influence of her second marriage. Kate, with whom Sylvia was a great pet, had out-scolded her prototype and namesake, and was now not upon speaking terms with any of the family, and had banished " Lem Dunn" into perpetual exile—until recalled. Sylvia, child-like, was delighted with her new dresses, new books, and new toys, and the prospect of a long journey and new scenes, and had no room in her heart for painful sensations.

*   *   *   *   *   *   *   *   *

The last evening of Madame D'Arblay's stay arrived.

"Oh ! Aunt Catherine ! Aunt Catherine !" exclaimed Sylvia, bursting into Kate's sanctum, " to-morrow we're going. I'm so glad. Mamma has just laid out my new blue pelisse and velvet hood, and my nice chinchilla muff, all ready for to-morrow at six "

"Yes, miss!" said Kate, severely, "you seem very much delighted to leave your poor, pale, sick mother, who is grieving herself to death at the idea of parting with *you*, who do not care for her."

A thunderbolt fell upon the child's gladness, and destroyed it all at once. She burst into tears.

"Oh! Aunt Catherine, *is* mamma sorry? Doesn't she want me to go? I thought she wanted me to go. I forgot I had to leave mamma; I only thought of the fun. I will run now and tell mamma that I won't go; no, *that* I won't." And Sylvia made for the door.

"Mr. Leslie will compel you, miss," said Catherine. The name that was a spell to all the household arrested the flying steps of Sylvia for an instant, then saying—

"I will speak with mamma," she ran out.

* * * * * * * * *

Mary Leslie, who had nerved her gentle heart to go through the impending trial, was in her own room, still engaged in laying out such articles of dress as would be needed by Sylvia for the next morning. Mrs. Leslie's tranquillity was entirely overthrown by the impetuosity of Sylvia, who now burst into her presence, exclaiming, as she threw herself into her mother's arms, "Mamma! mamma! I can't leave you; I don't want to go any longer, now I know you do not wish it. I *love you*, mamma, better than fine clothes, and grandmothers, and journeys; and so, mamma, I *cannot* go, and I *will not* go."

Mrs. Leslie was quite unprepared for this outburst; Sylvia had been so tractable and so cheerful up to this time. She repressed her tears with difficulty, and replied, with an effort—

"*Cannot* and *will not*, Sylvia! why, what manner of words are those, and where learnt you them? You will, of course, do as your parents wish you."

"Aunt Catherine says that if they send me away from you, mamma, it will break your heart, for that you don't want me to go"

"Catherine is mistaken; listen to *me*, my darling Sylvia
I *do* want you to go; and though I may be very sorry to part
with my dear little girl, yet I shall soon get over the grief,
because I know it will be for her benefit. And now," added
the mother, with an effort at cheerfulness, "let us talk about
the fine ride in the cars you will have, and look at the pretty
things I have put in your nice little travelling basket."

"No, no, mamma! No, no, mamma! I don't care for the
ride in the cars, and don't want the travelling basket. I love
you! I want to *stay* with you," exclaimed Sylvia, bursting
into tears. "Oh, mamma, *don't* let me go! don't, *please*
don't. I did not think about parting from you before, and I
know I can't! *indeed* I can't!"

There was grief, there was agony, on the mother's countenance, as she crushed back the rising emotions of her heart,
and choked back her tears. She struggled to speak, but
could not do so with the calmness requisite to soothe her child.
She could only press her closer to her bosom in silence.
Neither spoke for some moments; at length—

"Mamma, do you know the night you were married, when
I slept alone in my little bed? Well, mamma, I cried all
night; I could not sleep, because I was away from you. I
knew that I should see you soon in the morning, but still I
wept; yes, and I wept many nights, too, although you did not
know it, and although you were not further off than the next
room, and I could see you every day. Now, so many days
must come and go, and so many nights pass, and—and—no
mother to—to—" and Sylvia, breaking from her mother's
hold, threw herself, in a fit of hysterical sobbing, upon the
carpet.

"Oh! God, have mercy on me, and give me strength," exclaimed the mother, in strong emotion, as she went toward
Sylvia, stood for an instant to gain self-control, then took her
child in her arms, and, reseating herself, pressed her to her
bosom, smoothed back the shining ringlets of her hair, and

imprinted kiss after kiss upon her fair brow, as she talked
gently and soothingly to her, and, rocking her to and fro,
finally succeeded in subduing her emotion. Exhaustion, after
so much excitement, soon put Sylvia to sleep; yet still the
mother rocked and sung, even as she had done when the little
girl in her arms was a babe—thinking, perhaps, that it might
be the last time she should ever hold her thus. At last she
arose, and, laying Sylvia on the bed, sunk upon her knees,
and poured out her whole soul in prayer to her Creator—first,
that this trial might yet be spared her, "if possible ;" then,
that if it were not, she might have strength and resignation to
bear it cheerfully. How earnestly, passionately, fervently,
she prayed! And when emotion became so great that words
failed, the upturned, straining eye, the clasped hands, and
heaving sighs, bore up the silent prayer; and at last, when
the weary head sunk upon the folded hands, and thought no
longer took the form of words, the heart, the untiring heart,
still bore up the prayer, in one intense, absorbing yearning
after mercy. Unknown to Mary, there was one spectator to
this scene. Leslie was standing within the door. He had
entered, silently and unobserved, at the moment that Mary
had lain the sleeping Sylvia on the bed, and sunk down by
her side in prayer. The first words of the prayer arrested his
intention of coming forward or speaking. He had seen, and
had heard—and never before had the pure and holy heart of
his wife been so unveiled as in that prayer; and while it yet
ascended, in all its Christian beauty and eloquence, he quietly
withdrew from the room, murmuring, "The angel, the angel,
how blind I have been! I must save her this trial; there is
but one way, for I must save her without sacrificing Sylvia."
He passed to the door of Madame D'Arblay's room, and
knocked. The pleasant voice of the old lady bade him enter;
he did so, and merely saying—"Will you come with me to
Mary's chamber, Madame? She seems much distressed at
the thought of parting with her daughter to-morrow." He

accompanied her thither, and withdrew. Mary's voice was
still heard, but in low, interrupted, and quivering tones. Her
tears were falling like rain, and her hands wringing and
twisting over each other; but the *words* of Mary's prayer,
breathed, as she deemed, to the ear of God alone, unfolded
the most secret thoughts and feelings of Mary's profoundly
pious heart.

"Oh, God!" exclaimed Madame D'Arblay, "I did not
dream of this. Mary, Mary, my dear child, arise. Your
prayer is heard and answered."

Mary started in surprise to her feet, and was caught to the
bosom of the old lady. "Mary, my dear daughter," said she,
"your child shall not be taken from you, neither shall she
lose anything by remaining with you. Oh! Mary, how little
did I know you! How unjustly have I judged you, when I
condemned the indifference with which you seemed to regard
a separation from your child. But, Mary, how could you
suppose that I would have taken my granddaughter away,
had I not thought that you were willing, nay, anxious, for
her removal to my abode? Forgive me, Mary, but I fancied
that your second marriage had unnaturally alienated your
heart from your child; I was therefore the more anxious to
receive her. But, Mary, why did you not make me acquainted
with your feelings on the subject?"

Mary, who during this long speech had had time to collect
herself, replied,—"Mr. Leslie, Madame, had determined that
Sylvia should go with you. He thought that her residence
beneath your roof would be a solace to you, and an advantage
to herself. I could not seek to thwart his purpose, by making
an appeal to your sympathies, you know, Madame."

"You were right, my daughter, perfectly right. You have
won my deepest love, my highest esteem, Mary Leslie! You
have won it by your self-control. You have established yourself firmly and permanently in your husband's respect and
affection; more than that, you have proved and known the

power of faith and prayer. Never forget it, my child! Now, Mary, I must tell you my improvised plan. Though I will not take Sylvia away, neither will I leave her. I am glad this has happened. I like you so much, Mary, I want to live with you. I have been so solitary; and, after all, a little girl is not company enough for an old woman. So, Mary, if you will give me an easy chair by your fireside, and a place at your table, I will even spend the close of my life with you. I will do everything for Sylvia here, that I would have done at home; and when I die, I will leave her all I possess; and if she marries before that event, I will dower her handsomely. What say you, Mary?"

"Oh, Madame!" exclaimed Mary, seizing her aged hands, and pressing them to her bosom and her lips, "if I have been silent, it has been from deep emotion. Words will not convey my thanks. It will take a lifetime to live my gratitude." At this moment the supper-bell rang, and its alarum awoke Sylvia from her deep sleep, who, when informed of the change in her grandmother's project, was delighted beyond measure; and, after bestowing many caresses on her grandmother and her mamma, ran to tell "Aunt Catherine" the good news. What effect the "good news" had upon Kate may be gathered from the following circumstance: Kate took pen and paper from her desk, and wrote a note. Meeting the errand-boy on the stairs as she descended to supper, she gave him the note, telling him to carry it to Captain Dunn, on board the store ship Endymion, promising to give him a half-dollar if he returned with an answer very quickly. Kate's note ran thus—

"CAPTAIN DUNN: Will you be so kind as to call at Harpers', and get 'Forest Days' for me. It is just out. Bring 't to me *this evening*. Yours, &c.

C. GLEASON.

"*Friday Evening*"—

for Kate, with all her impetuosity, exercised a precaution which

3

I would recommend to all young ladies, and would not commit herself, by writing love-letters or billets-doux; for she said, "I might change my mind, or he might change his; and then— there!" Captain Dunn answered the note in person, and took his seat with the happy family at the supper table. Kate's good-humour was entirely restored. She welcomed back her exile with affectionate frankness. Sylvia's bright eyes were glancing and flashing from one face to another, each counte- nance seeming to reflect its own gladness. Madame D'Arblay regarded the scene with a look of quiet self-complacency, that seemed to say, "I have made them all happy!" Mary's coun- tenance expressed quiet and grateful happiness. Leslie's eyes were occasionally fixed upon the face of his wife, with looks of ineffable and holy tenderness. Leslie never subjected her love to another trial. He was deeply moved by the gentle resigna- tion, the tender submission, with which she had yielded up the dearest object of her affections and her most cherished wishes, to be dealt with according to his good pleasure. That submission had given her a place in and an influence over his heart, that no beauty, grace, or accomplishments—no, nor in- tellectual nor moral excellence *without it*—could have secured.

A month from this time, a gay party was assembled at Mr Leslie's to honour the nuptials of Captain Lemuel Dunn, U. S. N., and Miss Catherine Gleason.

The married life of Kate Gleason, who entered upon her duties with views and feelings so opposite to those of Mary, which we have endeavoured to illustrate, will form the subject of another chapter.

THE MARRIED SHREW:

A SEQUEL TO

THE WIFE'S VICTORY.

Oh! when she's angry, she is keen and shrewd;
She was a vixen when she went to school;
And though she is but little, she is fierce.—SHAKSPEARE.

KATE DUNN entered the gay world of fashion first as a married woman, and decided was her success. Kate's life with her grandfather, and afterwards with the Leslies, had been very domestic, and, as she expressed it, very *triste;* she had gone but little into society. Now she was resolved to have compensation, since no greater obstacle than "Lem Dunn" intervened.

Formerly she was prevented from going to balls and parties by want of proper chaperonage; now her state as a married woman rendered her independent of that. Kate was now resolved to combine all the pleasures of the maiden with the privileges of the matron; consequently, in fashionable society, where her resplendent beauty and sparkling wit drew many admirers, she was always surrounded by a circle of young men, who were very well pleased to carry on a flirtation with a pretty woman, without the fear of a suit for breach of promise before their eyes. There was one man, however, who was constantly banished from her circle, and that man was her husband.

(57)

"There are hundreds of intelligent men and pretty women here to-night; go and amuse yourself; I shall not be jealous;" was the *kind* address of Kate to her husband, as he lingered by her side.

Captain Dunn walked off, and *took an extra glass of wine.*

"Can you not comprehend that, as we are married now, your attendance can be dispensed with; nay, more—that it is *outré*, absurd, to remember that you have a wife in the room?" was the petulant speech with which she received him when he returned after an hour's absence.

"Decidedly, Captain Dunn, you are making yourself and me appear very ridiculous by this Darby and Joan exhibition of conjugal affection. Positively we shall be cited as a 'pattern couple;' and I know nothing that could be more scandalous or alarming," said Mrs. Dunn to the Captain, as they entered the carriage to return from a large party one evening.

"I don't understand *your* opinions and feelings upon this subject, Catherine, but *I* don't like this fashionable manner of waiting upon any other woman but my own wife, and seeing her attended by any other man except her own husband."

"Oh, indeed, Captain Dunn, you make me quite sick, talking so foolishly about 'own wives' and 'own husbands;' the fact of our marriage is incontrovertible; there is no need to emphasize it so often."

"Kate's head is a little turned by her French romances, but I feel sure her principles are really sound. I will not make myself 'ridiculous,' as she would call it, by fretting and fuming, nor will I annoy her by useless remonstrance now. Give her folly its full way; it will soon wear itself out, or"——Captain Dunn paused in his mental soliloquy, *poured out and swallowed a glass of wine.*

* * * * * * * * *

A few weeks from this time, Captain Dunn was ordered to sea, and made preparations, with a reluctant heart, to leave his bride. A few days previous to joining his ship, he seated

himself by the side of Catherine, and, passing his hands caress-
ingly through her ringlets, said:

"You will be very lonesome in this large house when I am
gone, dear wife."

"Oh! no, I shan't; I shall fill it with company; don't
tumble my curls, please, Captain."   Captain Dunn folded his
hands, and a sigh escaped him.

"I have been thinking, Kate, of inviting my mother to
take up her residence here during my absence."

"To watch your wife, I presume, sir, and to look after your
interests, of which you think me incapable."

"Kate! how can you——; I had no thought beyond giving you pleasure, by providing you with a desirable companion."

"Then, Captain, I beg you will not trouble your mother to
leave her own home, to come to me; it might greatly inconvenience her."

"Not at all.   Since my sister's marriage and departure for
Europe, my mother is quite alone, and very sad; she would
be more cheerful here with you."

"I do not think so—old people are seldom contented out
of their own homes."

"Yes, but with my mother it is different; she has an
excellent heart and most serene temper, and is prepared to
love you as a daughter. *Besides*, her support has hitherto
been my most agreeable duty; but I cannot now sustain the
expense of two establishments; so you see the propriety, nay,
the necessity, that obliges me to offer her a home here."

"I thought it was all on *my* account," sneered Kate;
"however, you may be sure she would be much better off in
a good boarding-house."

"Madam!" exclaimed Captain Dunn, in angry astonishment; but, quickly controlling himself, and looking seriously
in his wife's face, he inquired, "Am I to understand, Catho-

rine, that you are opposed to my mother's presence in this
house?"

Notwithstanding all her assurance, Kate's eyes fell, and her
cheeks glowed under the gaze that was fixed upon her. She
was determined to have her own way, however, though it
would require some hardihood to tell the frank and noble-
hearted man before her that she *was* opposed to having his
mother under their roof. She replied with assumed firmness,
but without raising her eyes—

"I have a great respect for your mother, Captain, and will
show her every attention in my power; but I *do* dislike the
idea of a mother-in-law in the same house with me; I cannot
conquer my repugnance to your proposed measure; and you
know, Captain, with such feelings on my part, your mother
and myself could not get along comfortably together."

"I certainly shall not insult her with the proposition," said
Captain Dunn haughtily, as he left the room.

"I have conquered again," thought Kate. "Now, I really
did feel like giving up once, but it won't do—such feelings
must not be encouraged—they would soon enslave me. Men
are naturally inclined to be tyrannical, particularly over their
wives. Oh! yes, decidedly, I was right in the affair of the
mother-in-law. Good heavens! I could not brook a prying,
fault-finding mother-in-law in the house." Could Kate have
followed with her eye her husband's steps that evening, through
the various scenes of dissipation to which he resorted to drown
thought, she might have exclaimed, with the conqueror of old,
"Another such victory would ruin me."

*   *   *   *   *   *   *   *   *   *

Captain Dunn was absent three years, during which time
Kate led a very gay life, despite the affectionate and repeated
remonstrances of Mrs. Leslie and Madame D'Arblay. She
thought several times of writing to or visiting Mrs. Dunn,
senior; but, unhappily, she did not know her address, being
ignorant what arrangement Captain Dunn had finally made

for her. The subject had never been mentioned between them
since the evening it was first broached. Kate's summers were
usually spent at some fashionable watering-place, and her
winters in a round of visiting and amusement.

The evening of Captain Dunn's expected return home, it
chanced that a brilliant ball was given by Madame la Baronne
V——, the lady of the French ambassador. "The beautiful
Mrs. Dunn" was among the most admired of the guests.

It was after having gone through a waltz with a distinguished
foreigner, that Kate sat down, when a note was placed in her
hand, that read as follows:

"DEAR CATHERINE: Come home; I am waiting for you;
I should hasten to you, but I may not intrude.
                                    "L. D."

"Tell Captain Dunn I will be home in an hour or two,"
said Catherine to the footman who brought the note.

"Very well, Thomas," said Captain Dunn, on receiving this
cool reply; "bring me the morning papers, and *a bottle of
port.*"

Notwithstanding the provoking coolness of her message,
when Catherine returned, a few hours after, the door was
opened by Captain Dunn, who received her in his arms, and
strained her to his bosom.

"Good Heavens! Captain," exclaimed Kate, releasing herself, "you take my breath away—and just see how you have
crushed my dress and dishevelled my hair. Pray, don't be
so energetic."

"You are looking in high health and beauty, my peerless
Catherine," said Captain Dunn, as he gazed upon her with
pride, not noticing her petulance.

"Do reserve your gallant speeches for other women, Captain,
and don't waste them upon your wife."

However deeply pained Captain Dunn might have been by
his wife's coolness and levity, nothing of mortification or dis-

pproval was apparent in his manner. Captain Dunn liked to leave all his bad weather at sea.

Some twelve months succeeding this event, Mrs. Dunn presented her husband with a son and heir. "And now," thought the happy father, "my wife will love her home for her child's sake." But Captain Lemuel Dunn "reckoned without his host"ess, as a very few days demonstrated.

"Where is the young sailor?" inquired he, as he took his seat by his wife's easy chair, a few days succeeding the birth of his son.

"Mrs. Tenly has got him."

"Mrs. Tenly—who is she?"

"A young woman whom I have engaged as a wet nurse."

"Now, is it possible, Kate, that you mean to let your child be nursed at the bosom of another woman?"

"Yes; it is both possible and positive—now, don't put on that disagreeable look—it is not usual for ladies of my station"——

"Your station—a rough sailor's wife"——

"Well, don't tease me! my delicate health forbids"——

"Your delicate health! Why, Kate, you have the finest constitution of any woman I know. You enjoy high—I had almost said rude—health."

"Well, then, if you must have it, I don't intend to spoil my figure by nursing a child. And I have no idea of going about the house in a slovenly wrapper, or ill-fitting corsage, for the sentimental nonsense of nursing my own baby."

"Ha! ha! ha! that's the most amusing reason of all—for you to give, Kate, who go about the house all the morning 'n a loose gown, with your hair in papers!"

"Captain Dunn, you're a bore."

"Well! this nurse—has she lost her own child?"

"No; she is raising it by hand."

"Then you are really cruel, as well as silly."

"Captain Dunn, please leave the room; this interview has fatigued me," said Kate, affecting languor.

If the reader will forgive the digression, I will describe a small, mean dwelling, not far from Captain Dunn's handsome house. In the basement story of a dilapidated old house—in a miserable room, with broken-down doors, and cracked and fly-stained window-glasses—on a poor straw bed, covered with a thin, faded counterpane, lay a shivering babe. A coloured girl, in tattered garments, was trying to coax a few embers to burn in the mildewed fireplace. At a cry from the awakened child, the girl gave over her hopeless efforts, and, taking the infant up, she sat down upon a low stool, and commenced rocking it backward and forward in her lap, to still its cries.

At this moment the door opened, and Mrs. Tenly, the fine ladies' nurse, entered, drew near her infant, and, while the tears coursed down her cheeks, looked upon it in silence. The little creature was now lying languidly across the girl's lap; its small limbs hung flaccidly, its tiny features were sharpened and attenuated, and its slumbers were interrupted by distressing moans.

"How has she been, Nelly?" she asked of the negro girl.

"Her has been cryin' a dreat deal, ma'am."

"Poor baby! poor little one! Oh, it is wicked, it is cruel, to give your nourishment to another child—your own nourishment, that nature has provided for your own poor little feeble self—to give it to another babe, and let you perish." The mother wept convulsively, as she took the babe from the little negro.

"Clare t' de Lord, I wouldn't do it, mam;" exclaimed the little girl, as she busied herself making the fire, and heating some water.

"Ah, Nelly, I've tried every other way at getting bread!"

Mrs. Tenly, after washing her little one, and dressed her in her night clothes, indulged herself by rocking her a few moments in her lap. "This will not do for me, though," said she; "that other chi'd will wake and cry, and Mrs. Dunn will be displeased." Pressing her child to her bosom once again, she laid her upon the bed, and prepared to go.

"Oh! Nelly, take *good* care of the baby, and I will bring you something pretty—will you, Nelly?"

" I alluz does take care of her, ma'am."

" And keep the panado warm in the corner, and give it to her when she wakes and cries in the night."

" Yes, ma'am."

Mrs. Tenly turned back to kiss the child again, and tucked her warmly up; then stopped the broken pane of the window, and left the house, her eyes streaming with tears.

This is no exaggerated picture. There are many such cases "I speak that I do *know.*" Mrs. Tenly had come over to this country in an emigrant ship, in company with her husband and some hundred others. They had suffered much from sickness and privation, and many of them were provided for as paupers. But Mrs. Tenly and her husband had found a home in this wretched cellar, where, within a week after their arrival, on the same day she thanked God for the birth of her first child and wept the loss of its father. Upon her recovery from her confinement, she tried, but in vain, to procure needle-work or washing. Her efforts to find a place at service were equally unsuccessful. At this time, the opportunity being presented, she put her child from her bosom, and went out as a nurse.

Mrs. Tenly could at least have gone for a while to the almshouse, which, though humiliating to the poorest and lowest, was yet better than the sacrificing of an infant's life, by cruelly and dishonestly depriving it of its natural rights.

There is but one circumstance that can exempt a woman from the duty of nursing her own children—and that is, ill health; and even then she has no right to engage a nurse, if, by so doing, she deprives another babe of its mother.

*   *   *   *   *   *   *   *   *   *

One morning, soon after Mrs. Dunn got about again, her nurse entered the room and said, weeping,—

"Will you have the goodness to take charge of your little boy, to-day?"

"Why? What is the matter?"

"My child is dying."

"Indeed! I am very sorry to hear it. Yes, certainly you must go; but what ails your child?"

"I do not know, madam; ever since I left her to come here, she has pined away."

"I am very sorry," said Kate; "I will call over and see her; or—no, I could do no good. I will give you a note to my sister, Mrs. Leslie; she will visit and assist you; it's all in her line. But get a physician, and tell him to send his account to me; and—stay, here is your month's wages."

Thanking Mrs. Dunn for her kindness, as she received the note and the money, Mrs. Tenly withdrew.

An hour after this, Mrs. Leslie stood by the bed of the sick child.

"Oh! Mrs. Leslie, is she dying?" sobbed the mother.

"Not dying, surely not dying, and not in any immediate danger, I think—I hope."

"Oh! Mrs. Leslie, ma'am, God bless you for saying that If my baby only lives, I shall never think anything else a trouble in the world. I'd slave for her all my life."

"We must get her into a sweet, clean, airy room, and then, with the doctor's prescription and *her mother's nursing*, she will recover."

"Oh! ma'am, if I only knew how to thank you; but she won't nurse, ma'am."

"You've tried her, then."

"When I first came home I did, but she couldn't; and then I gave her the powder, and she went to sleep."

"She is awake; try her now."

Mrs. Tenly took the child in her arms, and placed it to her breast.

The babe looked up into her mother's face with a sort of

sickly inquiring smile, then let her head sink upon her mother's bosom with a sigh of intense satisfaction.

"Poor little thing, she is happy now," said her mother smiling through her tears.

"Oh! she will soon get well," said Mrs. Leslie, cheerfully. "And now, Mrs. Tenly, as I too have a little family to look after at home, I must leave for the present, but I will send my daughter over this afternoon."

"I have a commission for you, daughter," said Mrs. Leslie to Sylvia, as she laid aside her walking-dress.

"And I have a commission for you, too, dear mamma; but what is yours?"

"You must get up all your little sister's last winter's clothes, and tie them into a bundle; then tell Martha to put on her bonnet and attend me in the pantry, bringing a large basket with her; finally, get on your pelisse and hood, to accompany her to see a sick child."

"Oh! yes, mamma, I understand;" and Sylvia flew to obey, but, dashing back in an instant, she said—

"Oh! I forgot, mamma, to tell you my commission, or, rather, uncle's. Uncle Harry has been here, and says, will you please find him a housekeeper; he wants one directly."

"Ah! I am very glad he does, Sylvia; I think we can find a very good housekeeper for uncle."

The basket of necessaries was packed and sent. The next day Mrs. Tenly and her sick child were removed into comfortable lodging; and a fortnight after, when the latter was recovered, she was put into the cars, and sent twenty miles into the country, to a farm owned and occupied by Mr. Harry Gleason.

*   *   *   *   *   *   *   *   *   *

A month succeeding these events, the Leslies and Madame D'Arblay were spending a day at Captain Dunn's. The party were assembled at dinner Suddenly the door was thrown open, and Uncle Harry Gleason stalked into the room, in a great heat, exclaiming—

"*Well*, Mrs. Leslie, my admirable niece! I always took you for a model of propriety. The veriest demirep could not have made a more glaring solecism in morals than you have done!"

The company all glanced in astonishment from Uncle Harry to Mary, who was looking aghast.

"Yes, ma'am," continued Uncle Harry, "a pretty mess you have made of it. I had a good opinion of you, Mary! I send to you, rather than to an intelligence office; I ask you to find me a proper housekeeper. And what do you do? Whom do you send?"

"I earnestly hope," said Mary, recovering her self-possession, "that Jane Tenly has in no particular discredited my recommendation. She was well thought of in her humble sphere. I always thought her a very good soul."

"And am I to have every good soul in the world thrust upon me? I *hate* good souls. No, ma'am! I didn't *want* a good soul, nor a good soul's *baby*, neither. I wanted a *housekeeper*—meaning a staid, serious, settled old body, who could tuck me up at night, and read me to sleep with Congressional speeches and the President's messages, and so on."

"Well, couldn't Jane do that, uncle?"

"Oh! of course *she* could, beau-*ty*-ful-ly," sneered the old man.

"Of what do you complain, then, sir, and how can we further serve or satisfy you?" inquired Leslie.

"Of what do I complain?" exclaimed Uncle Harry. "I complain of a blue-eyed woman, sir, and a baby, sir. I sent to Madame Propriety, there, for a housekeeper; and what does she send me, sir! A rosy-cheeked woman, and—and —a baby, sir! What will the neighbours say? A man of my age! a gentleman of my integrity, sir! A woman with bright brown hair and a baby, sir!———Well," said

the old man, suddenly dropping his voice, " there was but one
thing to be done, and that I *did*."

No one replied.

"*And that I did*."

Still all were silent.

" Why the devil don't some of you ask me *what* I did ?"
cried Uncle Harry, losing patience.

" Sent her away again ?" suggested Mary.

"*No*, ma'am, I didn't. I never sent a woman away again
in all my life, and never mean to. No, no; you know what
I did well enough, although you affect stupidity, because you
think it will be a mortification to me to tell it of myself. But
it ain't, though! not a bit. Guess I'm old enough to judge
for myself. Should like to know what right *any* body
has to find fault with what *I* do. Well! why *in the devil*
don't some of you ask me what I did ?"

" What did you do, sir ?" asked Mary, coaxingly.

" I married Jane Tenly and the baby—that's what I did."

" Oh ! uncle, no !" exclaimed Mary, in a tone of vexation
and distress.

Kate drew herself up, and regarded her uncle—scorn
writhing her lip, and anger flashing from her eyes.

Leslie, after an involuntary expression of surprise and displeasure, was silent.

Captain Dunn broke into a hearty and good-humoured
laugh, as he sprang from his seat, and seized and shook Uncle
Harry's hands, exclaiming—

" Well done ! that's right ! wish you joy with all my heart.
God bless you !"

" Ah ! Dunn, *you've* got some heart. You see, Dunn, the
old man *did* want some one to love. Here are my nieces, to
be sure; but I am only a fourth or fifth-rate person in their
affections; so, Dunn, you know, the old fellow wanted some
one to love, who would be always in his sight; and that poor,

meek, blue-eyed woman wanted a friend; and so you see, Dunn"——

"I see! I see! It was the best thing you ever did in your life. You have given a worthy young woman a comfortable home, a respectable position, and, above all, an excellent husband; and you have secured for yourself a handsome, good, and *grateful* wife. I shall be always happy to receive you both at my house."

"Captain Dunn has been indulging too freely in wine, sir, else he would have added—in the *basement* story, as visitors of her late friends, the housemaid and cook !"

"Catherine !" exclaimed Captain Dunn, sternly.

Uncle Harry Gleason bowed to the ground with great ceremony, and withdrew.

*   *   *   *   *   *   *   *   *

"I fear that Captain Dunn *does* indulge too freely in the use of wine," whispered Mary Leslie, when she found herself alone with Leslie that evening.

"I *know* he does," was the reply.

"What can be done ?" asked Mary, sadly.

"Very little, I fear. Something, however, we must attempt. I will speak to Dunn. I will be in his company more than hitherto. And—you must remonstrate with *Catherine*. I fear she does not make herself or her home agreeable to her husband."

"I *know* she does not," sighed Mary.

The entrance of Madame D'Arblay and Sylvia, attended by a servant with lights, arrested the conversation. The ladies gathered around their work-table with their sewing, and Leslie, opening a book, read aloud while they plied their needles. A far different scene was enacting at Captain Dunn's.

When the departure of their guests had left the Dunns alone—

"I am grieved and astonished, Catherine," said Captain

Dunn, "that you should have treated your uncle so disrespect-fully and cruelly."

"I am grieved, but *not astonished*, Captain Dunn, that you have so far forgotten what was due to yourself and me, as to have invited that woman here. A man whose faculties are always obscured by the fumes of wine cannot astonish me by *any* act of absurdity or wickedness."

"What do you mean by *that*, madam?"

"I mean, sir, that you are never sober, and therefore cannot be considered a responsible human being."

"Catherine!"

"Don't you understand me *yet?* You are more stupid than I supposed even. In common parlance, then, you are always *drunk*—and generally, by consequence, a *fool*."

"This is not to be endured!" exclaimed Captain Dunn, rising hastily, and pacing the floor with rapid strides; then pausing before his wife, he said severely—

"You presume, Catherine, upon your sex, and your feeble-ness. But have a care; where weakness and womanhood do not imply delicacy and gentleness, they lose their claim upon our forbearance."

"*Do you threaten me, sir?*" whispered Catherine, in a low, smooth, contemptuous tone of irony. "But of course, why need I be surprised? A man who can connive at the marriage of his cast-off mistress with an honoured relative, and then insult his wife by inviting the abandoned creature to his house, is capable of any act of meanness."

Exasperated to frenzy by the false and monstrous charges contained in this speech, delirious with anger, Captain Dunn raised his hand, and a blow rang sharply upon the cheek of Catherine; and seizing his hat, he rushed madly from the room and the house.

A few minutes after, Mrs. Dunn's maid found her in strong hysterics, and in that condition she was conveyed to bed.

*   *   *   *   *   *   *   *   *

"What in Heaven's name *is* all this dreadful business. Captain?" inquired Uncle Harry, as he entered a private parlour in the —— Hotel, occupied temporarily by Captain Dunn.

"I have disgraced myself—that is the amount of it," replied Captain Dunn, bitterly.

"Been drinking?"

"No, no; at least, not much."

"Been forging?"

"I have acted the part of a poltroon."

"*Not* received an insult or a blow, without knocking the dealer of it down—*not that?*"

"Worse, far worse than that; I have struck my wife."

"Hallelujah! glad on't—better late than never. Hope you gave her a good sound drubbing while you were at it. She's wanted it a long time, the huzzy; she'll treat you all the better, now she's got it, 'specially if she has any fear of the discipline being repeated. Never you mind—*I'm* her uncle, and her natural guardian; and *I* approve of it—*I* uphold you in it," quoth Uncle Harry, his thoughts reverting to Kate's treatment of himself the day previous. "Mind, *I* give you leave, and *I'm* her uncle."

"Pray, do not talk so upon this subject, sir. Believe me, I am sunk very low in my own opinion. I have long dreaded this. I would to Heaven my patience had held out a few days longer, until my ship sailed. Then this rupture might have been delayed, or might never have occurred. Great God! that I, that *I*, should have raised my hand against a weak, defenceless woman!"

"Well, what of it? I don't see why weak, defenceless women are not to be punished when they deserve it, as well as weak, defenceless children," exclaimed the old monster. "Would you feel any great compunction for having chastised a weak, defenceless child, if he deserved it?"

"Your opinions are extremely revolting, Mr. Gleason; but I sent for you to request your good offices with Kate. She

4

refuses to see me, and returns unopened all my notes I wish
you to see her, implore her forgiveness for me, and bring me
her answers. Will you do this?"

"No, I sha'n't; for that would neutralize the good effect
of the drubbing."

"Then I must see Mrs. Leslie immediately. Will you ex
cuse me?"

"Yes, and accompany you."

The two gentlemen then left the house, and took their way
to Leslie's together.

The earnest efforts of the Leslies failed, however, to bring
about a reconciliation between the parties. Catherine remained
in her own room, outraged and indignant; and Captain Dunn
at his hotel, busily preparing for his voyage.

*   *   *   *   *   *   *   *   *

The last day of Captain Dunn's stay arrived. His ship
was to sail the next morning. He had made a last ineffectual
effort to see his wife. She delighted to afflict him to the last
safe moment, yet designed to have a full reconciliation before
his departure. "Yes," said she, "to-morrow morning I will
see him, and forgive him. It will not do to let him go away
in despair; for during three years' absence, he may cease to
love me—and now this evening to shine the most resplendent
star in the constellation of beauty to be assembled at Madame
Le Normand's ball. It is very fortunate, by the by, that this
shocking affair has not got wind yet."

That night, Mrs. Dunn, superbly attired, seemingly in high
beauty and spirits, entered the magnificent saloon of Madame
Le Normand.

That night, at the same hour, Captain Dunn took his melancholy way towards his now desolated home. Before leaving
his native shores, he wished to look again upon the face of his
infant son. The whole front of the house looked dark as he
approached it. Entering and groping his way through the
gloom, along the dark passage and up the stairs, he reached

the nursery door, and entered the room. A small lamp was sitting on the hearth; its feeble rays revealed a scene that sent all the blood from the father's cheek. Straight up in the bed sat the infant, in an attitude fixed and immovable as marble —his cheek blanched—his eyes wide open in a frightful stare —his lips apart with horror, while his gaze was fixed in deadly terror upon a dressed-up bugaboo at the foot of the bed. In an instant, seizing the bundle of sticks and rags that composed this figure, Captain Dunn threw it out of the window, and turned to his boy. The removal of the figure seemed to have dissolved the icy chain that bound the boy; for he now fell back in the bed, in violent convulsions. Seizing the bell-rope Captain Dunn now rang a peal that presently brought every remaining servant in the house to his presence.

"Thomas," said he to the first one that appeared, "run immediately for Doctor Wise. William," said he to the other man, "where is Mrs. Dunn?"

"At Madame Le Normand's ball, sir."

"And her nurse?"

"Gone out to a tea-drinking, sir."

"And the housemaid and cook? Gone, too, I suppose?"

"Yes, sir."

"You may leave the room. Stay, call me a carriage."

"Yes, sir."

Captain Dunn now turned to his son, whose spasms were over, and having placed him in a comfortable position, awaited the arrival of the physician.

At length, the Doctor entered, and, having looked at the child, ordered a warm bath, wrote a prescription and sent it off.

"And now, Doctor, is there any chance of his recovery?" inquired Captain Dunn, after having given the Doctor a full account of the causes that led to the child's seizure.

"For his full recovery, very little—this will be likely to affect him through life."

Dunn groaned.

"Doctor, could he be removed with safety, by a steamboat journey, some ninety or a hundred miles up the river ?"

"With perfect safety," said the Doctor.

"Then, sir, I will trouble you, if you please, to write at length your orders for his treatment on the journey, as I shall take him away to-night."

The physician, with a look of surprise, complied, and soon after took his leave.

Captain Dunn, raising the sleeping infant in his arms, threw a cloak around him, descended the stairs, entered the carriage, which had been some time before the door, and was driven towards the steamboat wharf.

At the same moment of time, Catherine Dunn, radiant with beauty and gayety, was led, smiling, to her place at the head of the cotillion forming in Madame Le Normand's saloon.

*   *   *   *   *   *   *   *   *   *

Day was dawning when Mrs. Captain Dunn drove up to her own door, and, wearied out with the night's dissipation, would have immediately sought her pillow, when her maid placed a note in her hand. She took it listlessly, and ran her eyes over its contents. They were as follows:

"Farewell, Catherine; farewell, infatuated woman, unduteous wife! neglectful mother! I leave you to the retribution that I pray may overtake you—that I pray may overtake you, in the hope that it may bring you to repentance, happily to reformation. I take your child where he may find, what he has never yet possessed, a mother's care and love—our child, whom your neglect has possibly made an idiot for life."

Frightful was the picture of passion presented by the wretched Catherine! Tearing the paper to atoms, she threw the fragments upon the floor, and would have ground them to powder with her heel. Her bosom heaved with fierce convalsions—her eyes scintillated—then pressing her hands suddenly to her mouth, she sank upon a chair, and thence upon the floor, a stream of dark blood trickling from her lips. Her maid in great alarm raised and placed her upon the bed; then, summoning her fellow servants, sent off for Mrs. Leslie and the physician. Both soon appeared. Mrs. Dunn had broken a blood-vessel, and the long-continued hemorrhage left her in a state of utter prostration, with her life in imminent danger.

On the afternoon of that day, as Catherine lay prostrate, placid, snowy, "like a broken lily on its icy bed," her ear, rendered supernaturally acute by her condition, heard the physician's whispered injunction to her attendants—

"She must be kept perfectly quiet; complete rest is absolutely necessary. She must not be permitted to raise a hand, scarcely to lift an eye-lid, or hear a sound. Even with the best precaution, a second hemorrhage will be very apt to ensue. Her life hangs upon a cobweb shred."

"And is Death hovering so near?" thought Catherine; and in an instant, as though invoked by the powerful magicians, Conscience and Fear, the errors of her past life arose before her. Catherine, like most young people in high health, had never contemplated the possibility of death approaching herself, except at the close of a long, long life, at a remote, out of sight distance. Late at night, Mrs. Leslie, who had never left Catherine's side since her attack, was stealing from the room. The quick senses of the invalid detected her.

"Oh! do not leave me, dearest Mary, to die alone here, with the servants."

"Dearest Catherine, I must go home a few moments, to attend to some little family matters. I will return very soon."

"Ah! go, go; I must not detain you from your family. I have no claim upon you, nor upon any human being now. There was one upon whose love I had every claim. He would have worn out his life in watching by my side—but him I have outraged, him I have alienated——"

"Oh! Catherine! Catherine! *do* be quiet, love; I will stay with you; but you must be perfectly quiet."

The injunction came too late. The hemorrhage broke out again, and the patient was brought immediately to the very verge of the grave.

* * * * * * * * *

At early dawn, at the same hour of Catherine's attack, a steamboat stopped for a few moments, to land a passenger, near the beautiful town of C., on the west bank of the Hudson. Captain Dunn, leaving the boat with his boy in his arms, took his way towards a white cottage, nearly hidden amidst the trees, on the bank of the river. Passing quickly through the white painted gate, and up the neat gravel walk bordered with roses, he paused and rang the door bell. Early as was the hour, the inmates of the cottage were astir. He was met by a cleanly maid servant, who showed him into a neat parlour, and went to summon her mistress. An old lady, in the dress of the Friends, entered the room, and embraced the visiter, saying:

" Welcome, welcome, my dear son. How hast thou been these many days?"

" Indifferent, mother; indifferent! but," said he, uncovering the infant, " I have brought you my son; if you love me, dear madam, take charge of him during my absence."

" But thy wife, Lemuel? Where is she? How is she?" inquired the lady, as she received the child, and proceeded to disencumber him of his outer garments.

" I know not! I care not!"

" What meanest thou, my son?"

" Listen to me, dear mother; I have but an hour to spend with you—I must be on shipboard by noon to-day—so I must be brief with my explanations." Captain Dunn here gave a rapid account of the troubles of his married life. When he concluded, breakfast was placed upon the table, and the old lady arose to pour out the coffee, merely saying, by way of comment upon her son's story—

"Oh! these young people! these young people! One would think, with health, and youth, and competence, they would feel happiness to be a duty; but with their pride and their passions, their petulance and haste, they cast away God's richest gifts with ingratitude, as things of nought."

Twenty-four hours from this time, Captain Dunn, bearing an aching heart in his bosom, had left the shores of his native country.

*   *   *   *   *   *   *   *   *

Two months succeeding this event, Catherine Dunn sat up in bed for the first time since her illness. Her thin and snowy face, with the blue tracing of the veins on her temples and forehead, the languid fall of the long eyelashes, the gentle drooping of the whole figure, gave to her beauty a delicate and spiritual air it had never possessed before, while the deprecating softness of her manner silently appealed to the sympathies of all around her.

An elderly woman, who had been her faithful nurse for many weeks past, and to whose skill and unwearied attention, under Providence, she owed her life, now entered the room.

"If you please, Rebecca, I will lie down now; I feel faint."

"Yes, dear," said the old woman, as she tenderly placed her patient in a recumbent posture, inquiring kindly if she "felt comfortable."

"Very comfortable," answered Catherine; then looking affectionately at her nurse, she said:

"How much I owe you, dear Rebecca—not only my life, but the knowledge of that truth that makes life of value!"

"Thy gratitude is due to thy Creator, my child, and not to the feeble instrument he has been pleased to use. Thou wouldst not thank the cup, Catherine, for the coffee thou hast just taken."

"Ah, why will you not let me thank you, my dear friend —
friend indeed, as well as well as Friend by profession? Think
—when you came to me, I was as a shipwrecked mariner on
an ocean rock—all, all lost—my life not worth a moment's
purchase—or, if possibly spared, objectless and aimless. Rebecca! Rebecca! though my first, best gratitude is due to
God, I must thank you too, I must love you too."

"I had an interest, dear child, in thy recovery, and in
thy spiritual health," said the nurse, looking steadily at
Catherine.

"Tell me your matron name," gazing earnestly in her face.

"I am thy husband's mother, Catherine."

The dreaded mother-in-law! The hated mother-in-law!
Catherine looked in the sweet face of her nurse, and burst into
tears.

"There, my child, drink this, and compose thyself," said
the old lady, pouring out a glass of water. Then she continued: "Yes, Catherine, thou wilt think it strange that a
woman of my sober class and age should be masquerading in
this way; but it came to pass after this manner. Nearly two
months ago, hearing that thou wert ill, I came down to visit
thee. Finding thee in great need of a mother's care, I determined to remain with thee. As thy state was very precarious,
and any surprise would have killed thee, I agreed with Mary
Leslie not to make myself known, but to attend thee as thy
nurse under my given name only. Thou knowest many of
my sect are called only by their given names. Thence it came
more natural."

"Ah! dearest madam! I will try to repay you with a daughter's love and duty; but the debt is stupendous. And now,
dear madam, will you tell me about my boy? I guessed that
my husband, that the Captain, had carried him to you."

"Thy infant is restored to health, Catherine; but for the
better salubrity of the air, I left him at home, in charge of a

careful and trust-worthy woman, who has been my own personal attendant for *many* years."

"And my husband—was he very much embittered against me?"

"He left thee in high displeasure, Catherine."

"Ah! yes! it could not have been otherwise; and yet I loved him, mother. Wild and passionate as I have been, I loved them both—my husband and child. Yet I never dreamed how deeply until now, that they are gone from me."

"Thou shalt see thy boy soon, dear Catherine. When thou art able to travel, I propose to take thee to my country house on the Hudson. There, the pure air, the quiet scene, and the company of thy boy, will effect thy complete restoration to health."

"But will my husband ever forgive me?" sighed Catherine.

"He should not be obdurate, for he has something to forgive in himself. A little more firmness on his part would have saved you much misery, had that firmness been exercised in the first days of your marriage."

"It would have taken a great deal of firmness, though, mother; for in those days, although I loved the Captain, there was a perverse devil always prompting me to *try* him, to see how far I *might* go with impunity—a wish to drive him to extremity—and I never loved him better than when I saw him in a thorough rage. This must have been insanity; was it not, mother?"

"No, my dear; I think, as thou saidst, it was Satan," said the placid Quaker. "And now I cannot allow thee to talk a moment longer; there is a fever spot already on thy cheek; so I shall draw the curtains, and leave thee to repose, my child."

*   *   *   *   *   *   *   *   *

Three years from the time of the commencement of Catherine Dunn's acquaintance with her mother-in-law, on a winter's evening, the white cottage at C. was lit up brightly. In the cozy parlour the cloth was laid for tea. In a large arm-chair, in one corner, sat an old lady, knitting. Upon an opposite lounge sat a young lady, employing herself with her needle, and in trying to keep awake an urchin of some five years old, who was hanging about her. But, ever and anon, she would start up and peer through the window-blinds or out of the door.

At last, going out upon the piazza, she remained some time, gazing down the moonlit river. Returning to the parlour, shivering with cold, she said:

"Do you not think the boat is very long, dear mother?"

"No, my dear; it is thy impatience."

"But it is after seven, madam."

"Our clock may be fast, dear."

"Mamma, I'm so sleepy," said the child.

"Ah, Lem, do try to keep awake, that's a dear boy! See here, I'll draw you a horse on the slate. Don't you want to see papa?"

"I don't believe papa is coming to-night, and I don't want a horse."

"Hark, mother! I hear the steamboat paddle," said Catherine. "Listen!"—and the colour rushed to her cheeks, and the light to her eyes, as she stood breathlessly waiting. Meantime, the steamboat puffed and blew and paddled past the town. There were no passengers for C. that night. Catherine sank down in her chair, the picture of disappointment and dejection.

"Thou must learn to bear these disappointments with more equanimity, Catherine. Thy husband will probably be up in the morning boat. We must rise very early to receive him; and, in order to do so, let us take tea and go to bed."

Catherine went to bed, and tried to sleep, for she wished very much to be in good looks to receive her husband; and Catherine knew that anxious vigils are bad cosmetics. Saying the multiplication table backwards, and counting a thousand slowly, equally failed in their usually soporific effect. At length, ere the dawn had peeped through the windows, the distant sound of the steamboat paddle struck upon her ear. Starting from her bed, and quickly throwing on her dressing-gown, she went into the parlour. Finding old Mrs. Dunn and her waiting-maid already up and dressed, and busy with their preparation for breakfast, Catherine hastened back, and, quickly performing her toilet, soon rejoined them, leading little Lemuel

"Now, dear, thou wilt not be disappointed—there is the bell—there are passengers for C. this morning," said the old lady.

Catherine flew to the door, and looked out; then, fluttering in again, she said quickly, while her colour went and came—

"Yes, indeed, mother; he is hurrying up the——Oh! After all, how will he receive me ?"

"With love, my poor child; with joy; do—don't tremble so. Rachel, bring in the coffee." A step was heard upon the threshold—a hand upon the lock—and Mrs. Dunn and Catherine turned to greet—*Mr. Leslie.* The blank expression of disappointment upon the features of each of the ladies, was far from flattering to their visiter. But the anxious and sorrowful expression upon Leslie's countenance soon awoke other feelings.

"What is the matter ? How is Mary ?" exclaimed both ladies in a breath.

."Mary is well," said he, taking the hand of each anxious questioner ; " but, my dear friends, summon all your fortitude, all your piety; I have come on a most painful errand; I am the messenger of the most afflicting news. Mrs. *Dunn*, your son—Catherine, your husband, has ceased to exist."

"Oh, God! support thy handmaid in this trial!" groaned the old mother, sinking into her chair.

A spasm, for an instant, convulsed the frame of Catherine, but left her perfectly still—her face blanched to marble white-ness—her eyes fearfully dilated. Her calmness was frightful.

"Now, tell me all about it," said she, in a voice of supernatural steadiness, "for I have a presentiment, I have a presentiment"——

"Yes, Catherine, I will; for so I have been *charged*, so I have promised to do. You are aware that your husband was in the habit of indulging freely in the use of intoxicating liquors."

"I was the cause of it; I drove him to drink," said Catherine, in the same unaccountable tone.

"This habit increased upon him fearfully after he sailed; and while in port, at one of the West India islands, *he died* in a fever of intoxication."

"And he died without ever guessing how I loved him; he died without knowing my bitter repentance; he died without forgiving me! But who cares? who cares?" said she, as her eyes grew wildly bright, and she broke into a loud maniac laugh, and, springing up, threw herself—into a pair of arms that pressed her fondly, while a pleasant, manly voice exclaimed:

"Why, dearest Kate, you have been dreaming frightful dreams."

And so she had.

Kate raised her head from the bosom that supported it, and looked up in bewilderment at the face of the speaker. It was Captain Lemuel Dunn, in his uniform, whose arms were around her. With a scream of joy, she buried her face once more in his bosom, and twined her arms around him. An impatient rap was now heard at the door, and Uncle Harry Gleason's voice exclaimed, quickly:

"Come! come! come! be quick with your kissing, Dunn; we *all* want to see her. Kate," he shouted, "get up; we are all here, Mary and all."

"Yes, Kate, get through your toilet quickly, dear one, for they are all here, the whole tribe of Manasseh"—meaning all Leslie's folks and Uncle Harry's family—"all come to pass a few days with us, and to take us back, they insist, to spend Christmas with them."

"I will not leave the room until I have obtained your forgiveness," said Catherine, with tears in her eyes; "and if you knew how sorry"——an embarrassed "I know, I know," from "Lem Dunn," cut short her words, as they passed into the parlour. Kate soon embraced her sister and the little ones, shook hands with Mr. Leslie, and offered her cheek to Uncle Harry, who drew himself up primly, and said:

"No, I thank you, ma'am; I've reformed my morals since my marriage; I don't kiss other men's wives now. I have got one of my own."

"Now, children, come to breakfast," said old Mrs. Dunn, taking her place at the head of the table.

There have been merrier reunions, but there never was a happier family party than the one that, in responding to the old lady's summons, sat down at her plentiful and hospitable board.

SYBIL BROTHERTON;

OR,

THE TEMPTATION.

———◆———

God is faithful, who will not suffer you to be tempted above that
you are able; but will with the temptation also make a way to escape.
1st CORINTHIANS x. 13

Thou dwell'st on sorrow's high and barren place,
But round about the mount an angel-guard,
Chariots of fire, horses of fire, encamp
To keep thee safe for Heaven.—MRS. ELLET.

THE HOMESTEAD—THE FAMILY.

IN one of the lower counties of Maryland, and in one of
the first settled neighbourhoods, surrounded by forest-crowned
hills, and embosomed in trees, stood the mansion of the
Brotherton family. It was a queer, old-fashioned house,
with many gable ends, and a very steep roof, and windows of
diamond-shaped panes set in lead sashes. These sashes, with
the bricks of which the house was built, had been imported
from "the old country."

It was the pride of the Brotherton family that they had
come over with Lord Baltimore; but whether as friend or footman to his lordship, tradition saith not. I can go no further
back than Hubert Brotherton, who flourished about a hundred
years ago. He was a notorious fox-hunter, and a celebrated
bon vivant in general; gave great hunts, great dinners, and
great balls and discovered a great talent for the manufactur-
ing of wings wherewith his acres might fly away. His wings
"worked extremely well," as inventors and patentees say, so

well that Hubert Brotherton, who at twenty-one could stand upon the highest point in his native county, and, looking around, call all the land in sight his own, died at forty, a poor man. It is a good illustration of the vicissitudes of life, the fact that the descendants of Hubert Brotherton, who in 1747 owned nearly a quarter part of the whole State of Maryland, in 1848 do not possess a foot of land in any country; and that the children of James Howlet, a domestic of the Brotherton family, have risen to the highest places in the Army, the Navy, and the Senate; but then the former sunk through idleness, sensuality, and extravagance; the latter rose by energy, industry, and sobriety.

Brotherton Hall had been some years in chancery at the time our story commences. The sole representatives of the Brotherton family were, now, Mrs. Judith Brotherton and her granddaughter Sybil. That dear old lady was a character! Heaven bless her! I fear I shall caricature the portrait in trying to portray her excellent, but somewhat complex nature Just as when I was a little girl, and would have some beautiful ideal face haunting my imagination, and, taking a pencil to draw it, would produce some hideous monstrosity, and throw away pencil and sketch in disgust.

Mrs. Brotherton had been very handsome in her youth, and was still a fine-looking old lady. She had a tall, stately figure, with singularly small feet and hands. Her high forehead and small Roman nose were relieved from hauteur by the tender expression of her deep-blue eyes, and the beautiful contour of her mouth. Now, don't sneer, young ladies and gentlemen; I have seen both old men and old women with very beautiful and attractive faces, albeit somewhat gray and wrinkled, and, when I was a school girl, I was very near falling in love with an old gentleman of sixty, for his beautiful smile and musical voice, and the fervent soul breathing through both.

But to my story. Mrs. Brotherton, to complete her portrait, generally wore a black satin dress, with a fine white muslin handkerchief folded over her bosom, and a plain cap of lace on her head. Mrs. Brotherton's character was very remarkable for three qualities—high family pride, warm benevolence of heart, and great romance of mind. Her benevolence always kept her pride in check, so that it never became arrogant, but was only manifested in her great solicitude in keeping her children from forming acquaintances or connexions with the *nouveaux riches* of the neighbourhood. Her benevolence had made great inroads upon her small fortune, and, for her thirdly-mentioned distinguishing trait, her romance of disposition, so far swept her flights of fancy, that, at the age of sixty, she would look upon her beautiful Sybil, and wish she could send her "home," as she fondly termed Old England, where she felt sure her lovely child would captivate some baron, earl, or duke. There was one rare feature in her mind more charming than even her benevolence. It was the simple, child-like trustfulness of disposition, that led her to reverse the rule of the worldling, and to believe every man and woman to be perfectly good, until she had experimentally found them to be otherwise.

Sybil Brotherton was a slight, fair girl, with a broad white forehead, large pensive blue eyes, and a sweet smile; a child of gentle and graceful movements, of low sweet tones, and of loving and pious heart. Sybil, too, was fanciful—she could not have been otherwise—and so, gently as she treated her partners at the village dancing-school, she thought them all sadly unlike the courtly Sir Charles Grandison and the stately Lord Mortimer; and she set down this world of reality to be a marvellously "flat, stale, and unprofitable" place to live in, and life itself, without a handsome and rich lover, to be a very dull story founded upon fact.

5

THE MESSENGER—THE NOVEL READERS.

IT was evening, the ground was covered with snow, and the last rays of the setting sun lit up into blazing splendour the icicles pendant from the pine trees that crowned the hills surrounding Brotherton Hall. In a quaint old wainscoted parlour, before a blazing hickory fire, sat Mrs. Brotherton and Sybil. The old lady was employed in knotting a valance, the young one in tambouring a muslin apron. Before them stood a little, round, spider-legged tea-table, covered with a damask cloth, and set out with a service of grotesque old China.

"It is growing dusky, my dear child; ring for Broom to bring in the lights," said Mrs. Brotherton, as she rolled up her valance, and put it in her basket.

Sybil complied by putting away her own work and ringing a little silver hand-bell that stood upon the table. There were no bell wires running through the house, like nerves through a human body, in those days, reader.

The door opened, and, in answer to the summons, an old gray-haired domestic appeared, with a candle in each hand. "Making a reverence" as he entered, he sat the light upon the table, saying, as he did so—

"Madam, a man from Colonel John Henry Hines is waiting without. He brings a message for you."

"Bring him in, Broom."

"Yes, madam," and, with a second obeisance, the old man left the room.

There was this peculiarity about Mrs. Brotherton and her household, that, from a limited intercourse with the world, and a familiar acquaintance with stately old dramas and novels of the last century, the old lady had acquired a somewhat stiff and courtly manner of speaking and acting, except when thrown off her guard by strong feeling. This stately manner was particularly admired by her two old servants, Katy and Broom, who copied it upon all possible occasions.

"Sarvint, madam—sarvint, miss," bowed the smart footman of Colouel Hines, as he entered the presence of the ladies

"I understand you bear a message from Colonel Hines," said Mrs Brotherton.

"Yes, madam; Colonel John Henry sends his 'spects, and says, with your permission, he will do himself the honour of calling, with his sister, in his carriage, to take Miss Brotherton to the ball to-morrow evening."

"Convey my grateful acknowledgments to Colonel Hines, and inform him that I shall be pleased to consign Miss Brotherton to his guardianship for the evening."

Overawed by the dignity and bewildered by the eloquence of the old lady, the man bowed and left the room, followed by Broom.

"Broom!" said he, "what the old 'oman mean by that? She going to let the gal go?"

"Mr. Trimble!" said Broom, drawing himself up stiffly, "in de first place, *my* name is Mr. Broomley, and not Broom; *my lady* is Madam Brotherton, and no old woman; and my *young* lady is Miss Brotherton of Brotherton Hall, and no gal."

"Well, then, but what am I to tell the Colonel? That she is going to let the gal—I mean the young lady—go?"

"Bress your stupidity, Mrs. Brotherton is pleased to 'sign Miss Brotherton to his garden for the evening."

"'Fore de Lord, I don't know what that is; but I shall tell Colonel Hines that she is going to let the gal go."

"Look here, you man in livery, you green and yellow poll parrot, if you call Miss Brotherton a gal again, I'll cane you; so be off with the message, now," said old Broom, flourishing his black-thorn stick.

The man went his way, and old Broom went into the kitchen to carry in tea. Having set supper upon the table, and seen the ladies seated, he took his stand behind the chair of Mrs. Brotherton.

"There, you may leave the room now, Broom If we should need anything, Miss Brotherton will ring."

The old man went out.

"Now, my dear Sybil," said the old lady, "but for the kind attention of Colonel Hines, I should not permit you to attend this ball, for I do not wish the face of my granddaughter to be seen too often at these village balls."

"Indeed, dear grandmother, if Colonel Hines is to attend me there, I would rather not go."

"And *why* my dear? What objections have you to Colonel Hines? Is he not very polite and attentive?"

"Yes, madam, oppressively so."

"Then, permit me to inform you that the attentions of Colonel Hines are a distinguished honour, even to Miss Brotherton."

"Yet, indeed, dear grandmother, I would fain dispense with the honour."

"Explain your antipathy, if you please, Sybil."

"Why, in the first place, dear grandmother, he is quite an old gentleman, near thirty, is he not?"

"Colonel Hines is forty-seven years of age, quite in the noon of life."

"And I, in the morning twilight," said Sybil, sadly.

"Any other objection, Sybil?"

"Then he is short and thick, and has a broad red face, and a bald head, and a big—that is, a large—I mean a stout—in a word, he is a round old gentleman, who gets into a great heat when he dances—"

"Miss Brotherton, I am shocked, I am humiliated, at your language," said the old lady, trying to look severely at her pet. "Now, do me the favour to ring for Broom to remove the tea-equipage."

When the table was cleared and the fire replenished—

"Now, Broom," said Mrs. Brotherton, "bring in the box of books that last arrived from Baltimore, and open it" The box was brought in, and the lid forced off, and the wealth of entertainment displayed, all in handsome bindings.

Old Broom was on his knee at the box, officiating as gentleman usher to the books.

"There, Broom, hand me that book in red—ah! 'The Romance of the Forest.'"

"Oh! Grandmother, let us read that—that must be very interesting."

"Here, my child, take it," said the old lady, forgetting he displeasure. "Hand me those others, Broom—'The Bandit's Bride,' ah ha!" "Oh! Grandmother, that! that! let's read *that* to-night." "Stay, my love, let us look further. You are too excitable," said the old lady, continuing her examination with intense interest. "'The Young Protector,' 'The Royal Captives,' 'The Children of the Abbey'"—

"Indeed! oh, grandmother, that! that! we ve heard so much about that—*do* let's read that to-night."

"Very well, then, my dear, lay it by. Here, Broom, take these books up stairs, and put them in the book-case; and then go and tell Katy to bring in half a dozen eggs and a bottle of port (we will have some mulled wine before we retire to rest, darling," said she in a low voice to Sybil), "and then, Broom, if you and Katy wish, you can come in and listen to the reading." Much pleased, the old man hastened to execute his mission. Now, do not think, gentle reader, that there was any inconsistency between Mrs. Brotherton's pride and her practice of admitting her old domestics to her evening readings. Her people, as she called them, had grown up with her —they were old and tried servants, perfectly faithful and respectful. And she had long observed with what greedy ears they would linger in the room and listen while she read.

Well! old Katy soon brought in her knitting, and old Broom followed her with his cards and wool, and one sat on a low seat in one corner of the fire-place, and the other on a cricket in the opposite corner, quiet, attentive, and pleased.

Mrs. Brotherton and Sybil sat before the fire, with a work-
stand between them, upon which stood a brightly burning
lamp, work-basket, scissors, snuffers, &c.   The old lady wiped
her spectacles, put them on, opened her book, and commenced
reading, amid profound silence, to most attentive and interested
auditors.   Sybil employed herself with her tambour frame.
When Mrs. Brotherton grew weary of reading aloud, she
would pass the book to Sybil, and take up her knotting
Miss Brotherton would then lay aside her work and read for
an hour; and in that way they would agreeably relieve each
other until it was time to retire to rest.   Then old Broom
would mull the wine, lay the cloth, and set out a few light
sponge cakes.   After Mrs. Brotherton and Sybil had partaken
of the refreshments, the remainder was carried into the kitchen,
for the solace of the old servants.   Family prayer concluded
the evening, and the little circle separated for the night.

THE BALL AND THE BEAUX.

THE next day was a busy one with Mrs. Brotherton and
Sybil.   At length, at seven o'clock, Miss Brotherton was
arrayed for the festival.   As I have never minutely described
Sybil Brotherton, I had better do it now, while she is in her
"best bib and tucker," when Katy declared she "looked like
any angel" (angels don't wear white satin, mechlin lace, and
pearls, Katy).   Sybil Brotherton was rather below the middle
stature, with a slender frame, yet full formed, with rounded
and tapering limbs, and a grace so natural that every movement expressed the poetry of motion.   Her forehead was
broad, high, and white; her eyes large, clear, and blue; her
lips full, glowing, and beautiful.   Her complexion was of that
delicate and transparent white, so seldom seen except in con-
sumptives, and in her cheeks was burning that fire of death
that so resembles the rich rose of health.   Her dark brown
hair fell in long and shining ringlets upon her graceful neck

ind rounded bosom. Her pure and delicate beauty was set off to advantage by the rich dress of white satin and mechlin lace, and the bandeau of pearls contrasted well with her dark hair. The carriage of Colonel Hines drew up before the door at eight o'clock, and Sybil, carefully wrapped in her velvet mantle and hood, was handed in, and driven off. On the morning after the ball, Mrs. Brotherton and Sybil were seated at breakfast, when the former said—

"You must now tell me, darling, whom you saw at the ball, and who were your partners in the dance."

"Well, dear grandmother, there was the same old set. The Etheringtons, and the Somervilles, and the Kinlocks, and the ——Oh! by the way, Hector Kinlock presented the Hon. Meredith Mills, one of our Representatives in Congress. He is from the lower part of the county, but he has purchased Blocksley Place, and is coming to reside in this neighbourhood."

"Ah! Meredith Mills. What sort of a person is he, my dear?"

"Why, he is a young man, talented, I rather think—agreeable—and—not married, grandma, if you mean that," said Sybil, with a sly smile.

"I am sorry to see you rather disposed to levity, my dear Sybil; pray avoid it. Meredith Mills—the name is familiar. Oh! yes; certainly, I know the family; a very old family, originally from Lincolnshire; came over with the Calverts; certainly, the Mills's of Meredith Place; and coming to live in our neighbourhood; and not married"——

"And very much smitten with Sybil Brotherton, and coming to see her this morning."

"Sybil!" exclaimed the old lady, gravely looking over the top of her spectacles.

"My dear grandmother, you know one must be merry the day after a ball, if they are not fatigued."

"And is Mr. Mills coming here this morning?"

"He said that he would do himself the honour of calling on us this morning."

"And what did you reply?"

"Why, that Mrs Brotherton would be happy to receive him."

"That was correct. Did you form any other new acquaintances, Sybil?"

"N—n—o, madam, none except"——

"Except whom?"

"Nobody, in fact, but"——

"But whom?"

"But a young gentleman who came with Mr. Mills."

"And who was he?"

"A young artist."

"Humph! you are reserved, Sybil. What was his name?"

"Middleton."

"And he was very agreeable."

"Dear grandmother, I never said so."

"And you were very much pleased with him."

"Dear grandmother! pleased with a gentleman at the first interview! I thought you had a better opinion of me."

The old lady smiled.

"Oh! a gentleman, was he? I thought you said he was a painter."

"An artist, grandmother, an artist; and surely an artist is a gentleman, if any man is."

"Humph! that depends upon whether he paints for money or amusement. But I shall not in future trust you to the care of any one. When I cannot attend you myself to public places, you must remain at home."

They were interrupted by a knock at the hall door and the entrance of old Broom, who informed the ladies that two gentlemen, Mr. Mills and Mr. Middleton, had called and were waiting in the drawing-room.

"Go in and see them, my dear Sybil. I will come presently," said Mrs. Brotherton.

As Sybil entered the drawing-room, Mr. Middleton advanced and led her to a seat, with the courtly grace of "sixty years since," hoping that Miss Brotherton had suffered no inconvenience from the fatigue of the preceding evening, or from the ride through the night air.

Miss Brotherton had suffered no inconvenience, and was much obliged.

Sybil then addressed herself to Mr. Mills, and trusted that he would find the neighbourhood pleasant and the neighbours agreeable.

Mr. Mills was pleased with the neighbourhood, and anticipated much pleasure from a more intimate acquaintance with its residents.

At this moment the door opened, and Mrs. Brotherton entered. Both gentlemen arose from their seats, and Sybil named Mr. Mills—Mr. Middleton—Mrs. Brotherton. The latter gentleman met Mrs. Brotherton, led her to the sofa, and took a seat near her. Mrs. Brotherton expressed to Mr. Middleton her gratification at forming his acquaintance. Mr. Middleton bowed reverently, and expressed his deep sense of the honour conferred upon him. The conversation then became general. Mr. Middleton quite won the heart of Mrs. Brotherton, by descanting upon the beauties of Brotherton Hall, its antique look, its picturesque situation, its pleasant locality, &c. Mrs. Brotherton, in acknowledgment, begged that he would frequently honour the Hall with his presence. All this time, Miss Brotherton was trying to amuse the Hon. Meredith Mills, and was in no small degree astonished and pleased at the wondrous *penchant* her grandmother had conceived for "the portrait painter" The problem was soon solved. The gentlemen arose to take leave. Madam Brotherton hoped they would soon repeat their visit. The gentlemen declared that they should feel so happy in accepting her invitation, and they bowed themselves out. When the sound of their horses' feet had died away—

"Well! what do you think of our visiters, grandma?" asked Sybil, gayly.

"Why, my dear Sybil, I think Mr. Meredith Mills a remarkably handsome, intellectual, and polished young gentleman. Of Mr. Middleton, I had not much opportunity of judging. He, as I regretted to see, had his attention entirely engrossed by yourself during the whole time of his visit. One thing, however, did strike me. I never saw a fairer illustration of the fact that good blood will show itself through all disguises. Now, observe—those two men—they were both equally well dressed, perhaps equally well educated, and received in the same society; but now observe the difference. In Mr. Meredith Mills, you saw the high-bred air of a gentleman of family; in Mr. Middleton was equally visible the *mauvaise honte* of a low person. Mr. Mills was easy, graceful, and conversable; Mr. Middleton shy, awkward, and embarrassed. I never saw a fairer illustration of high-bred aristocracy and of upstart vulgarity."

Sybil listened to this disquisition, with eyes and lips wide open with astonishment.

"Why, my dear grandmother!" said she, "are you not under a mistake? Which of the gentlemen did you suppose to be Mr. Mills?"

"Why, of course, the Hon Meredith Mills was the gentleman who conversed with *me*, while you were so much occupied with the other young person.'

A smile flashed into the eyes and curled around the lips of Sybil for an instant, and vanished, as she said, seriously—

"My dear grandmother, it's all owing to my awkward presentation, I suppose; but you have made the most amusing mistake. The tall, handsome, graceful, accomplished, and high-bred man, who led you to the sofa, and who charmed you so much by his intellectual conversation, and whom you have so highly approved and praised, was Harold Middleton, the portrait painter; and the little drab-coloured gentleman, in light hair and a gray coat, was the Hon. Meredith Mills, of Meredith Place."

"I hope you do not jest with me, Miss Brotherton," said the old lady, looking curiously, between surprise, pique, and embarrassment.

"Or rather, you hope I *do* jest, dear grandmother, but I speak truth; however, your rule, I suppose, still holds good. This is but an exception."

The old lady seemed consoled, and remarked, with a smile—

"There is one thing, however, that pleases me, my dear Sybil. It is, that you kept that young man, Middleton, at a proper distance, while you showed fitting respect for Mr. Meredith Mills."

Sybil smiled, but there was something sad, almost remorseful, in her smile.

"MY GRANDFATHER, LORD MAINWARING."

A FEW weeks passed away. Sybil met young Middleton often in society. Indeed, he even came often to the house, where Mrs. Brotherton, in consideration of the pressing invitation extended to him on his first visit, continued to treat him with civility, if, indeed, the charming manners of the young man had not put it out of her power to treat him otherwise. Then, his unembarrassed manner to Miss Brotherton led off the suspicion that his affections were interested in her. The following circumstance opened the eyes of Mrs. Brotherton to the real position of the parties.

Colonel Hines had proposed for the hand of Miss Brotherton; Mrs. Brotherton had made known his wishes to her granddaughter, who received the news of the revival and pressing of the obnoxious suit with so much agitation and distress, that Mrs. Brotherton perceived that her heart was no longer free, and, by her questions, soon ascertained who had become its master Upon the same evening, it happened that young Middleton called, and was received by Mrs. Brotherton alone and coldly. Sybil was weeping in her own room. Young Middleton, perceiving the change in her manner, suspected the truth, for he had become well acquainted with the old lady's foible; he therefore soon arose to take his leave, remarking, as he did so,

"This is probably the last opportunity I shall have of paying my devoirs to the ladies of Brotherton Hall; for my grandfather, the Earl of Mainwaring, has written to command my immediate return to England."

"Sir! did I hear aright? Your grandfather, the Earl of Mainwaring!" exclaimed the old lady, thrown off her guard.

"Yes, madam," said young Middleton, quietly. "Permit me to wish you a good evening. Pray present my most respectful regards to Miss Brotherton. Good evening, madam."

"No, no; do not go yet. You must take leave of Sybil—and—pray do me the favour to touch the bell. Perhaps you would take some refreshments."

The young man complied with her request, and—

"Broom!" said she to the old servant who answered the summons, "go and give my compliments to Miss Brotherton, and ask her *why* she keeps us waiting thus, and desire her to come down; and, Broom, serve refreshments. Mr. Middleton has ridden far, and would like something. Mr. Middleton, *do* be seated."

A sinister smile flitted across the young man's countenance as he sat down. Greatly wondering at the summons, Sybil entered the room, followed by Broom with refreshments. The young man's hurry seemed now to have evaporated, as, eventually, did the strong necessity for his going to England. It was late when he left the house. Sybil pleaded fatigue, and retired soon to bed. Many a fine aerial castle did Mrs. Brotherton build that evening for her pet.

"Humph! indeed!" soliloquized the old lady, as she walked

restlessly about her chamber floor. "Who would have thought it? Lord Mainwaring! I wonder whether young Middleton's father is the eldest son of the Earl, the heir to his titles and estates. I should like so much to know. Dear me! the Earl of Mainwaring! The Earl and *Countess* of Mainwaring! Lord and Lady Mainwaring! I will go to England with them —my *granddaughter,* Lady Mainwaring!" said the old lady, ringing all the changes on the coveted title. "I must have a wedding. I will get Otto, the great Baltimore confectioner, and Sampson, the French cook, to provide the breakfast. Then we must go to Baltimore ourselves, and speak to Madame Modiste to furnish the bridal dress and veil, and we must consult her upon the trousseau generally"——and "Countess of Mainwaring!" muttered the old lady, as she sank to sleep that night. "How well a coronet will grace that angel brow!"

"God help old madam!" said Katy to Broom that night at the kitchen fire, "she has been talking to herself all the evening."

Young Middleton's return to England was indefinitely postponed, and, before the trees had put forth their leaves, or the snow was melted off the ground, Sybil Brotherton was the wife of Harold Middleton. The young couple, much to the comfort of Mrs. Brotherton, had concluded to spend the first year of their married life at Brotherton Hall. Mrs. Brotherton had ascertained that the father of her son-in-law was the *third* son of Lord Mainwaring, and that at least three persons stood between him and the Earl's coronet. But at least he was the grandson of a peer, and that was much.

THE YOUNG WIFE.

How soon was the sweet dream of Sybil broken! How soon the beautiful illusion of Sybil dispelled! How soon "the veiled prophet" of her idolatry stood forth in all his hideous deformity! A few months after their marriage, Harold Middleton began to absent himself from his young

wife all day, and sometimes all night. The playful and loving
expostulations of Sybil were kindly taken at first, and explanations, which she received with confiding affection, were
given of his absence. But even this disguise was at last
thrown off.

About twelve months after her marriage, Sybil was sitting
reading with her grandmother, in their little parlour. Earlier
than usual, the old lady complained of fatigue and drowsiness
and retired to rest. Sybil did not seek her chamber, but,
desiring Broom to bring some refreshments, and sending
Katy to her chamber for his dressing-gown and slippers, she
drew her chair to the fire, to await the coming of her husband
She could not read, she laid her book down, her very face
breathed joy. Sybil had ascertained that she would become
a mother, and, with the confiding love of a young wife, she
wished to make her husband a sharer of her joy. Long did
Sybil wait, but not impatiently, for her face was still beaming
with gentle happiness, when the sound of a horse's feet, followed by an impatient rap at the door, caused her to start
joyfully up, and go to open it herself, exclaiming, as she met
her husband—

"Oh! dear Harold, how glad I am that you have come at
last! I have been waiting so long for you!"

Repulsing her offered caress, he said, sternly and angrily—

"I have before this intimated my desire that you should
retire to rest at your usual hour, instead of sitting up for me,
Mrs. Middleton. Do not give me occasion to repeat the injunction."

A woman of more spirit would have resented this; a woman
of less sensibility might not have felt it. Poor Sybil, from
the very manner of her education, as well as from her native
temperament, was the victim of a morbid sensibility. This
was the first occasion upon which Middleton had spoken unkindly to her, and she felt it deeply. Pale and trembling,
she sank into her seat; Middleton threw himself upon the

sofa The coffee grew cold, the oysters became turbid in
their liquor, the candles burned low, the fire died out, and
Sybil's sweet news remained untold. Silent tears were stealing down her cheeks. This seemed rather to harden the heart
of her husband, who now said, sternly—

"This course of conduct looks very like a wilful disregard
of my wishes, Mrs. Middleton. Perhaps they were not explained with sufficient clearness?"

Sybil started as the first angry tones of his voice fell upon
her ears, then looking into his face with an expression of
distressing inquiry, and meeting nothing there but sullen
anger, she arose from her seat, and, taking her night-lamp,
was about to leave the room. Seeming to take a second thought
when she reached the door, she turned back, and, setting down
her lamp, approached her husband, and putting her arms
around his neck and pressing her lips upon his brow, she
murmured—

"Do not be angry with me, dear Harold. I will not stay
up for you another time, if you will love me now."

This caress was received in sullen silence, and not returned.
The gentle words of Sybil remained unnoticed. Unclasping
her arms, after a few moments, she withdrew to her chamber,
and sought her pillow, where, like a child as she was, she soon
wept herself to sleep.

"A poor, pale, whining creature," muttered Middleton,
looking after his wife as she left the room. "If I had known
that this old place was in chancery, I would have seen her in
Jericho before I would have married her. Strange! that I
never happened to hear it until to-night. And you, Inez!
my bright, my beautiful, my dark-browed girl of Italy!
Was it for this, I cast you away? No matter; fetters not
riveted with gold fall easily from my wrists, bright Inez!
And if this property should slip from its present possess-
ors"——

Middleton fell into a deep revery, so that it was near morn ing when he retired to his chamber.

A few months passed, and the case in chancery was decided against the Brothertons, and a suit entered to eject them from the premises. From this time, the mask of hypocrisy assumed by Middleton, and which had occasionally slipped aside, was now laid by for ever. With what funds he could wrest from his gentle wife, or, through her, from Mrs. Brotherton, he would frequent L——, the county seat, and spend whole days and nights in dissipation. Sybil grew pale and melancholy, and, having lost all esteem and respect for her husband, took no further comfort in her love; and, indeed, with her delicate health and timid temper, she generally felt rather relieved, when, after she had given him all the money she could raise, he would take himself off for a week, for then she felt secure, at least, from personal violence and danger to herself and her unborn babe; for, alas! Sybil Middleton, the delicate, the sensi-tive, and the refined, had felt the weight of her husband's hand in anger, had trembled for her life in his presence. But these scenes of violence would generally occur after Middleton had been drinking freely. And Sybil had another sorrow; she perceived, with grief and dismay, that her beloved grand-mother was falling into premature dotage. The trials of the old lady's age had been too great for her to bear. The loss of the Brotherton estate, the unworthiness of her son-in-law, the misery of her darling granddaughter, and the prospective ejectment from the home of her youth, all pressed upon the old lady's mind, and at length broke it down.

THE YOUNG MOTHER.

"STAY with me to-night, dear Harold; I am ill, and I am frightened. Stay with me to-night," pleaded Sybil, timidly taking the hand of her husband as he was about to leave the house.

"I am not a physician, Mrs. Middleton," replied he, coldly.

"Yet you are more to me—the only one who can give me comfort and strength in my coming trial. I am weak and fearful. I know I am a fool, yet bear with me a while, and —stay with me to-night."

"You have your grandmother with you."

"Alas! my poor grandmother! she herself needs care and attention She is incapable of giving me comfort. Oh! do not leave me!" exclaimed she suddenly, catching his hand, as he was about to go. "Stay with me to-night."

"You are importunate, Mrs. Middleton," said he, releasing himself, "and I regret to say that I cannot comply with your request. Good-evening." And he left the room.

Sybil turned aside to weep, but wiped her tears hastily away, as she perceived her poor grandmother totter into the room.

"Weeping again, Sybil, my poor child?" said the old lady, sinking into a chair, and holding out her arms to her grand-daughter. "Come to my bosom, my dear child. What is your grief, Sybil?"

"Nothing, my dear grandmother, only I am not very well," said Mrs. Middleton, pleased, yet wondering at the temporary revival of the old lady's intellect.

"No, my poor child; you are far from well. I see that. You must go to bed, Sybil, and I will send for a physician. Katy! tell Broom to saddle a horse, and ride over to Doctor Hall's, and ask him to come over directly; that Mrs. Middleton is ill; and, Katy, do you carry an armful of wood up into your young lady's chamber. Lean on me, my dear Sybil, and come up stairs."

Lean on her! Poor old trembler! There was something inexpressibly touching in her protection of Sybil, while she herself so much needed support.

Mrs. Middleton gained her room, and was assisted to bed. Mrs. Brotherton took her seat in a large arm-chair by her side. Sybil repressed her complaints, that she might not give pain

6

to the tender-hearted old lady. The physician lived en miles
off; the night was far advanced, and he had not yet arrived.
Sybil lay perfectly quiet and silent, except when she would
entreat her grandmother to go to rest, and leave old Katy to
watch.——

"No, no, darling; no, no, my poor child," would be the old
lady's answer.

Sybil at last said—

"Dear grandmother, I would like to go to sleep, but I cannot sleep while I see you there. Will you not retire to bed?"

"Are you better, then, my love? I am so glad! Well,
as soon as I see you asleep, I will go!"

"Good-night, then, dear grandmother!"

"God bless you, darling!"

Sybil closed her eyes and affected to sleep. After a few
moments, the old lady arose and looked over her, but she
could not see by the dim light of the taper the corrugated brow
and the clenched hands of the sufferer.

"She is asleep!" murmured the old lady. "Bless her,
poor thing, I was afraid she was going to be sick." And she
glided from the room, telling Katy that she would dispense
with her services for that night, and charging her to sleep by
the bedside of her young lady, in case she should need any
thing.

In an hour after, Sybil Middleton pressed her first-born
child to her bosom.

"Thank God for my beautiful boy! Thank God for my
spared life!" fervently exclaimed the exhausted mother, as
she received the babe in her arms.

"Now, my dear young lady, as you are comfortable, hadn't
I better wake madam?"

"No, Katy; let her sleep, and I must rest now. How
proud Harold will be of his son! How happy poor grandmother will feel that my trial is safely over!" was the last
thought of Sybil, as she sank to rest.

"Oh! my dear young lady! my dear young lady!" exclaimed old Katy, bursting into the chamber of Mrs. Middleton at early dawn.

"Why, what is the matter, Katy?" inquired Sybil, in affright.

"Your poor grandmother! your good old grandmother!"

"Katy! what *is* the matter? What of my dear grandmother?"

"Dead in her bed! dead in her bed!"

With a smothered shriek, Sybil fell back on her pillow.

Old Broom, who, unable to find the Doctor, had returned late at night, was despatched to Colonel Hines's. The Colonel and his sister quickly obeyed the summons, and hastened to Brotherton Hall. The family physician also arrived early in the morning, and a messenger was despatched to Mr. Middleton, at L——. In the mean time, Colonel Hines and his sister Rachel took the direction of affairs; and truly the kind offices of these good Samaritans were needed, for Mrs. Brotherton had expired during the night in a fit of apoplexy, and Mrs. Middleton was lying extremely ill and delirious. Mr. Middleton returned late in the evening. On the fourth day from her decease, the funeral of Mrs. Brotherton took place. It was attended by all the gentry of the neighbourhood. The wild delirium of Mrs. Middleton had been subdued, but she lay in a stupor, insensible to all that was passing around her. Miss Rachel Hines kindly volunteered to remain at Brotherton Hall to nurse the invalid.

At length Sybil was raised from her bed of illness, and, in a fortnight from the day on which she first sat up, she left her room. Miss Rachel Hines had returned home It was evening, and Sybil said to herself—

"I will surprise Harold, and please him, by joining him at tea."

And wrapping her shawl around her, she descended to the parlour. Old Broom was just setting tea upon the table as

she entered. In answer to her inquiry, the old man told her
that Mr. Middleton was talking with a strange man in the
entry. Desiring Katy to go up and remain with her infant,
and telling Broem to be in waiting upon the table, Sybil took
her seat. Middleton entered, and, as he sat down in his place,
remarked—

"I am glad to see you out of your chamber, Sybil, for we
shall be obliged to get out of the house very soon."

"As you please, dear Harold. I am ready to accompany
you, when and where you please."

Harold Middleton smiled darkly.

"But it is not as I please, Mrs. Middleton. Let me tell
you, it is far more easy to get rid of one handsome establish-
ment than to find another."

Not comprehending the cause of his ill-humour, but seeing
from his inflamed face that he had been drinking, Sybil answered gently and soothingly——

"Dearest Harold, believe me, I am willing to do just as
you see fit. I had as lieve remain here as go elsewhere, if you
prefer it."

"You are dull, Mrs. Middleton; you do not seem to comprehend that a writ of ejectment has been served upon us, and
that we *must* go."

"Oh! it is sad, indeed, to leave our home upon compulsion.
But, dearest Harold, do not call me Mrs. Middleton, and speak
so coldly to me. You know I have no one to love me now
but you."

"You are irritable, and not very agreeable, this evening,
Mrs. Middleton. I think you have left your chamber too soon;
I advise you to return to it."

Sybil left the room.

On the morning succeeding this conversation, Middleton
left home for Baltimore, and was absent about a week. At
the end of that time he returned, and, entering the parlour,
where his wife sat at work, informed her that he had received

a letter from his father requiring his immediate presence in
London to attend a lawsuit; and that he should go in the
next packet, which would sail in two weeks.

"Very well, dear Harold, we must make some provision for
the two poor old people in the kitchen, and I shall be so glad
to go. I like the arrangement very much. I shall be delighted
to cross the ocean, and so happy, so very happy, to know your
father and mother. I shall find parents again in them; and
they will be *so* pleased, will they not, to see our babe, their
grandchild? Oh! yes; I shall be quite ready in a week."

"Well! have you done, Sybil?"

Sybil raised her large, tender eyes to his countenance with
an inquiring glance, and remained silent.

"I never contemplated taking *you* to England, Sybil; at
least when I go. I do not indeed know how you would be
received by my family. It will take, I fear, some considerable
diplomacy to reconcile my father to this somewhat inconsiderate marriage of mine."

The blood rushed to the face of Sybil, and the tears to her
eyes; to conceal which, she stooped and raised her babe from
the cradle.

"But this is my design. I will attend promptly my father's
summons; meet him in London, and, after the hurry of business is over, I will endeavour to reconcile him to our marriage,
then send or come for you and the child."

Mrs. Middleton was reassured by his words, especially as
his manner was kinder than usual, and he had called her
"Sybil" through the conversation. She inquired—

"And how long will it be, dear Harold, before you send?"

"Oh! in a few months from this—in the fall, probably;
and, in the mean time, I will take a house for you in Baltimore for the summer."

"It seems a long time until the fall; but then I suppose I
am weak to feel so," said Sybil, repressing a sigh.

The next few days were employed in selling off the furni-

ture and plate at Brotherton Hall. A few family portraits
and some pieces of old-fashioned furniture were reserved for the
use of Mrs. Middleton during the summer.

Two weeks from this time, Sybil found herself the occupant
of a small cottage on the suburbs of Baltimore. Katy was
retained in her service, upon reduced wages; and old Broom,
who had "saved a penny," went to live with some of his relations.

It was the morning of Middleton's departure. His trunks
were all on board, and the packet was to sail with the first
tide.

At early dawn, Middleton and Sybil stood at the cottage
gate.

"And will you *indeed* send for me in the fall, dear Harold?"
said Sybil, sadly.

"Why, *certainly*, Sybil; why do you doubt me?" said Middleton, smilingly.

"I do not doubt you, but I love to hear you promise again
and again."

"Well, I must be gone; farewell, Sybil."

"Good-bye! good-bye!—Oh! come back; let me take a
long, long look into your eyes—a look that will last me till
we meet"——

"Well! will that do, Sybil? There—there—I must go.
Be cheerful; farewell. I will send for you soon."

And they parted; he with a lie on his lips, rejoicing in his
release; she to her lonely hearth, profoundly grateful for his
seeming kindness, and building many bright hopes upon his
faithless promises.

KATY'S MISHAPS IN THE CITY.

THE leaves were falling, and the cold north-west wind was
blowing them in drifts about the cottage of Mrs. Middleton.
Old Katy was roaming about the garden, gathering sticks to

make a fire; in the course of her gleaning, she passed into the
front yard. Seeing the figure of an old man leaning on a stick
at the gate, she dropped her bundle and hastened forward, joyfully exclaiming—

"Lor' a' mercy upon me, Broom! Is this *you?* *Is* this
you? Bless your ole soul, I am *so* glad to see you once again
in this worl'! Come in, come in; how have you been this long
time?"

"Thanky, Katy, thanky; I'm so-so, 'cept the rheumatics,
and the phthisic, and the asthma and lumbago, and the liver
complaint, and the consumption, except that I enjoys pretty
good health in general."

"'Deed! I'm glad to hear you're so hearty. It's more than
I am; I'm trouble with a stiff neck."

"Yes! you were always stiff-necked, Katy."

Now, Broom, that was a libel on Katy!

"Well, Katy, how is the young madam and the little child,
and when is she going to foreign parts?"

"Ah! poor dear child! I think she's in a 'sumption,
Broom. She used to be purty as a picter, Broom; now she's
all pale and thin, and her eyes are hollow. She's never hearn
a word from that vilyun (God forgive me) that she married.
She's gone to the pos' office now, poor dear heart, to see if
there's a letter for her. She seen in a newspaper how the ship
that *he* went out in has comed back, and so she's gone. But
come in, Broom, out o' the cold; you shall see the child, poor
little cretur, by the kitchen fire—no! by the kitchen fire-place
—no fire there! Dunno when there will be."

"Why, you don't go to make out how the young madam
wants for anything, do ye?"

"Don't want for nothing, don't she? I tell you, Broom,
that vilyun (mercy on me) never left her a single dollar—made
out he'd want all the money to carry him to foreign parts. *I*
know, 'cause, you see, she wanted tea and sugar the day after
he went away; and so she sent her silver spoons to be sold—

sent 'em by me; and by the same token, the silversmiff where
I took them took the spoons away from me, and sent for a
cons'able, and had me 'rested on 'spicion of stealing them;
yes! and 'rested me there all day, till the young lady could be
sent for. Lor', Broom, how my feelings were hurted that day!
that ever Catherine Ann Gallagher should be 'rested for
stealin' silver spoons! You don't know how I was hurt!"

"I can 'magine, Katy; I can 'magine. You know, though,
you used to hear the ole madam say, as none of the people in
cities ever come ober with Lord Baltimore, so how can you
'spect better from them?"

"Well, I was going to tell you, Broom—but come in out
of the wind—there's the baby! The very image of the old
madam, aint he? There! don't wake him; sit down. I was
a-going to tell you, that after that, the young madam always
wrote a line when she sent me to sell anything; and she sold
almost all the silver she had, to buy things and pay rent; for
only think, Broom, people here have to pay for living in
houses!"

"Pshaw! I could have told you that long ago."

"I didn't know it. Well, there's nothing left to sell, now,
but the blade of the butter knife and her thimble—that's *silver*,
I mean; and what we are to do, now the winter's setting in,
the Lord knows. We been living on black tea and rye bread
all this summer. The poor child wanted me to go hire
out where I could get wages and better living; but no, I says;
if I've got a black skin, I've got a white soul; and I ain't a-
going to 'sert her in her 'fliction."

"No, no more I wouldn't, Katy. Dear, dear, dear," sighed
the old man; "this is *very* 'stressing, very! But couldn't
the young lady teach the pianner, or paint pictures, or diskiver
some rich relations, like the 'stressed ladies in the story books,
she used to read to us about?"

"Well, I often thinks o' that myself; and I thinks, what's
the good o' larnin' unless it helps people to get along in the

world. But, poor thing! her mind is 'sturbed enough. Sometimes she does walk about a whole day, looking for needlework; but she is a stranger, and gets no luck, and she comes
home, and mopes, and mopes. I 'vises her to smoke a pipe;
but she won't take 'vice. I tells her, if it hadn't a been for
smoking a pipe, I should have gone ravin' 'stracted mad, when
Colonel Hines (Heaven forgive him) sold my poor dear gal to
Georgy. My poor gal! my poor gal! your poor old mother
will never see you again in this world. My poor dear gal! all
the child I had in the world!" Here the poor old soul lost
recollection of everything but her own sorrow, and sobbed
hysterically.

"Don't cry, Katy! don't cry! that's a good 'oman!"

"Hush, Broom, hush! you never had no child sold away
from you."

"No, Katy, because my wife was sold away from me the
first year we were married, and I never had the heart to marry
again."

"My poor gal! my poor child!"

"Come, Katy, don't take on so; don't, that's a dove!"

When the old creature had exhausted herself with weeping,
she wiped her eyes. Then Broom said to her—

"You never told me, Katy, how it was that you were free
and your child a slave."

"Why, you see, Broom, I was left to Colonel Hines by his
uncle, but I was left to be free at twenty-five; and I had my
little gal before I had served my time out, and so she was a
slave. I had been living with Mrs Brotherton ever since I
was ten years old, and I was there when my poor gal was sold.
She tried to prevent it, but couldn't. You were gone with
Colonel Brotherton to the wars then. Don't ask me any more,
please, Broom;" and the old creature fell to weeping again.
At last, wiping her eyes. she said—   .

"Well, well! well, well! may be it will all come right in
another wor'd. Give me that bundle of chips, Broom; I

must make a cup of tea for Mrs. Middleton, against she comes. I wish I had a little wood, to make a fire in her room."

"Now, you stop, old 'oman. How long before she'll be back ?"

" An hour or so."

"Well!" said the old man, brightening up, "I'll just tell you what I goin' to do. I goin' after a load of wood and a basket of good things; and I'll just have 'em brought home, and don't you let on who sent them, 'cause the young lady might feel bad at 'ceiving a favour from the likes o' me, 'cause that's a little worser than anything we ever heard about in the books at night."

The old man was as good as his word. In an hour a blazing fire was kindled in Sybil's room, and the tea-table spread with nice white bread and fresh butter, while a pot of fragrant hyson was drawing on the hearth. The babe was awake, sitting on the carpet, blowing a whistle with great glee. At last Sybil entered, pale, languid, and weary, and, dropping into a chair, held out her arms to the babe, who crawled fast upon his hands and knees to reach her lap.

" Ah! she's got no letter," thought old Katy, as she came in to set the tea on the table.

"The silversmiff has been here, ma'am (Heaven forgive me for lying," muttered she to herself).

"The silversmith, Katy!"

"Yes, ma'am; and he fotch two dollars, as he said was due on the spoons; and so I took the money, ma'am, and bought some wood and some other things; (Heaven look over fibbing.")

" Very well, Katy, that was a Godsend, indeed; but you left the babe to do this."

"No, ma'am; old Uncle Broom 'rived this morning, and I got him to go."

" Poor old man! Has he travelled all the way up here? Send him in to see me, Katy."

"'Scuse me, Mrs. Middleton; but did you get a letter, ma'am?"

"No, Katy; but to-morrow I will go and see the captain of the vessel; perhaps he has a letter or a message for me."

THE CAPTAIN'S NEWS.

THE next morning, after an early breakfast, Sybil put her babe to sleep, and went her way in search of the captain of the packet in which her husband had left America. In going towards the vessel, she had to pass through crowds of coarse women and rough men, whose ribaldry caused her nerves to tremble and her cheek to burn with shame. At length, finding it difficult to reach the vessel, which was lying off the shore, she inquired where the captain was likely to be found, and was directed to his lodgings in the city. She hurried thither, was so lucky as to find him at home, and was shown into his presence. He was a fat, red-faced, self-satisfied looking man, who arose to receive her with rather an insolent leer.

"You are Captain Blackston, I presume?"

"At your service, miss."

"I am Mrs. Middleton."

"Ah! I beg your pardon, madam."

"My husband, Mr. Harold P. Middleton, went to Liverpool in your ship about six months since. I have come to inquire whether you have any letter or message from him for me, and whether he was in good health when he landed."

"Whew!" whistled the captain.

"Will you please to tell me, sir?"

"Why, madam, here seems to be a great mystery. Mr. Middleton, certainly, was my passenger to Liverpool; but he took with him a lady whom he called Mrs. Middleton, and whom I supposed to be his wife. Heavens! ma'am, don't faint here in my room!" exclaimed the captain, seizing the bell rope, and ringing an alarm.

"William!" cried he, energetically, to the man that answered the bell, "call a hackney coach for this lady."

Sybil mastered her emotion by a great effort, and entered the coach that had been called for her, for indeed her trembling limbs refused to convey her home. It took Sybil's last dollar, the produce of the sale of the butter-knife, to pay her fare. For many days, Sybil remained almost stupefied with grief, sometimes wandering restlessly about, sometimes sitting for hours in one mournful position, sometimes catching up her infant, and weeping passionately over it. Poor old Katy was distressed almost to death, but could not guess the cause of her acute sorrow. A few weeks from this time there was an arrival from Liverpool, and a few days after, Sybil saw a letter advertised for her in the paper. Too weak to go herself, she hurried old Katy off to the office. Poor old Katy was always sure to fall into adventures, when she was sent into the city. When she arrived at the post office, and was asked by the clerk what she wanted, she answered—

"That letter, if you please, sir."

"What letter, aunty?"

"Why, the letter from foreign parts, if you please."

"Yes; but whose letter?"

"Why, hizzen, sir, hizzen."

"What name, old woman?"

"Why, Mr. Middleton, the gentleman as went to foreign parts."

The clerk looked over his list, and answered—

"There is nothing here for Mr. Middleton."

"The letter ain't for Mr. Middleton, sir."

"For whom then, old woman?" said the clerk, growing impatient.

"Miss Sybil that was, sir—Miss Sybil Brotherton, of Brotherton Hall, come over with Lord Baltimore, sir," said Katy, curtsying at every clause.

"There is no letter here for Miss Brotherton."

"She's not Miss Brotherton now; she's Mrs. Middleton."

"Why, what a stupid old beast is this! Here, here is your letter."

"Thanky, sir! very kind of you, indeed, sir; thanky, kindly. I wouldn't take a golden guinea for this letter."

It was raining hard when Katy left the office, and she looked around in despair—for Katy had no umbrella. A hackney coach was standing near, and Katy looked longingly at it Observing this, the driver said, jeeringly—

"A hack, ma'am?"

"Thank you, kindly; yes, sir, if you please."

Finding a customer, the driver changed his tone, and let down his steps, and handed the old woman in with respectful alacrity, put them up again, jumped into his seat, and drove off.

"Dear me!" said old Katy, as she sat back in the carriage. "This is very nice and comfortable—so much better than sploshing through the mud and getting wet to the skin. I love the motion of a carriage, too—it tintillates one's feelings so pleasantly. What a very polite young man, to offer me a ride—so different from other people. Ain't he got manners? I shouldn't wonder if his family didn't come over with Lord Baltimore. What nice soft cushions!"

The end of this soliloquy brought Katy to Mrs. Middleton's door. The "very polite young man" jumped from his seat, and, letting down the steps, handed Katy out.

"I am very much obliged to you, indeed, sir, for your kindness, sir. I'll do you a favour whenever I have a chance."

"Very well; you're quite welcome; your money is just as good as anybody's else. It's a dollar."

"Sir?"

"It's a dollar."

"What's a dollar?"

"It's a dollar you owe me for bringing you home in my hack."

"Why, you invited me to ride in your hack, I never asked you; it was your own offer, and I thank you kindly. But you're not going to charge me, now, I hopes."

"Come, that's rich."

"Good-morning; I thank you kindly; I must go in now."

"Look here, old woman; none of your nonsense; hand me that dollar."

"I shan't do no such a thing! I shan't do no such a thing! You 'vited me to take a ride, and I rid; and now I know it was all to cheat me out of a dollar."

"See here, you old devil, if you don't pay me that dollar, I'll put you in the hands of a constable for swindling."

"Now, the mercy upon me; where am I to get a dollar from?"

Words now grew so high between the belligerent parties, that the noise drew Mrs. Middleton to the door; and great was her perplexity when she understood the cause of dispute —for poor Sybil was penniless. Telling Katy that she was in the wrong, and explaining to the hackman Katy's mistake, and promising to pay him the next day, Sybil separated the combatants, and, receiving her letter, she retired to read it. She opened it eagerly. There was no enclosure; and merely remarking that little Hubert would go without his flannel some time longer, she began to read. Her cheek grew pale and paler as she read, the letter dropped from her hand, and she sat as one stricken with epilepsy. Presently, the blood rushed back in torrents to her face, and, clasping her hands to her throbbing temples, she started up and paced the floor with irregular steps, exclaiming—

"Oh! the fiend! the fiend!—yet not the fiend, either, for there is something large about the devil, after all—the reptile! the reptile, rather! Coldly to tell me he does not care for me— falsely to tell me that he suspects my fidelity—to renounce his wife, to disown his child, and slander both, to colour his base- ness! Where sleeps the justice of God? What stays the thunderbolt, that it does not strike him down in his rampant wickedness?" And Sybil threw herself, writhing, upon the bed. The scathing thunder and lightning of passion passed, and the rain fell. Sybil wept as she murmured—

"Oh, Harold! Harold! I never thought to have felt towards thee thus! I never thought to have spoken of you so!"

Sybil sat, pale, exhausted, and alarmed, at the typhoon that had passed through her gentle soul

"Great God!" said she, "this, then, is passion! this, then, is anger! Oh! now, indeed, I know there is no need of a lake of burning fire; our bosoms may be a hell, as mine has just proved; our own passions may be tormenting fiends, if there be no others.'

Sybil sunk upon her knees and prayed; and from this moment may be dated the commencement of her true knowledge of God, of herself, of the value of life and the use of suffering, of the reality of another and a happier state of existence. Amid the confusion, the storm, the whirlwind of her excited passion, arose "the still small voice" that whispered, "Peace, be still," and "Be not afraid; it is I." Sybil arose from her prayer, calm, composed; prospects became clearer before her mental vision, and she thought—

"Though it is all over now with me and my husband, yet, now that I know the worst, I can bear it! I have no further thoughts of going to him. I must bestir myself to find some means of support for myself and child. I will trust to God's blessing on my best exertions. I will work and pray; and I shall succeed, I know I shall."

With newly inspired courage, Sybil put on her bonnet and shawl, and went to the door; but the rain, that again came down in torrents, arrested her purpose of going out.

Sybil was a good performer on the piano and harp, and she sought to obtain pupils in her art; but she was a stranger, without letters of introduction, and her efforts of course failed of success. She then thought of writing to her relative, General Bushrod Brotherton, the successful litigant in the suit in chancery, and the present possessor of Brotherton Hall. She wrote, and, telling him of her destitution, requested him to obtain for her the testimonials of some of her former neighbours.

———

GENERAL BUSHROD BROTHERTON.

A WEEK from this time she went to the post-office, hoping to receive her expected packet of testimonials. Before she came home, a storm of wind and snow arose and raged with great violence. Old Katy stood at the cottage gate, looking the picture of dismay, and whispering to herself—

"Poor thing! she'll catch her death; and then all her troubles will be over!"

In the midst of Katy's lamentation, a travelling carriage drew up before the door, a servant jumped off from behind, let down the steps, and an old gentleman, with a military air, alighted and walked towards the house.

"Well! bless the Lord! if here ain't General Bushrod Brotherton himself!" exclaimed Katy, in a low voice, as she hastened to open the gate.

"Well, old woman! *Katy*, are you not?"

"Yes, sir—Katy, sir—yes, sir," answered the old woman, curtsying at every two words.

"She's gone out, sir; she'll soon be home, sir. Will you come in?"

General Brotherton followed the old servant into the house, and in half an hour after, Sybil came home. Katy was on the watch for her, and, meeting her, said—

"Oh! Mrs. Middleton! who you think is here, ma'am? General Brotherton is in the house. Come round the kitchen way, to change your dress. I stole your best gown out of your room, for you to put on there."

Be it known to the reader, that there was no getting into Sybil's chamber but through the parlour; hence Katy's little piece of finesse. Sybil changed her dress quickly, and went into the parlour.

"My dear Mrs. Middleton, or my sweet cousin Sybil—if you will permit me to call you so—how pleased I am at this opportunity of making your acquaintance!" cordially exclaimed General Brotherton, advancing to meet her. General Brotherton was a tall, stout man, with a broad, rosy, good-humoured face, and gray hair. Sybil was rather prepossessed with his appearance, and received him kindly and gracefully. After a little unimportant conversation, and a few remarks that led to the subject, General Brotherton observed—

"I hope, my dear little cousin Sybil, you will do me the justice to believe that I would never have molested Mrs. Brotherton in the possession of her home during her life."

"Had she lived," replied Sybil, "Mrs. Brotherton would have acknowledged the kind intention, as I do, with deep gratitude."

"There is more I wished to say to you, my dear cousin Sybil; but I am a blunt old man, and may not know how to approach the subject with the necessary tact and delicacy, perhaps; and I may offend when I desire to please. If I do, you will forgive me, will you not, my dear cousin? Well, this is what I wished to say: First, I have received your letter, and that has brought me to town. Of that, more anon. Well; at the time my attorney entered suit for possession of the Brotherton property, I had heard that Mrs. Brotherton was dead, and that you, Sybil, had been some time married to a wild young fellow, the son of a man of wealth and family, and that you were both soon going to England. Hence the suit. But within a month, my dear cousin Sybil, I have heard another story—that my cousin's husband was an impostor and a villain; that he has left her and her child in poverty and want,

7

excusing his base desertion by charging her with conjugal in-
fidelity."

Sybil covered her burning face with her hands.

"Oh, Lord!" she groaned, "I did not know, I did not
dream, any one but myself knew of this!"

"It is all over our neighbourhood; but, of course, no one
believes the wicked lie."

"You need not tell me that, sir," exclaimed Sybil, suddenly assuming the air of an outraged empress. "It is not
within the wide range of possibility that my bitterest enemy,
even were he the most credulous of fools, *could* believe such
a thing! And I only wonder that any one should allude in
my presence to such a story."

"There, there," muttered the General, seemingly much mortified, "I knew I should offend—I am such a rough old wretch
—I blurt things out so."

His manner touched Sybil, and produced a reaction in her
feelings. She hastened to say—

"Forgive me, my dear sir; much trouble has made me
very irritable, and I cannot bear the least allusion to that
subject."

"Very well! All's right! Now, to come to the point and
purpose of my visit. He has left you—that is plain. He
has taken a foreign girl out with him—one Inez—Inez de—I
forget! but I heard all about it. Well! I have no nearer re-
lation than you in the world; and if you will return with me
to Brotherton Hall, and live with me and my old wife, and be
our daughter, and if you will apply to the Legislature for a
divorce, and have your son's name changed to that of Brotherton, I will execute a will, leaving, at my death, all the Brotherton property to you for your lifetime, and afterwards to your
son. Come, Sybil, what say you?"

The vision of wealth, comfort, ease, and her child's interest,
arose before her "mind's eye," her heart beat quickly, her
face flushed.

"Come, my dear little cousin! what say you?"

The "still small voice" whispered the moral bearing of the question, and Sybil's heart paused in its violent beatings to listen—the flush died away from her face.

"Come, my dear Sybil, your answer."

"Will you give me a few days to think of this, my dear sir? and in the mean time believe me most grateful, most deeply grateful, for your kindness."

"Selfishness, pure selfishness, dear Sybil. My wife and I are lonesome in the old house; we want company. Think of my proposition a whole week, if you will—I don't like hasty decisions myself; but give me an answer at the end of that time. But mind, cousin Sybil, my conditions are positively unalterable—for I know very well, if *one* condition is not insisted upon, that just as soon as my old head is laid low, and you in possession of Brotherton Hall, that fellow would be sneaking back, and then you'd receive him. I know—oh! I know you women so well. He'd be so penitent! and you so forgiving! and in five or six years the Brotherton estate would be lost at the faro table, and you would be beggared. Oh! I know—I know so well!" So saying, the old man took leave, entered his carriage, and was driven off.

Now, this proposition would not have tempted Sybil, had a single spark of affection or esteem for her husband remained in her bosom; but it was not so. Her regard for Middleton had rather been a girlish fancy, than a woman's deep affection; though, with a woman of Sybil's domestic tastes and affectionate heart, this regard would have deepened into love, had not all respect been so soon lost. It was not his dissipation, nor his brutality, nor even his desertion of her, that had alienated the heart of his wife, but the cold, fierce, determined malignity of mind—the unmixed, unredeemed, unredeemable depravity of heart manifested throughout their entire married life, but most plainly discovered in the only letter he had ever written to her. Sybil's heart, therefore, was not defended against the

solicitations of self-interest and maternal love by any affection
lingering there. The test of principle could therefore be
fairly applied to her unguarded, unsupported heart.

When the old man was gone, Sybil sat down to consider
She was a stranger and friendless; her money was all spent,
and her plate and jewelry all sold; her store of fuel and provisions nearly exhausted, and winter coming on. Lastly, and
worse than all, she was deficient in that spirit of enterprise and
energy required to meet the difficulties of her situation. Yet
her mental debate was not very long; for all her early impressions and all her religious principles were against the proposed measure. In a few hours, therefore, Sybil's mind was
fully made up.

The winter set in very cold. The air was frosty and nip-
ping; snow-clouds darkened the sky. The day on which Sybil
was to give her answer to General Brotherton dawned. It
was intensely cold. As Sybil arose from her bed, shrinking
and shuddering from the biting air, she covered up closely her
sleeping boy, saying—

"God bless thee, poor little one! You will freeze if I take
you up to-day."

She passed into the parlour, where Katy was attempting to
open the shutters. They were so bound with ice and blocked
up with snow, that it required considerable effort to push them
open; and then the dreary aspect abroad, the ground deeply
covered with snow; the sky, gloomily darkened with clouds,
was rendered still more dreary by the severely felt privations
at home.

"My dear Miss Middleton, you're shivering from head to
foot; let me go get your shawl," exclaimed Katy, with chatter-
ing teeth.

"Do, Katy. But, Katy, is there no wood left to make a
fire?" asked Sybil, shuddering.

"There's one blessed long log left. I going to split it up

now. 'Deed and 'deed, Miss Middleton, if I was you, I'd take
the child, and I'd go settle down on some o' my relations."

" Without an invitation, and perhaps without a welcome
either, Katy?"

"I dunno, I dunno, Miss Sybil! Cross looks don't bite
like this cold."

"No, Katy, but worse; one bites the fingers and toes, but
the other gnaws at the heart."

Katy made no reply, but went out, and soon returned with
her arm full of split wood, of which she made a fire.

"Now, Katy, what have we for breakfast?" inquired Sybil.

"One blessed pint of flour, and one teaspoon full of black
tea."

"Then, Katy, get it ready, and we will eat our last meal
by our last fire."

The poor meal was scarcely over, and the table removed,
before there came a knock at the door, followed by the entrance of General Brotherton, who, taking a seat at the fire,
unceremoniously exclaimed—

"Oh! my dear little cousin, this is dreadful weather for
travelling; yet we'll have to venture it; for when it moderates,
and this snow melts, the roads will be impassable for a fortnight. Come! can you get ready by to-morrow morning? I
wrote a week ago to the old lady, to look for us to-morrow evening."

"My dear cousin," said Sybil, "you must not think me ungrateful, if I decline your kind offer."

"Decline it! Upon what ground? Upon what ground?"

"I am not able to comply with its conditions."

"Which one? which one?"

"That of the divorce."

"Oh! is that all? Yes, you can; nothing is more easy.
It is only to apply to the Legislature, and"——

"Understand me, my dear sir. I cannot conscientiously

take any step towards the accomplishment of such a measure," said Sybil, gently.

"Um—hum-m—ah ha! I said so; I knew it; just like all other women—fools! stick to a bad man through thick and thin; and if he runs away, wear the willow fifty years for his sake. But look here, Sybil—my poor Sybil—don't weep; look at your child; look at him, and have a little mercy on his tender frame and his many wants," said the old man, pointing to little Hubert.

Sybil *did* look at her thinly clad and shivering child, and the appeal reached her heart; yet, mastering her rising emotion, she answered—

"I have! I have! I have thought of all that; and yet—and yet I cannot, *indeed* I cannot, do as you recommend."

"Then God help you!" exclaimed the old man, rising in pique; "I have no more to say. Good-morning, my dear."

"Won't you sit longer, cousin?" asked Sybil, timidly.

"No! no, I thank you. I shall be very busy all day to-day. I shall leave to-morrow."

The fire was dying out, and the room was getting chilly, so that Sybil did not press her invitation. She extended her hand cordially to the old man, as she said—

"You will remember, dear General, to get those letters for me."

"Yes, yes; I'll do that," said he. "Good-bye, cousin Sybil; farewell, little one," said he, shaking hands with Sybil, and caressing the child.

"Never mind," thought the old gentleman, as he entered his carriage, "I'll let her alone a while, and I'll bet before the month is out she'll be writing to me, revoking her decision."

The old man was gone, the fire had burnt out, and Sybil and her boy were left alone before the cold hearth. Sybil caught up the boy to her bosom, and wept bitterly. Suddenly she thought of the preacher whom she had heard the preceding

Sunday. The hopeful and comforting words of his discourse came back to her mind with a soothing influence. They did more; they inspired her with courage and energy.

"Yes," said she aloud, "that minister! why did I not think of him before? I *know* he is a good man, and he will advise me in what manner to set about procuring pupils. I will go to him at once."

THE PASTOR.

MRS. MIDDLETON arrived at the pastor's house, and was shown up into his study, and informed by the servant that Mr. Livingston would be with her in a few minutes. Sybil had changed very much since her first presentation to the reader. Though not yet twenty years old, the rose of youth had faded from her pale cheek; yet her fair complexion—large, clear, blue, serene eyes—her sweet serious lips—her gentle manner—and low sweet voice, and her mourning-dress, rendered her far more interesting than in her days of health and happiness. Sybil wanted self-possession, and she trembled slightly as she entered the pastor's study. The ten minutes, however, that elapsed before his entrance, enabled her to regain composure.

Mr. Livingston, the pastor, now entered. He was a man of about forty years of age, tall, slender, with dark hair and eyes, and strikingly handsome, notwithstanding a pale complexion and hollow cheeks. Mrs. Middleton was reassured by the kindly manner and gentle tones with which this Christian pastor greeted her.

"I hope you will pardon the liberty I take in calling upon you, Mr. Livingston. I am a stranger in this city, and I wish to open a small school, by which to support myself and child; and I have come to-day to solicit your assistance in my project, or at least your advice as to what steps it will be proper to take towards its accomplishment."

"You are a widow, I presume, madam?" said the pastor, glancing at Mrs. Middleton's mourning dress.

"No, sir," murmured Sybil, a burning blush mounting to her brow.

The pastor looked at her in doubt; then said—

"You are probably able to produce good references?"

"Sir?"

"You are provided with testimonials of moral and intellectual fitness for the profession you wish to enter upon?"

"I have no such testimonials, sir, just now; but I hope to receive some in a few days, from my native place."

"They are indispensable to your success, my dear madam, and I trust you will be able to procure them; if you do, I shall take pleasure in rendering all the assistance in my power towards the accomplishment of your object."

A quick flush passed over the pale cheek of Mrs. Middleton. She felt humiliated. She knew that she was suspected. She did *not* know that such was the case with every poor, needy, and friendless woman, especially if she be young, pretty, and a stranger. Sybil arose and took leave. Her parting look of suffering resignation smote upon the heart of the minister. He stepped after her, and said, gently—

"Give me your name and address, madam; I will call and see what can be done in your case to-morrow."

Sybil now recollected, with confusion, that she had not given her name. She did as he requested, and went her way home reassured, thinking—

"I was not mistaken, after all, in Mr. Livingston—such a calm and holy smile—such a sweet, soothing voice—and then his general manner, so gentle, though I saw he did not think justly of me; but my awkwardness and confusion impressed him unfavourably at first."

The next day the minister called. Sybil was in her chamber, putting her boy to sleep, so that the minister sat in her little parlour some ten minutes, before she made her appearance Mr. Livingston *had* been favourably impressed with Sybil; he was now confirmed in his good opinion by the appearance of her home. There is something about a dwelling, or the furniture of a dwelling, that will impress one favourably, or otherwise, with its occupant. Sybil's little parlour told her story. The furniture was a portion of that brought from Brotherton Hall, telling of decayed gentility. There was the rich old Turkey carpet, somewhat worn, that covered the floor; there were the crimson damask curtains, somewhat faded, that hung from the windows; there were the old-fashioned stuffed chairs—the large, unwieldy sofa—the heavy mahogany tables; and last, and most eloquent, were the fine old family portraits, all choice specimens of art, that hung upon the walls. There was a portrait of old Mrs. Brotherton, of Sybil's father and mother, and one of Sybil herself. One very characteristic thing I neglected to mention. It was three hanging shelves, containing Sybil's library of novels and romances. The observant eye of the pastor noted and drew conclusions from everything; but the portrait of Sybil in her blooming happy girlhood, arrested and fixed his attention. He was gazing upon it, in deep thought, when Mrs. Middleton came in.

"My dear Mrs. Middleton," said he, turning to meet her, "I must beg your confidence; you have told me that you are distressed; I see that you are reduced. I wish to devote my poor energies to your service; but, in order to serve you effectually, I would know more of your circumstances and expectations."

Sybil looked in his face. The noble frankness of the expression inspired her with confidence. She thanked him, and, with a flushed cheek and averted eye, she told her story. The minister listened with deep attention, and at the close of her narration he sought to direct her attention to the Great Source of strength and joy. Feeling her religious sympathies drawn out, Sybil related the emotion she had felt upon the receipt of her last letter, the whirlwind of anger that had shaken her

soul, her subsequent alarm and repentance, and the peace and
hope that had filled her bosom since.   To this *naive* confession
the pastor listened with deep interest; for by that glimpse
into the soul of Sybil he recognised a nature capable of the
highest religious and intellectual culture, and one therefore
likely to be refined in the seven times heated furnace of affliction.   Moral philosophy was the pastor's favourite study; and
men and women, with their trials and temptations, were the
books he read upon the subject.   The refined, the strong, the
tempted and struggling soul of Sybil Middleton attracted him
forcibly, and he resolved to watch, to shield, and strengthen
it in its contest.   But, of that, more by and by.   He did not
for a moment lose sight of the immediate object of his visit
—the temporal welfare of his intended *protegé*.   He discovered Sybil's musical proficiency, and advised her to com-
mence by instructing a few young ladies in that accomplishment,
and volunteered to go among his parishioners, and seek out
pupils for her.   Mrs. Middleton expressed her gratitude, and
the pastor arose to take leave.   His eye fell upon Sybil's book-
shelves, filled with romances, and a slight smile curled his lip,
as he asked—

"Is this your favourite reading, Mrs. Middleton?"

"In my days of ease and cheerfulness, I used to delight in
these books," answered Sybil; "but now"——

"But now you require the most precious thoughts of the
most holy writers to comfort and sustain you—books that you
can feed upon.   Shall I send you some such?"

"If you please, Mr. Livingston; I shall be very grateful.
But, indeed, you are too kind to me—to me, who have no
claim upon you, or any one else."

"Pardon me; you *have* a claim upon me, and a claim upon
society; and the claim is mutual.   Society demands of you,
that you cultivate all your natural gifts to the utmost, and use
them for its benefit.   You, then, have a right to demand of
society, *happiness*."

The minister took leave, and the same day went about among the members of his congregation to solicit pupils for his new *protegé*. The Rev. Stephen Livingston was more than popular among his parishioners; he had a rising name, and they were proud of him. Any enterprise, therefore, favoured by their pastor, was very likely to be highly successful. Mr. Livingston's *protegé* was enthusiastically taken up and excessively patronized by his congregation. A class of fifteen pupils was soon made up for Mrs. Middleton. Many of them, at Mr. Livingston's instance, paid in advance; and in that way Sybil's immediate wants were relieved. From this time, the light of hope sparkled again in the eyes of Sybil, the rose of health bloomed again on her cheeks. Her new profession introduced her among an intelligent and cultivated circle of acquaintances, some of whom, who were not too aristocratic to notice their children's teacher, eventually became warm friends. Mrs. Middleton became deeply yet healthfully interested in the progress of her pupils; and when her list of fifteen increased to thirty, nearly all her time in the day was taken up in attending upon them. The day would thus pass quickly and pleasantly away; for my heroine, reader, was of a cheerful and grateful temper, and did not call her daily occupation *toil*, nor her interest in it *anxiety*. Then upon her return home in the evening, she would find a blazing fire, and tea prepared in her little parlour, and perhaps a new book left by the pastor, awaiting her. When the weather would permit, little Hubert would be at the gate waiting, and would totter forth to meet her. At such times, the mother's heart would bound to meet her boy, and, catching him up in her arms, she would hurry into the house, and, sitting down, would strain him to her bosom, covering him with kisses the while. Katy, since she was no longer pinched with hunger or chilled with cold, was as blithe as a bird, and sung at her work all day long; while old Broom, who had run his visit into a permanent stay, employed himself in sawing and packing away wood for the

winter's use; in clearing up the garden, which he meant to
put under cultivation in the spring; and in attending to little
Hubert.

THE PACKET.

ONE cold, damp evening, near the spring, Sybil returned
home later than usual. It had been drizzling all day long,
and towards evening the rain had fallen in torrents. Sybil
had remained with the pupil whom she had last visited until
near dark, hoping that the rain would cease. At last, borrow-
ing an umbrella, she set out for home. How cheerful looked
her little cottage, with the lights gleaming through its parlour
windows! She entered the house, and, throwing aside her
cloak and hood, looked around for little Hubert. Not seeing
him, she passed into her chamber, where he lay asleep; kissing
him softly, and murmuring a blessing, she returned to the
little parlour. Everything was comfortable there; the wood
fire was blazing cheerfully; the tea-table was set, and Sybil's
work-stand and basket placed in the corner, with her rocking-
chair and footstool near it. Sybil sat down at her workstand
while Katy brought in tea.

"The parson been here, ma'am," said Katy; "waited for
you a good while; just gone away; left this book for you in
your work-basket."

Sybil took up the book, murmuring to herself—

"'Paley'; oh! Mr. Livingston is so kind! No one was ever
so kind to me before, except my poor old grandmother. But
what is this, Katy?" said she, about taking up a packet directed, in a strange hand, to herself, and bearing a ship stamp:
"who left this?"

"That! Yes, ma'am; he brought that, too, from the pos'
office for you."

Sybil tore off the envelope. It was a London paper. She
unfolded it, and read with astonishment and grief the follow-

ing notice, to which her attention was directed by a couple of pen strokes:

"DIED, at his residence in Portman Square, on the thirtieth of October, Harold Preble Middleton, son of the Hon. Fenton Preble Middleton, and grandson of the Right Hon. the Earl of Mainwaring."

The paper dropped from her hands, and Sybil fell into thought. She did not reflect upon the man who had oppressed, deserted, slandered her; she thought only of the lover of her youth, the father of her child, and her tears began to flow faster than she could wipe them away.

"Well, I declare, Mrs. Middleton," said Katy, coming in, "you have not touched a mouthful of supper. I took such pains with them sponge cakes, too; and the tea is best 'perial."

"You may take the table away, Katy," said Sybil, and, arising and passing into her chamber, she fell weeping upon the crib of her child.

GENERAL AND MRS. BROTHERTON.

To say that Sybil was the "inconsolable" widow of a man whom she had married upon a slight and insufficient acquaintance; who had remained with her comparatively but a short time; who had abused her even unto personal violence; who had forsaken her at her utmost need; aspersed her character, and disowned her child—to say this would be an incredible libel on her sanity. "Some natural tears she shed, but wiped them soon." She remained at home a fortnight, and occupied herself with making up her mourning, without thinking of the necessity of sending notes of explanation to her patrons, who were left by that omission to conjecture the cause of her protracted absence from her pupils. These conjectures at length reached the ears of the pastor, and he resolved to call and see Mrs. Middleton. He found Sybil calmly at work with her needle, while her little boy played upon the carpet. No change

in Sybil's looks warned him of what had occurred, so he said
to her playfully—

"My dear Mrs. Middleton, I have resolved myself into a
committee of inquiry, to ascertain the cause or causes of your
self-immersement."

In their lively moments, Sybil had always answered his
smiles with smiling, and his quibs with quiddities, but now
her grave countenance seemed to rebuke his jesting. Request-
ing him to be seated, she arose from her chair, and, taking
from her writing-desk the London paper, put it into his hands,
and, pointing to the obituary notice, said, while the tears arose
to her eyes—

"The knowledge of *that event* has kept me at home for
some time past. Will you please inform my patrons of it?"

Her large, tender eyes were raised to the pastor's face as
she spoke, and she observed with surprise and displeasure the
sudden, the involuntary flush of—*something* that lighted up
the pastor's face as he read. Well! I own it; for my part, I
do "expect perfection from human beings," at least from some
of us, and especially from Christian ministers; and I feel humiliated to be obliged to acknowledge the existence of a single
human weakness in Mr. Livingston; but so it was, the Rev.
Stephen Livingston, the fervent Christian, the beloved pastor,
the rising divine, had not lately, with his *whole soul*, worshipped one God, but in the temple of his heart *one niche* was
occupied by an idol. Little did he suspect this, however,
until, in perusing the paragraph, he discovered the real nature
of his regard for Sybil, by the sudden recollection of the possibility of its gratification. Reproaching himself immediately
and bitterly for this feeling, he returned the paper to Sybil,
saying coldly, as he arose to take leave—

"Mrs. Middleton, you may, and I hope will, command my
services in this distressing affair, whenever they may be required."

Sybil thanked him, and returned his cold " Good-evening, madam," with a distant " Good-night, sir."

" And now," thought the pastor, as he turned from the door, " I do not see that I have effaced *one* error of sinful exultation, by another error of studied coldness. Poor child! at the very moment that she required consolation, advice, and assistance, to leave her so abruptly, without offering a single word of comfort. I must certainly see her again soon, and make amends for this."

Mrs. Middleton also indulged in a soliloquy to this effect—

" I am afraid, after all, that I have a very bad, or at least a very conceited mind ; to think that I should be so vain as to suppose that Mr. Livingston was—that he felt—that the pastor thought"—Sybil durst not finish the sentence, even mentally, but, with a feeling of self-abasement, endeavoured to force her thoughts from the subject, after saying to herself—

" Yes, yes ; I have done the good pastor foul wrong by my vain suspicions. Well, well ; I will be more reasonable when he comes again, if, indeed, he *ever* comes, after my cold ingratitude."

The next day the pastor called with more *friendly* offers of assistance, and his visit passed off in the easy manner of their first acquaintance. At his suggestion, Sybil resolved to do many things, very necessary to be done, but which, with her limited knowledge of life, she would not else have thought of doing. For instance, the obituary notice was sent to some of the Baltimore papers ; a letter was written to General Brotherton, informing him of her widowhood ; and another letter was written to the Earl of Mainwaring, inquiring the particulars of Mr. Middleton's decease. Having assisted Sybil in all these matters, Mr. Livingston refrained from visiting her again. It was now, by missing it, that Sybil began to estimate the society of the pastor at its full value ; she also divined the cause of his absence, though no word or glance had hinted it—such is the mental free-masonry of affection.

A few weeks after this, when the spring had well opened, Sybil received a visit from General and Mrs. Brotherton. They had come to renew their generous proposal to Sybil, and, in the event of her rejecting it, to invite her to pass the first year of her widowhood at Brotherton Hall. In thinking of Mrs. General Brotherton, and in hearing her called by the General "the old lady," and "the old wife," and "my old lady," Sybil had pictured to herself a venerable woman, not unlike her departed grandmother. What was her surprise, then, when the General introduced her to a handsome, fashionable-looking Frenchwoman, really forty-eight, but apparently about thirty-five years of age. Sybil had heard, it is true, that General Brotherton, during his service in the old French war, had been taken prisoner, and, during his captivity, had fallen in love with and married the daughter of a French officer, but she had lately forgotten it. General and Mrs. Brotherton remained in Baltimore a fortnight, and, during that time, the old proposition to Sybil was renewed. As there now existed no obstacle to its acceptance, Sybil gratefully acceded to it, and began making active preparations for a removal to Brotherton Hall, the General superintending the packing *up* and *off* of the furniture, while Madame busied herself among milliners and mantua-makers, compelling Sybil to go with her on all her excursions. Though no two people could be more opposite in temper than the lively Frenchwoman and the thoughtful Sybil, yet (for this very reason, perhaps) they were strongly attached to each other. Sybil had parted with all her pupils, and taken leave of all her friends, and so she felt and looked very serious as she entered the carriage with General and Mrs. Brotherton, on the morning of her departure; so that Madame said to her—

"Come! *ma belle*, you put on a look of fortitude quite gratuitous, under the circumstances; for really, I cannot see

that it requires so much moral courage to reconcile you to a
black dress, when it becomes you so extremely well. If *I*,
now, with my dark complexion, were compelled to make myself hideous in widow's weeds, it might be a matter of regret;
but *you*—a fine girl like *you*—could not wear a more becoming
colour; therefore, leave that look of resignation, for I shall
neither pity nor praise you on account of it."

Sybil raised her eyes to the face of Mrs. Brotherton in
simple wonder.

"Ah! ah! *mignonne*," exclaimed Madame. "Your eyes
are quite large enough, and very beautiful, just as they are;
do not try to stretch them any larger; for, *en verité*, I think
your look of wonder even less attractive than your look of
martyrdom."

"She's not mad, cousin Sybil; at least, not *raving* mad,
although you may fear it. I assure you there is no danger.
Madame is a harmless lunatic," said the General, seriously

Sybil laughed, in spite of herself. The object of her two
relatives was effected; they had rallied her into cheerfulness.
It was in May. It was late at night, and the full moon was
shining brightly when they arrived at Brotherton Hall, and
Sybil re-entered the home of her childhood.

SYBIL'S DREAM OF HAPPINESS.

A YEAR had passed since the arrival of Mrs. Middleton and
her child at Brotherton Hall—a year during which she had
won the affection of her relatives, who esteemed her as a
daughter—a year dotted with a few bright days, the occasions
upon which her sometime pastor had blessed Brotherton Hall
with his visits.

Her letter to the Earl of Mainwaring had not been answered;
but then a voyage across the Atlantic, fifty years ago, was not
the afternoon excursion that it is now; so that Sybil waited
five or six months without anxiety At the end of that time,

8

she had written again, and, to insure the safe delivery of her
·etter at its destination, she had enclosed it to the American
Minister at the Court of St. James. She was now expecting
an answer to this last letter. The spring of 1800 opened
beautifully. The sunshine abroad was not more bright, warm,
and genial, than the sunshine of the breast enjoyed by Sybil
Middleton. At no period of her short life had Sybil been so
happy. By a judicious attention to the laws of physiology,
her early constitutional tendency to consumption had been conquered. By free exercise in the open air, and frequent bathing, she had attained high health ; and, during the course of
her acquaintance with Mr. Livingston, her intellectual faculties
had become greatly unfolded ; and now Sybil Middleton, in
the full developement and high enjoyment of mental, moral,
and physical life, dreamed that she was about to attain the
acme of human happiness; for one who had assisted her in
difficulty, advised her in prosperity, sympathized with her in
sorrow—one who had developed and cultivated her intellect,
enlarged and elevated her moral sense, enlightened and exalted
her Christian faith—one whom she loved and worshipped next
to God himself—had received her promise to become his wife.
It was with the candour of pure affection that Sybil expressed
the full joy she felt in giving him her hand. It is true that,
for some months past, Sybil had expected this proposal ; yet,
now that it had been made, she could scarcely believe in the
reality of her happiness. That Livingston, upon whose words
she had hung with such deep joy—that he from whose instruc-
tions she had derived such strength and comfort—he upon
whom she constantly depended for guidance—he whom she
revered and honoured first upon earth, and whom she had
lately grown to love with the whole strength of her earnest
soul—that he should take her to his bosom, to pass her whole
life with him, to bear his honoured name, to share his blessed
labours—oh ! this seemed a happiness too full for earth, and

Sybil trembled amidst her joy, as the day of their marriage drew near.

"In one short week, my own dear Sybil!—in one short week we meet again, to part no more on earth. Oh! the joy, the joy to feel that this is our last brief separation! for I have grieved to leave you, even for a few days, my Sybil!" exclaimed Mr. Livingston, as he folded his betrothed bride to his bosom.

"Oh! yes, in one week more," murmured Sybil; "yet, ah! my own love, I grow superstitious, and tremble lest this joy be too full to last."

She raised her head from his bosom, and looked into his face; their eyes met in a long, full, earnest gaze; again he pressed her to his bosom in a silent embrace. Ah! if they could have died in that embrace! They parted.

THE AWAKENING.

MR. LIVINGSTON, on his arrival at the parsonage late that night, found letters awaiting him. The first that arrested his attention bore a foreign mark; it was evidently from an acquaintance of his in London, and in answer to a letter of inquiry, written on the part of Mrs. Middleton. He took it up, opened the seal, and began to read. Did a basilisk blast his sight? Had he plucked up a mandrake to drive him mad? The paper fell from his cold hands; dashing his clenched fists against his burning brow, he groaned out—

"My God! my God! This is too much for humanity to bear! Let me die now!"

He rushed out into the air, and up and down, through the cool streets he walked, without calming the fever of his blood, or cooling the fire in his brain—up and down through the silent streets, muttering half-smothered words of despair and grief—up and down through the dark streets, with a strange light gleaming in his eyes, until morning dawned; then hurrying to his house, he shut himself up in his study, saying—

"No, no, I must not see her in this state of mind! I must strive to conquer this. Good God! shall I, who pretend to strengthen and console others, go mad, or die myself?"

When the sun arose, and shone into the study of the pastor, its beams fell upon a face that seemed to have grown old in a night. He was sitting at a little table facing the window; his face was pale and haggard, his eyes hollow, his gaze strained upon a text in the open Bible before him, his thoughts concentrated upon a point—long he remained so; at length his head drooped upon the book—he prayed; it was the first time he had dared to pray since the opening of the fatal letter; he was strengthened; he became composed—though all day long he remained in his study without refreshment, reading, praying, and meditating—though all night long he kept a vigil there, yet upon the following day, which was Sunday, he preached with his usual power and perspicuity. It is true that his congregation were shocked at his haggard countenance and shaking frame, and many of them made anxious inquiries concerning his health. Their pastor confessed that he was not well, and finally succeeded in escaping from his officious friends, and regaining the privacy of his home. Early on Monday morning, the pastor arose, and, having saddled his horse himself, mounted, and took his way towards Brotherton Hall. He was again changed. Not a vestige of emotion was visible in his face or manner. His countenance was sorrowful, but calm, resolute, and still. His manner gentle and serious, yet determined.

That day Sybil was sitting alone, at work, singing in the overflowing joy of her heart. The little boy was trundling a hoop in the yard, and ever and anon, his merry laugh and shout came in at the open windows. General and Mrs. Brotherton were out taking a ride. Presently, there was a sound of a horse's feet in the yard, a familiar foot-step in the hall, a hand upon the lock, and Mr. Livingston stood before Sybil.

His face was pale, and wore the impress of desperate sorrow, yet inflexible resolution.

Sybil had sprung to meet him, yet stood transfixed by his looks.

"Good heavens, dearest! what is the matter? Has anything happened?" exclaimed she.

"Sit down, Sybil," said he, gravely; at the same time taking a seat himself.

"Yes—I will—but, oh! indeed something *has* happened—I see it by your looks. Dear love, what *can* it be?" exclaimed Sybil, anxiously.

"Yes, Sybil, something *has* happened—something to change the whole current of our future lives. You are growing pale, Sybil; summon all your Christian fortitude, or, if your strength fail, call on Him who giveth freely. I have received a letter from my London correspondent on the subject upon which I wrote to him six months ago—you remember"——

"Yes! yes!—well? well?"——

"Well, Sybil!—my poor Sybil, we have been labouring under a fatal mistake—your husband is living!" Sybil fell back in her chair, deadly pale and faint. Mr. Livingston poured out and handed her a glass of water, which, when she had drank, she murmured—

"It is over— it is over—that happy dream."

Deceived by her quietness, the pastor went on to say—

"This was the way in which the mistake originated, Mrs Middleton"——

"You need not tell me! It is of no use! We do not care to know how the poison was distilled that has sapped our lives! We do not inquire where the dagger was wrought that is sheathed in our hearts"——

"Sybil! Sybil!—Oh, Heaven support her—her hands are icy cold—her breath comes thick and short. Sybil!—Oh! my poor Sybil—bear up under this; be resigned to the will of Heaven."

"Commonplace! commonplace! You'd say the same to a mother whose only child was about to be hung! 'Be resigned!' 'Bear up!' And have I *not* borne up? Have I *not* been resigned? *I*, that have suffered as no one ever suffered before me! *I*, that have been tried as no one ever was tried before me! Resignation! fortitude! What have they done for me, but to provoke upon my head a reiteration of trial, as if Heaven were making the experiment of how much sorrow a human being could bear, without going mad!"

"Now, may Heaven forgive your wild words, Sybil! Oh! Sybil! suffer me to pray with you, as in days past?"

"Pray!" exclaimed she, bitterly; "to whom, and for what? *Pray!* I've prayed all my life; and here I sit, a tortured, a blighted, a miserable woman! I would I were annihilated!"

"Oh! Sybil, if this were the *only* life, *still* you would have no excuse for such a frantic arraignment of Providence. But, oh! bethink you, this dark, this thorny, this sorrowful road, if we tread it firmly and patiently, will lead us to"——

"'Another and a happier world,' perhaps. I know nothing of it! I do not see it! I do not hear it! Away with it! I will none of it!——Give me—oh! give me happiness in *this* world, that I know." And Sybil, extending her arms pleadingly towards her lover, burst into tears. Struggling with a powerful emotion, the pastor turned abruptly, and walked to a window, at the opposite end of the room, where he remained a long time, apparently gazing out upon the landscape.

Laughing, jesting, and joyous, General Brotherton and his wife now entered the room, from their drive. Sybil slipped out, and fled to her chamber to conceal her emotion, while the pastor turned tranquilly to meet them.

Very early on the next morning, Mr. Livingston descended to the parlour. He was to leave Brotherton Hall after the family breakfast—to leave it with the probability of never returning—yet he resolved, before going, to put in execution a plan which he had matured during the night He had been.

very much shaken by the despair of Sybil. He knew her disposition better than she knew herself. He knew that there could be no risk in the plan he resolved to propose, in order to rouse all the energy of her soul, to throw off the weight of her sorrow. Through all this seeming stoicism, the pastor ever felt the wound that was festering in his own heart. The pastor had not been down many minutes, before Sybil entered. She was very, very pale, gentle, and subdued. Sinking, trembling, in a chair, she said, in a low, sad voice—

"Give me the letter now, my friend; I can read it now."

The pastor placed it in her hands. She read as follows:

" MY DEAR FRIEND : I have made inquiries concerning the person of whom you wrote me. The obituary notice in the London paper referred to the honourable Harold Preble Middleton, the grandson of the Earl of Mainwaring, a gentleman who has never left England, and who, besides, has left a widow and children in Portman Square. I have since learned that there is a relative of the family, bearing the same name, who spent three years in America. This person is represented to be a sort of genteel loafer, or aristocratic vagabond, who spends his time in ' going to and fro on the earth, and passing up and down in it;' a sort of amateur artist, and is now at Rome, studying the old masterpieces of painting. With him is an Italian woman, who passes for his wife—one Inez or Inice di Silva."

The letter was long, but it here left the subject of so much interest to Sybil; so, folding it up slowly and calmly, she returned it to Livingston. Sybil was composed, but it was the composure of despair, the quiet of weakness—the feebleness of nature was upon her. Her heart seemed melting, dying in her bosom ; and indeed she thought, and welcomed the thought, that this weakness was unto death. The pastor saw this, and felt the urgent necessity of rousing her.

" I am much relieved to see you have regained composure, dear Sybil."

"Yes—I have regained composure"—said she, sighing. "But, oh! my dear friend, I have lost your good opinion—I know it—I feel it; through the ravings of my despair, I have lost your esteem for ever."

"No, dear Sybil, my esteem for you remains undiminished; I never supposed you to be an angel, and I am not surprised to find you a woman."

"But you were so firm, so self-possessed, so calm."

"Yes, Sybil, after two nights of moral tempest; and my calmness was perhaps as much the effect of exhausted nature, as of reason or religion. We have both sinned, Sybil, not *hitherto* in our attachment—for that was involuntary, inevitable—but in the terrible arraignment of Providence of which we have both been guilty."

"Yes, yes. Oh! I feel that," said Sybil. "It is well for us, indeed, that our Father in Heaven is so long-suffering and patient with us. Listen, my friend; when I fled to my chamber last evening, I was mad! The very elements of my being were broken up—all was storm, confusion, chaos! and this storm raged through my soul until it exhausted my strength I felt as though the very earth had rolled from beneath my feet, and I had forfeited my claim upon Heaven. Eternal night seemed to have fallen upon my soul; I was desolate, forsaken, *cursed*. I was mad! I was tempted! The thought of self-destruction flashed into my mind, and I said, I will leave life, I will fly to death; and with the sophistry of passion I added, I shall not be as a rebellious subject, rushing unbidden into the presence of his king—no, no, but as a tempest-driven child, flying for refuge to the bosom of her Father. I started up, my grasp was upon the lock of the door, when a gentle hand, a weak infant's hand, held me back. I turned, and little Hubert was standing by me, looking with wonder and grief upon me—while he murmured, ' *I* love you, mamma.' Oh! my friend, can you understand the revulsion of feeling that overpowered me? I sank down where I was, and, fold-

ing the babe to my bosom, I wept; and as my emotion subsided, I became penetrated with a sense of my ingratitude and
sin, and I prayed; but oh! my friend, *before* I prayed, simul-
taneously with the first dawning of penitence came a sense of
forgiveness. God meets us more than half way with pardon;
he does not wait for the bended knee; he does not stay for
the forming prayer; he meets the first impulse of penitence
with forgiveness. I do not pretend to account for the existence of suffering, I do not clearly comprehend the use of trial,
but I know that God is good; I feel that God is love; I
believe that we are not tortured in vain. But I am an egotist
—I have talked too long; yet you have been in some sort my
father confessor, Livingston," added she, with a sorrowful
attempt to smile. The short-lived animation that had borne
her through this speech was fast dying away.

"No, dear Sybil, you have given me comfort," replied the
pastor.

He still called her "dear Sybil," for he could not bring
himself to address the failing, fainting woman before him, in
any but the language of tenderness. She had relapsed into a
fearful apathy—her form was still as death—her face was
ashy pale even to her lips—the very torpor of despair seemed
to have stupefied her—the very elements of existence seemed
resolving into dissolution. The pastor saw this with alarm,
and hastened to rouse her attention by the proposal of his
plan

"Listen to me, dear Sybil; there is hope for us yet."

"Hope!" echoed Sybil, unconsciously.

"Yes, hope. Attend to me, dear Sybil, if you please.
You remember the proposition made to you by General Brotherton about two years ago—you remember, Sybil?"

"Yes," said Sybil, absently.

"When General Brotherton is informed of the contents of
this letter, that proposition will be renewed. Do you not
think so?"

"Possibly," replied Sybil, indifferently.

"*Probably*, nay, certainly. What if you were to accept the conditions, and free yourself?"

Starting, half raising herself, bending forward, while the light brightened in her eyes and the colour warmed in her cheek, she exclaimed—

" Mr. Livingston, my friend, do *you* advise me to this?"

"Nay, Sybil—I advise you to nothing. This is a matter, above all others, upon which you must not take advice; but I *do* say to you, that it is worth investigation; and I promise, that if, after you shall have examined the subject by the light of the Holy Scriptures, with the aid of sincere prayer, you may religiously as well as legally free yourself, and enter a second engagement, I will then entreat you to bless me with your hand."

"But," said Sybil, reviving, "even if our own consciences were satisfied, such a marriage might impair your usefulness"——

" It might secure our happiness."

"No! as heaven hears me," exclaimed Sybil, warmly, "I would not purchase happiness, *even for you*, at the price of the faintest shadow upon your Christian character."

"Dismiss that from your mind, Sybil. Let us strive to understand the will of God. Let us strive to do that which is right in the sight of God, and leave the consequences with Him."

"Then tell me what is right, my own dear guide and mentor. I do not wish to go beyond you for direction in this difficulty. I am sure you know what is right, for you have seemed to stand between my God and myself, interpreting his will to me."

' No, Sybil! my gentle one, this is between God and your own conscience; it would be sacrilege to interfere. You must ' tread the wine press alone,' looking to Him for fortitude who entered it *alone* before you."

"Alas! alas! and I have no father or mother to advise with me, no brother or sister to comfort me, no friend when you are gone to sympathize with me."

"Dear Sybil, you are of all persons the best fitted to judge of your own case, by the light of religion; no one knows the circumstances as you know them."

"I am very well aware that it is considered extremely ill-natured to intrude upon lovers; but when they choose the family breakfast room, early in the morning, for their *tete-a-tete*, and less happy folks are hungry, how can it be avoided?" exclaimed the jovial old General, as he bustled into the room.

How his merriment jarred upon the excited nerves of Sybil!

"When I was wooing, we used to take woodland walks on such fine spring mornings as this. Ask madame—here she comes. I'm telling these transported people, Gabrielle, when you and I were transcendentalated, we did not stay about the house putting sensible people to inconvenience by taking possession of their breakfast room, keeping them from their chocolate. No; when *we* were etherealized, and left eating and drinking to people that were 'of the earth earthy,' we rehearsed our dreams and visions 'amid the vasty solitudes of nature,' as cousin Sybil's books call mountains and forests. Come! old lady," added he, patting his wife affectionately on the shoulder, "make them stir about—stir about. As I have been shooting at water fowl and not at hearts, this morning, I am smitten with a rather exacting affection for coffee and toast."

The General had lately affected to call his wife "old lady," —a *sobriquet* which the pretty Frenchwoman never failed to receive with a toss of the head, at once haughty, petulant, and graceful, which shook down her ringlets in the most becoming fall.

Breakfast was served; and immediately after it was removed, the pastor arose to take leave. He shook hands with Mrs. Brotherton, with the General, and approached Sybil with a sinking, dying heart—with a reeling brain. Well he knew that this was the last, last time he should ever behold her. Truly he felt that he should never, *never* again, see her face, hear her voice, touch her hand—the woman towards whom his whole being tended with a force, by an attraction, almost impossible to be checked. His heart sank, his brain reeled, his voice quivered, yet his words were cold.

"Mrs. Middleton, farewell."

"Good-bye," said Sybil, as her cold hand fell heavily from his grasp.

That cold, conventional leave-taking, amid the merry group! and with their bursting hearts! Well, perhaps it was better.

"'*Mrs. Middleton!*' Well, I call Venus, Cupid, and Psyche, and all the Muses and Graces, to witness that I never called the old lady by any name than 'Flower,' 'Star,' 'Pearl,' 'Angel,' 'Seraph,' or '*Gabrielle*,' that meant each and all, from the moment of our engagement until some three or four weeks after marriage!"

Livingston was gone.

"Why, cousin Sybil, what do you intend to do with such an icicle as that? Decidedly, that man has mistaken his vocation. He was intended for a monk. Sybil! Heavens! What is the matter? Wife! come here; she's ill—she's got an inflammation on the brain—her hands are cold as ice, her head as hot as fire—her eyes are wild. Sybil! speak to your old cousin; how do you feel?"

"What is Good? What is Evil? Where is God?" asked Sybil, wildly.

"Oh; my good gracious; she's mad, raving mad. Old lady, I say! All owing to that strong coffee—destroyed her nervous system. All owing to coffee and novels—drinking strong coffee and eating—I mean *reading*—novels, I know."

"You know nothing about it. Leave the room, General— you're like a bear nursing a baby," said Mrs. Brotherton. coming in.

"Yes; but Gabe—I mean *old lady*," amended the General,
spitefully—"she's very ill, I tell you."

"She is not. It is a rush of blood to the brain—nothing
more. Leave her to me."

The General left the room, grumbling, "she's *my* cousin,
Gabrielle—not yours."

Madame looked after him with a fond, quizzing smile.
She understood the *pathology* and treatment of overwrought
passion as well as a Parisian doctor. Delicately refraining
from expressing any surprise, or asking any questions, she applied the necessary remedies, and soon restored her patient to
composure.

Livingston had succeeded, by an almost superhuman exertion of will, in subduing all outward demonstrations of emo
tion while in the presence of Sybil. Leaving Brotherton
Hall, he spurred his horse into a furious gallop, as though he
would ride away from himself, or win the race of sorrow; and
rustics, who saw him shoot past like an arrow, surmised that
he carried an express. Then, again, he would permit his
horse to fall into a slow walk, as though he were pursuing a
journey without object or aim; and those who knew his
person, might have conjectured that he was meditating his
next Sabbath's discourse. He was tempted—for he knew that
it was with himself—*himself*—that this question rested at
last. He knew that the woman whose mind he had developed,
whose heart was all his own, over whom he possessed un-
bounded influence, who never questioned his rectitude of principle, who seldom exerted her own moral agency, if *he* were
at hand to decide for her—he felt that this woman could not
fail to be won by his arguments to any course he should point
out to her; and he felt that he was responsible not only for his
own moral welfare, but for hers also—and he *loved* her moral
welfare, above all things he loved that, and he regretted the
feminine softness of character, that while it made her so
sweetly attractive, left her so much at his disposal; and he

wished that corrected, and he knew that this trial would effect
its cure, by calling out all the latent energies of her really
strong soul, by arousing the sleeping strength of her pure
moral sense; and he had no fears for the result; he knew the
features of her mind, as a mother knows the face of her child;
he knew that she would suffer, struggle, but *overcome*. And
he knew that her soul would come out from this struggle, pure
as gold from the furnace, strong as steel from the tempering,
healthful as a young giant from the wrestle. But, then, to
lose her—*to lose her!* Oh! those three words expressed for
him the very alpha and omega, the *all* of mortal agony—and,
at the thought, he would feel exasperated to spurn away all
his earthly usefulness and interests, to forego all his heavenly
hopes and aspirations, to possess her—and *would* have done
so, but for the *right-directed will*, the calm, the inflexible, the
unchanged, the immutable will—the regal will—that sat re-
straining, directing, governing, subduing, this revolt of the
passions, like an upright judge amid an excited populace.

The pastor reached home, and commenced preparations to
remove to the South. And thus it is—whenever two people
are disappointed in love, the man goes away somewhere, flies
to the North or the South Pole, or makes a balloon voyage to
spend a winter in the moon, and speedily effaces old impressions by new ones—while the woman, poor thing, is left to
brood over her disappointment, amid the very ruins of her
tumbled-down castle from the air, surrounded by all the asso-
ciations of her past joy—taking the same walks, and missing
one from her side—sitting in the same parlour, at the same
hour, logically looking for the same form, listening for the
same voice, "waiting for the steps that come not back." Decidedly, she would break her heart, but that some old aunty
reminds her that men are not worth breaking hearts for; and,
besides, broken hearts have gone out of fashion, and women
don't like to be unfashionable.

THE STRUGGLE.

But Sybil, poor Sybil, with her strong affections, her fervent aspirations after right, her feebleness of will, her nervous temperament, and her terrible trial!

When General Brotherton had read the letter that had been silently placed in his hands by Livingston at leaving, the old gentleman's rage exploded and scattered consternation throughout his household. You would have supposed, to have heard him, that he considered the continued existence of Middleton as the very climax of his crimes. If he ever dared to set foot in America, he would hang him up with his own hands, as he would a thieving cur. He wouldn't wait for that—he'd go to Rome, old as he was, that he would, and shoot the fellow like a mad dog. And the old gentleman drove the dogs from the room, kicked the cat, scolded the servants, and frightened the child, by way of convincing people that he meant what he said.

After a few days, having reconsidered the subject of setting Providence right in this matter of life and death, General Brotherton renewed his former proposition, and pressed Sybil to its adoption—using all the arguments that his clear, logical, worldly view of the affair could suggest. Sybil, whom the surges of emotion, that had swept over her, had left quiet and weak, replied, that she would *think* of it.

"She will 'think of it.' Gabrielle! do you hear? She 'will think of it;' that's a great point gained. It's easy to perceive that her desire for the crown of martyrdom is considerably diminished. I should judge the parson had set her right upon some points of Christian doctrine."

And Sybil did think of it—until her brain reeled and her reason tottered. She did not examine the moral and legal authorities upon the subject, for she did not possess a logical mind, and she said, properly enough, "They will only confuse my mind with their arguments and counter arguments, for half the time they are more desirous to conquer in controversy, than to find truth; but I will go to the fount of light and truth —I will go to the Bible;" and she went to the Bible, and she searched with care, with eagerness, with breathless avidity, *with an earnest desire to find that which she sought*—Christian permission to free herself; and she found that there is but one cause for which a man may divorce his wife, and *no cause, none*, for which a woman may divorce her husband and marry again. There is something in Bible truth that heals while it probes, that strengthens while it chastises. He who laid down this seemingly partial law understood the hearts of women, and knew the comparatively spiritual nature of their affections. He who delivered this stringent command was himself steeped to the lips in suffering, was himself "tempted in all things *as we are*." Never before had Sybil so *sympathized* (thus to speak) with the Saviour's sufferings, never had she *so* realized the Saviour's temptations, never had she so received the great lesson of the Saviour's life and death, as now, when, "searching the Scriptures" in sorrow and temptation, and in the tenderness of her melted heart, she breathed forth—

"Not all thy promises, oh! Saviour, affect me so much as thy example and thy sufferings. I will bear my cross, even so, Sufferer and Saviour, for it was thy way."

All emotion, even religious emotion, is short-lived, and not to be trusted. The only permanent safety is in a clear conception of duty, and a resolute determination to act up to it, looking to God for strength. So true is this, that through all their teaching, the Saviour and his Apostles seldom or never appeal to passion or imagination—generally to reason.

Sybil's religious enthusiasm subsided, and then came the temptation in its might—the temptation of a lifetime, the trial of principle, the test of faith, the crisis of character—the point upon which all that could blind to right, all that could tempt to evil, were brought to a focus. To every one who has passed unsullied through the lesser temptations of this world, to every one upon whom the common trials of life have had little influence, to every one who has attained a certain moral point of elevation, there comes once in life one trial of pre-eminent strength, one temptation of almost irresistible might, one test of infallible truth—a temptation, through the most powerful passion of the soul, of the weakest point in the character. This touchstone may be applied in youth, in mid-life, or in age; and the result is almost invariably *final*, giving the bent to character for time and for eternity. To one whose besetting sin is *avarice*, this test may come in the shape of some rare chance to secure a great pecuniary profit, at the cost of a slight departure from rectitude; and it may come in a time of great penury and severe privation, and it may offer affluence at the price of integrity. How severe his struggle then! Will he stop to inquire, "What shall it profit a man, if he gain the whole world, and lose his own soul?" To one of a higher grade, for whom wealth has but little attraction, but to whom the applause of men is as the breath of life, it may come, this touchstone, in the form of some golden opportunity of securing popular favour by a slight deviation from the straight line of duty—as when some great statesman, whose popularity is fluctuating, is tempted of his ambition to engage in some popular but unholy cause; it may come when his favour with men is at the lowest ebb, and it may place within his reach the very prize of his life-long hopes, the very god of his life-long aspirations—requiring of him only to overleap some obstacle of duty to reach it, to let fall some principle of justice to grasp it. Will he, the tempted, then feel that "the friendship of the world is enmity with God?" and will he remember that the most unpopular man on earth, during his life, was "Jesus of Nazareth, whom they *crucified?*"

And to those for whom neither the applause of nations nor the wealth of the Indies have attraction sufficient to draw from duty, but who are gifted with ardent affections, and whose

9

dearest and most importunate sin is to bestow love and worship, due only to the Creator, upon the creature—to them comes an opportunity of satisfying to the full the strong and craving affections, at a sacrifice of principle seemingly *so* trifling as not to subject them to the strictures of the most moral community, or exclude them from the communion of the most puritanical Christian church, but which the microscopic eye of a faithful conscience will detect and expose. Will the tempted then remember, that, if duty demand it, the right hand must be cut off, the right eye plucked out, *Isaac offered up ?*

In all her former sorrows, Sybil Middleton had been simply a passive sufferer, bearing meekly the troubles which she could not avert, but exercising no moral agency, practising no self-denial, achieving no victory. True, the mild virtues of patience and resignation had been brought out, but these were natural to Sybil hitherto; she could not have been otherwise than resigned and patient under suffering. But now there came a far greater trial—a duty demanding not self-immolation only —oh, no! that would have been comparatively a light grief, a slight test—but the sacrifice of one dearer than self, the casting out of the object of the heart's fondest affections, the hurling down of the idol of the soul's highest worship. The struggle was long and fierce; nights of watching, days of tears, weeks of sorrow, passed before Sybil could turn a deaf ear to the solicitations of affection and of interest, and resolve to be true to her present conceptions of duty. At last she took a pen, and wrote to Mr. Livingston as follows:

"Mr. LIVINGSTON : I have decided. We must meet no more. We must write no more. Let an ocean of silence and distance freeze up between us. Let us die to each other.
SYBIL."

Not until this letter was sealed and sent, did Sybil realize that all indeed was over. She threw herself upon the lounge —she buried her head in the pillows, as if to shut out all

sight and sound, writhing and quivering as though in the
extremity of mortal anguish—then starting from her couch,
and tossing her wild hair from her face, she walked the floor
with nervous and irregular steps, wringing and twisting her pale
fingers together; and when this passion had exhausted its
victim, she lay in the apathy of despair, content with the
silence, darkness, and repose of her chamber—dreading light,
sound, or disturbance—scarcely wishing for a change, though
that change might bring happiness. Alas! for the reward
of an approving conscience; alas! for the triumph of a
victory over temptation; alas! for the support of conscious
rectitude. She felt none of these consolations now—*none*.
It is not in the first moments of such a victory, the soul
exhausted with its struggles and prostrate with its sufferings,
that such comfort can be received. It is not at the instant
that the right hand is cut off, that the right eye is plucked
out, and the wounds are still smarting and bleeding, that one
feels it to be "better" so. It is not at the moment in which
the most cherished object of the affections, which has become
entwined with every fibre of the heart, is first torn away, and the
severed tendons are lacerated and bleeding, that they can clasp
any support, or repose on any pillow. The time of strength
and joy does come—and it comes in beauty, in glory, and in
permanency; but it dawns gradually as the morning after a
night of storms and darkness. Sybil gradually obtained composure, by degrees became interested in her daily avocations,
and eventually grew happy, realizing that happiness does not
consist in the accomplishment of our dearest wishes, but in
the cultivation and exercise of our virtues.

I have dwelt too long upon the trials of Sybil, trials which
were all comprised in the passage of a few years, which were
acutely felt only for a few weeks. She had received the
attacks of some severe troubles, and sustained the shock of
one terrible disappointment; yet, now that she has survived
the snows of seventy winters, now that her form is bowed, and

her hair is white with age and not with grief, you might look
upon that calm face, and believe that grief had never convulsed
it; upon that clear brow, and believe that care had never
clouded it; into that serene eye, and think that tears had
never dimmed it.   And more—you may hear it often observed,
that " Mrs. Middleton has a very young-looking face for her
age;" and the reply, " Yes, very; but then, she has never had
any trouble to make her look old"——and that is all *they*
know about it, reader !

And the pastor ! Livingston obtained a pastoral charge in
the South.   He became eminent as a theologian, a philanthro-
pist, and a moral philosopher; yet people said that in his
private life he was a cold, severe ascetic, proof against all
tender impressions—a very woman-hater; and that was all
they knew about it, reader !

Verily, " The true greatness of human life is almost alto-
gether out of sight "

THE IRISH REFUGEE.

———◆———

The only son of his mother, and she was a widow.—LUKE vii. 12

> Long years shall see thee roaming
>   A sad and weary way,
> Like traveller tired at gloaming
>   Of a sultry summer day.
> But soon a home will greet thee,
>   Though low its portals be,
> And ready kinsmen meet thee,
>   And peace that will not flee.—PERCIVAL.

IT was a lovely morning, that last Saturday in July, 1849. The sun had not yet risen, when our family party, consisting of Aunt and Uncle Clive, Cousin Christine and myself, took seats at an early breakfast table. A capacious carriage, well packed with presents for country cousins, stood at the door, ready to convey us to Virginia, to spend the month of August. We, a merry set of grown-up children, were too delighted with our prospective pleasure, to eat anything, and so we soon left the table, and put on our bonnets and hats, preparatory to a start. We entered the carriage.

"Now, then, are we all ready?" asked Uncle Clive.

"Yes," replied aunt.

"Has nothing been forgotten?"

"No.—But stay! Where is Cousin Peggy's cap, Chrissy!"

"There—pinned up in that paper, to the roof of the carriag⸲ Don't hit your head against it, uncle."

"Clive, where did you put the basket of bread, and butter, and cold chicken?"

"There—in the bottom of the carriage. Be careful now, my dear, or you will get your feet into it."

"No, I shan't. But hadn't you better put the band-box, with Martha's bonnet, inside here?"

"Indeed, mother," interposed Miss Chrissy, "there is no room for it; for cousin Peggy's bundle is on one side, and the keg of crackers on the other; my feet are resting on the caddy of tea, and the loaf of sugar and paper of coffee are in my lap!"

"There! let's get along," said Uncle Clive, impatiently. "I declare, the sun is already half an hour high, and a ride of forty-five or fifty miles before us. We shall not reach Willow Glade before ten o'clock to-night."

"Yes, and about nine o'clock we shall be going down Bloody Run Hill, and I never can go through the piece of woods between that and Gibbet Hill, after dark, without horror."

"Ever since the pedlar was murdered."

"Yes, ever since the pedlar was murdered, and before too."

Uncle Clive now jumped into his seat, and taking the reins, we set off at a pretty brisk rate.

"Clive, don't that horse look a little vicious? See how he pricks up his ears!"

"Pooh! Nonsense! He's as safe a horse as ever drew."

"What o'clock is it now?"

"Humph! half past five. I think the next time we wish to get off at sunrise, we had better arrange to start at midnight; then, perhaps, we may succeed."

Turning the corner of the street at this moment, the sudden sight of the river, and the wood on the opposite bank, glimmering and glistening in the light of the morning sun, elicited a simultaneous burst of admiration from our travellers. Then the prospective pleasures of the rural visit were discussed, the family and friendly reunions, the dinner parties, the fish feasts upon the river's banks, the oyster excursions and crab expeditions; and in such pleasant anticipations, the cheerful hours of that delightful forenoon slipped away; and when, at last, the heat of the sun grew oppressive, and our sharpened appetites reminded us* of the dinner basket, we began to cast around for a cool, dry, and shady spot, on which to rest and refresh ourselves. The road, here, was wide, and passed through a thick forest. A few more turns of the wheels brought us to a narrow foot-path, diverging from the main road, into the forest, on the left-hand side.

" Let's get out here, Clive, and follow this path; I know it. It leads to a fine spring, with an acre or two of cleared land about it, on which there was once a dwelling."

This was agreed upon; and we all alighted, and took the path through the wood. We had not gone many yards, ere a scene of woodland beauty opened to our view. It presented an area of about four acres of open land in the midst of the forest. From the opposite side, a little rivulet took its rise, and ran tinkling and splushing, in its pebbly bed, through the centre of this open glade, until its music was lost in the distance in the forest. But the most interesting object in sight, was a ruined cottage. It was very small. It could not have contained more than two rooms. In front, there had once been a door, with a window on each side; but, now, both door and windows were gone.

The solitary chimney had fallen down, and the stones, of which it had been built, lay scattered around. A peach-tree grew at the side of the cottage, and its branches, heavy with the luscious fruit, drooped upon the low roof. A grape vine grew in front, and its graceful tendrils twined in and out, through the sashless windows and the broken door. A bird of prey was perched upon the house, and, as we approached with a fearful scream it took its flight.

"Be careful, Christine, where you step; your foot is on a grave!"

With a start, and a sudden pallor, Christine looked down upon the fragment of a grave-stone. Stooping, and putting aside the long grass and weeds, she read: "The only CHILD of his mother, and she a widow."

"Whose grave could this have been, mother? The upper part of the stone, which should bear the name, is gone. O, how sad this ruined cot, and this lonely grave! I suppose, mother, here, in the heart of the forest, in this small cottage, lived the widow and her only child. The child died, as we may see, and she—Oh! was the boon of death granted to her at the same moment? But, who were they, mother? As your early life was passed in this part of the country, you surely can tell us."

Aunt Clive, who had been gazing sadly and silently on the scene, since giving the warning to Christine, said—

"Yes, I can tell you the story. But here comes your father, looking very tired and hungry; and, as it is a very sad tale, we will defer it until we have dined."

We spread our repast upon the grass, and seating ourselves upon the fragments of the broken chimney, soon became engrossed in the discussion of cold chicken, ham, and bread. As soon as we had despatched them, and repacked our basket, and while we were waiting for the horses to feed and rest, Aunt Clive told us the following tale of real life:

THE IRISH EMIGRANTS.

A SHORT time previous to the breaking out of the Rebellion in Ireland, a family of distinction came from that country to America, and purchased and settled upon a handsome estate near the then flourishing village of Richmond. Their family name was Delany. With them, came a Doctor Dulan, a clergyman of the established church. Through the influence of the Delanys, Doctor Dulan was preferred to the rectorship

of the newly established parish of All Saints, and subsequently
to the President's chair of the new collegiate school of Newton
Hall. This prosperity enabled him to send for his son and
daughter, and settle with them in a comfortable home, near
the scene of his labours.

It was about the fifth year of his residence in Virginia, that
the Rebellion in Ireland broke out, and foremost among the
patriots was young Robert Dulan, a brother of the Doctor.
All know how that desperate and fatal effort terminated.
Soon after the martyrdom of the noble Emmett, young Dulan
was arrested, tried, condemned, and followed his admired leader
to the scaffold, leaving his heart-broken young wife and infant
boy in extreme penury and destitution. As soon as she recovered from the first stunning shock of her bereavement, she
wrote to her brother-in-law, soliciting protection for herself
and child. To this the Doctor, who, to great austerity of
manners, united an excellent heart, replied by inviting his
brother's widow to come to Virginia, and enclosing the amount
of money required to supply the means. As soon as the old
gentleman had done that, he began to prepare for her reception. Knowing that two families seldom get on well beneath
the same roof, and with a delicate consideration for the pecu
liar nature of her trials, he wished to give her a home of her
own. Selecting this spot, for the beauty and seclusion of its
position, as well as for its proximity to his own residence, he
built this cottage, enclosed it by a neat paling, and planted
fruit trees. It was a very cheerful, pretty place, this neat,
new cottage, painted white, with green window shutters; the
white curtains; the honeysuckle and white jessamine, trained
to grow over and shade the windows; the white paling, tipped
with green; the clean gravel walk that led up to the door, the
borders of which were skirted with white and red roses; the
clusters of tulips, lilies, and hyacinths—all contributed to make
the wilderness "blossom as the rose;" and every day, the

kind-hearted man sought to add some new attraction to .h
scene.

One evening, the Doctor had been over to the cottage, superintending the arrangement of some furniture. On his return
home, a servant brought a packet of letters and papers.
Glancing over one of them, he said—

"Elizabeth, my daughter."

A prim, young lady, in a high-necked dress, and a close-
fitting black-net cap, looked up from her work, and answered
in a low, formal voice—

"My father."

"Your aunt and cousin have at length arrived at the port
of Baltimore. They came over in the Walter Raleigh. I
wish you to be in readiness to accompany me to-morrow, when
I go to bring them down."

"My father, yes," were the only words that escaped the
formal and frozen girl.

A week after this conversation, the still life of the beautiful
cottage was enlivened. A lovely boy played before the door,
while a pale mother watched him from within. That pale
mother was not yet thirty years of age, yet her cheeks were
sunken, her eyes dim, and her hair streaked with silver.
Truly, the face was breaking fast, but the heart was breaking
faster. But the boy! Oh, he was a noble child! Tall for
his age (he was but five years old), his dark hair, parted over
a high, broad forehead, fell in sable curls upon his shoulders;
his large black eyes, now keen and piercing as the young
eagle's, now soft and melting as the dove's. His dark eyes
wore their softest shade, as he stole to his mother's side, and
twining his little arms around her neck, drew her face down
to his, saying, with a kiss, "Willie is so sorry!"

"For what should Willie be sorry?" said the mother, tenderly caressing him.

"Because mamma is sad. Does she want Willie to do anything?"

"No, sweet boy, she wants nothing done that Willie can do."

"If mamma's head aches, Willie will hold it."

"Her head does not ache."

"If mamma wants Willie to stop teasing her and go to bed, he will go."

"You are not teasing me, dear Willie, and it is rather too early for you to go to bed."

The widow strove to chase the gloom from her brow, that she might not darken by its shadow the bright sunshine of her child's early life, and with an effort at cheerfulness she exclaimed—"Now go, Willie, and get the pretty book cousin Elizabeth gave you, and see if you can read the stories in it."

Willie ran off to obey with cheerful alacrity.

The Doctor was not able to do more for his sister-in-law, than to give her the cottage, and supply her with the necessaries of life; and to do this, he cheerfully curtailed the expenses of his own household. It was delightful to see the affectionate gratitude of the widow and child towards their benefactor. And that angel child, I wish I could do justice to his filial devotion. He seemed, at that early age, to feel as though he only lived to love and bless his mother. To be constantly at her side, to wait upon her, even to study her wants and anticipate her wishes, seemed to be the greatest joy of the little creature.

"Willie, why don't you eat your cake?" asked his uncle one day, when Willie had been sent over to the Doctor's on an errand, and had been treated to a large slice of plum-cake by his cousin Elizabeth.

Willie silently began to nibble his cake, but with evident reluctance.

"Why, you do not seem to like it! Is it not good?"

"Yes, sir, thank you."

"Why don't you eat it then?"

"My father," said Elizabeth.

"Well, Miss Dulan?"

"I think that Willie always carries every piece of cake he gets to his mother."

"But why not always prevent that, by sending her a piece yourself?"

"Because, my dear father, I think it may be wrong to restrain the amiable spirit of self-denial evinced by the child."

"Then you are mistaken, Miss Dulan; and recollect that it is very irreverent in a young lady to express an opinion at variance with the spirit of what her father has just said."

Elizabeth meekly and in silence went to the pantry and cut a piece of cake, which she carefully wrapped up and gave to Willie, for his mother. Willie received it with an humble and deprecatory look, as if he felt the whole responsibility and weight of the reproof that had fallen upon his cousin.

One Christmas eve, when Willie was above seven years old, the widow and her son were sitting by the cottage hearth. The closed shutters, drawn curtains, clean hearth, and bright fire, threw an air of great comfort over the room. Mrs. Dulan sat at her little work-table, setting the finishing stitches in a fine linen shirt, the last of a dozen that she had been making for the Doctor.

The snow-storm, that had been raging all day long, had subsided, though occasionally the light and drifted snow would be blown up from the ground, by a gust of wind, against the windows of the house. "Poor boy," said the widow, looking at her son, "you look tired and sleepy; go to bed, Willie."

"Oh! dear mamma, I am not tired, and I could not sleep at all, while you are up alone and at work; please let me stay up, but I will go to bed if you say so," added he submissively.

"Come and kiss me, darling. Yes, Willie, you may stay up as long as you like." "I will go to bed myself," added she, mentally, "so as not to keep the poor boy up."

"Well, Willie, I will tell you a story, darling, which will amuse you, while I sew."

Just at this moment the sound of carriage wheels, followed immediately by a jump from the box, and a smart rap at the door, caused the widow to start hastily from her seat. The door was opened, and Jake, the big black coachman of the old Doctor, made his appearance, a heavy cloak and a large muffling hood hanging over his arm.

"Marm," said he, "it has clarred off beautiful, and Massa has sent the carriage arter you, and he says how he would have sent it afore, but how the roads was blocked up with snow-drifts. Me and Pontius Pilate, and Massa John, has been all the arternoon, a clarring it away, and I thinks, Marm, if you don't come to-night, how the road will be as bad as ever to-morrow morning, with this wind a-blowing about the snow. Miss Lizzy has sent this hood of hern, and Massa has sent this big cloth cloak of hizzen, so that you need'nt ketch cold."

Mrs. Dulan did not immediately reply, but looked at Willie, and seemed to reflect.

Jake added :

"I hopes you'll come, Marm, for Massa and Miss Lizzy and Massa John has quite set their heads on having you with them, to spend Christmas, and Massa John told me to tell you how he had bagged a fine passel of water-fowl and wild turkeys, and I myself has made a trap for Massa Willie to catch snow-birds."

"Yes, we will go," said Mrs. Dulan. "Do me the favour, Jacob, to pour a pitcher of water on that fire, while I tie on Willie's cloak and mittens."

In twenty minutes more, Willie was seated on his uncle's knees, by his bright fireside, and his mother sat conversing with John and Elizabeth, and a few neighbours, whom the inclemency of the weather had not deterred from dropping in to spend Christmas eve. The old housekeeper stood at the beaufet, cutting up seed-cake, and pouring out elder wine, which was soon passed round to the company.

That Christmas was a gorgeous morning. The sun rose

and lit up into flashing splendour the icy glories of the landscape. From every roof and eave, from every bough and
bush, dropped millions of blazing jewels. Earth wore a gorgeous bridal dress, bedecked with diamonds. Within the
Doctor's house everything was comfortable as you could wish.
A rousing fire of hickory wood roared upon the hearth, an
abundant breakfast of coffee, tea, buckwheat cakes, muffins,
eggs, wild fowl, oysters, &c., &c., smoked upon the board.
The family were all gathered in the breakfast room. The
Doctor was serving out egg-nog from a capacious bowl upon
the sideboard.

"Cousin Elizabeth," said little Willie, taking her hand and
leading her away to the sofa, "what do ladies love?"

"What do ladies love? Why, Willie, what a queer question."

"Yes, but tell me what *do* ladies love?"

"Why, their papas, of course, and their brothers, and their
relations; it would not be decorous to love any one else," said
the prim maiden.

"Oh, you don't know what I mean; I mean what do ladies
love *to have?* You know boys like to have kites and marbles,
and traps to catch snow-birds, and picture books, and half-
pence, and such things. Now what do ladies love to have?"

"Oh! now I understand you. Why, we like to have a good
assortment of crewels and floss to work tapestry with, and a
quantity of bright-coloured silk to embroider with, and—"

"Oh! that's what *you* like, Cousin Elizabeth; but mamma
doesn't work samplers," said the boy, with a dash of pettish
contempt in his tone. "Uncle has given me a bright new
shilling, for a Christmas gift, to do what I please with, and I
want to get something with it for poor dear mamma."

"La! child, you can get nothing of any account with a
shilling."

"Can't I?" said he, and his little face fell for an instant,

but soon lighting up, he exclaimed, " Oh, ho ! Cousin Elizabeth,
I am brighter than you are, this time. A silver thimble is a
very little thing, and can be bought with a shilling, I am sure ;
so I will buy one for mamma. Poor mamma has an old brass
one now, which cankers her finger."

" Here, Willie," said Elizabeth, " I have not paid you my
Christmas gift, and you caught me, you know, take this shilling,
and now run and ask your uncle to take you to the village
with him, when he goes, and then you can buy your thimble.
You have enough to get one now."

Willie thanked his cousin with a hearty embrace, and ran
off to do as she advised him. The family now sat down to
breakfast, after which they all went to church, where the Doctor performed Divine service. A large party of friends and
neighbours returned with them to dinner, and the remainder
of the day was spent in hilarity and innocent enjoyment.

The next day the thimble was purchased, as agreed upon,
and little Willie kept it a profound secret from his mother,
until the first evening on which they found themselves at
home, in their little parlour, when the candle was lit, and the
little stand drawn to the fire, the work-box opened, and the
old brass thimble put on. Then little Willie, glowing with
blissful excitement, put his hand in his pocket to find his
present. It was not there. He searched the other pocket,
then his cap, then shook his cloak and looked about the carpet.
Alarmed now, he opened the door and was going out, when
his mother called to him.

"What is the matter, Willie? Where are you going?
What have you lost?"

"Nothing much, mother; I am only going out a minute,"
and he closed the door, and began an almost hopeless search
by the moonlight, for his lost treasure. Up and down the
walk he searched without finding it. He opened the gate, and
peeping and peering about, wandered up the road, until his
little feet and limbs got wet in the soft snow, and his hands

became benumbed; when, feeling convinced that it was lost, he sat down and burst into a passionate fit of weeping. Let no one feel surprise or contempt at this. In this little affair of the thimble, there had been disinterested love, self-sacrifice, anticipated joy, disappointment and despair, though all expended on a cheap thimble. Yet, Willie was but seven years old, and "thought as a child, felt as a child, understood as a child." I am a grown up child now, and have had many troubles, but the most acute sorrow I ever felt, was the death of my pet pigeon, when I was seven years old.

It was long before the storm in his little bosom subsided, but when at last it did, he turned to go home; he would not go before, lest he might grieve his mother with the sight of his tears. At last, weary and half frozen, he opened the cottage gate, and met his mother coming to look for him, and she who always spoke most gently to him, and for whose dear sake she was suffering, now by a sad chance, and out of her fright and vexation, sharply rebuked him and hurried him off to bed. "If dear mamma had known, she would not have scolded me so, though," was his last thought as he sank into a feverish sleep. The next morning when Mrs. Dulan arose, the heavy breathing, and bright flush upon the cheek of her boy, caught her attention, and roused her fears for his health. As she gazed, a sharp expression of pain contracted his features, and he awoke. Feebly stretching out his arms, to embrace her, he said:

"Oh, mamma, Willie is so sick, and his breast hurts so bad."

The child had caught the pleurisy.

It was late at night before medical assistance could be procured from a distant village. In the mean time the child's illness had fearfully progressed; and when at last the physician arrived, and examined him, he could give no hopes of his recovery. Language cannot depict the anguish of the mother, as she bent over the couch of her suffering boy, and, if a grain could have increased the burden of her grief, it would have been felt in the memory of the few words of harsh rebuke when he had returned half frozen, and heavy-hearted, from his fruitless search after the thimble, for the kind Elizabeth had arrived and explained the incident of the night.

It was midnight of the ninth day. Willie had lain in a stupor, for a whole day and night previous. His mother stood by his bed; she neither spoke nor wept, but her face wore the expression of acute suffering. Her eyes were strained with an earnest, anxious, agonized gaze upon the deathly countenance of the boy. Old Doctor Dulan entered the room at this moment, and looking down at the child, and taking his thin cold hand in his own, felt his pulse, and turning to the wretched mother, who had fixed her anxious eyes imploringly upon him, he said—

"Hannah, my dear sister—but, O, God! I cannot deceive you," and abruptly left the room.

"Elizabeth," said he to his daughter, who was sitting by the parlour fire, "go into the next room, and remain with your aunt, and if anything occurs, summon me at once; and, John, saddle my horse quickly, and ride over to Mrs. Caply, and tell her to come over here."

Mrs. Caply was the layer-out of the dead for the neighbourhood.

How tediously wore that dreary night away in the sickroom, where the insensible child was watched by his mother and her friend! The flickering taper, which both forgot to snuff, would fitfully flare up, and reveal the watchers, the bed, and the prostrate form of the pale, stiff, motionless boy, with his eyes flared back with a fixed and horrid stare. In the parlour, a party equally silent and gloomy, kept their vigils. Doctor Dulan, his son, and the old woman, whose fearful errand made her very presence a horror, formed the group. The old woman at last, weary at holding her tongue so long,

10

broke silence by saying, "I always thought that child would never be raised, sir—he was so smart and clever, and so dutiful to his ma. He was too good for this world, sir. How long has he been sick, sir?"

"Little more than a week; but I beg you will be silent, lest you disturb them in the next room."

"Yes, sir, certainly. Sick people ought to be kept quiet, though perhaps that don't much matter when they are dying. Well, poor little fellow, he was a pretty child, and will look lovely in his shroud and cap, and—"

"Hush!" exclaimed John Dulan, in a tone so stern that the woman was constrained to be silent.

Daylight was now peeping in at the windows. The Doctor arose, put out the lamps, opened the shutters, stirred the fire, and went into the next room. The widow was sitting in the same place, holding one of the boy's hands between her own, her head bowed down upon it. The Doctor looked at the child; his eyes were now closed, as if in sleep; he laid his hand upon his brow, and bending down, intently gazed upon him. The child opened his eyes slowly. Passing quickly round the bed, the Doctor laid his hand upon the recumbent head and said: "Look up, Hannah, your child is restored." With an ecstatic expression of gratitude and joy, the mother started to her feet, and gazed upon her boy.

"Kiss me, mamma," said Willie, opening his gentle eyes, in which beamed a quiet look of recognition and love. The mother kissed her child repeatedly and fervently, while exclamations of profound gratitude to Heaven escaped her. The Doctor went to the window, and threw open the shutters. The rising sun poured his light into the room, and lit it up with splendour.

I must transport you now, in imagination, over a few years of time and a few miles of country, and take you into a splendid drawing-room, in the handsome country-house of the Delany's, which, you remember, I described in the first part of this story, situated near the town of Richmond. On a luxurious sofa, in this superb room, reclined a most beautiful woman Her golden hair divided above a high and classic brow, fell, flashing and glittering upon her white bosom, like sunbeams on the snow. Her eyes—but who can describe those glorious eyes of living sapphire? Sapphire! Compare her eloquent eyes to soulless gems? Her eyes! Why, when their serious light was turned upon you, you would feel spell-bound, entranced, as by a strain of rich and solemn music, and when their merry glance caught yours, you'd think there could not be a grief or a sin on earth! But the greatest charm in that fascinating countenance, was the lips, small, full, red, their habitual expression being that of heavenly serenity and goodness.

Bending over the arm of the sofa, his head resting upon his hand, was a young man; his eyes earnestly, anxiously, pleadingly fixed upon the face of his companion, in whose ear, in a full, rich, and passionate tone, he was pouring a tale of love, hopeless almost to despair. The girl listened with a saddened countenance, and turning her large eyes, humid with tears, upon his face, she spoke—

"Richard, I am grieved beyond measure. Oh, cousin, I do not merit your deep and earnest love. I am an ingrate! I do not return it."

"Do you dislike me?"

"Oh, no, no, no, indeed I do not—I esteem and respect you; nay, more, I love you as a brother."

"Then, dear, dearest Alice, since I am honoured with your esteem, if not blessed with your love, give me your hand—be my wife—and ultimately perhaps——"

"Horrible!" exclaimed the young girl, leaving the room abruptly.

"What the d—l does that fool mean?" exclaimed Richard Delany, as an angry flush passed over his face. "One would think I had insulted her. Colonel Delany's penniless depend

ant should receive with more humility, if not with more gratitude, an offer of marriage from his heir. But I see how it is:
She loves that beggarly Dulan—that wretched usher. But,
death—death to the poverty-stricken wretch, if he presume to
cross my path!" and the clenched fists, livid complexion, and
grinding teeth gave fearful testimony to the deadly hatred
that had sprung up in his bosom.

At this moment, Colonel Delany entered the room, and
taking a seat, said—

"Richard, I have somewhat to say to you, and I wish you
seriously to attend. You know that I am your best, your
most disinterested friend, and that your welfare lies nearer to
my heart than aught else earthly. Well, I have observed,
with much regret, the increased interest you seem to take in
your cousin—your passion for her in fact. These things are
easily arrested in the commencement, and they must be arrested. You can do it, and you must do it! I have other views
for you. Promise me, my son, that you will give up all
thoughts of Alice."

Richard, who had remained in deep thought, during his
father's address, now looked up and replied:

"But, my father, Alice is a very beautiful, very amiable,
very intellectual—"

"Beggar!"

"Father!!"

"Unbend that brow, sir! nor dare to address your parent
in that insolent tone! And now, sir, once for all, let us come
to the point, and understand each other, perfectly. Should
you persist in your addresses to Alice, should you finally
marry her, not a shilling, not a penny of your father's wealth
shall fall on an ungrateful son."

Richard reflected profoundly a moment, and then replied:

"Fear of the loss of wealth would not deter me from any
step. But the loss of my father would be an evil, I could
never risk to encounter. I will obey you, sir."

"I am not satisfied," thought the old gentleman, as he le't his son, after a few more moments of conversation. "I am n't satisfied. I will watch them closely, and in the course of the day speak to Alice."

An opportunity soon offered. He found himself alone with Alice, after tea.

"Alice," he commenced, "I wish to make a confidant of you;" and he proceeded to unfold to her, at some length, his ambitious projects for his son, and concluded by giving her to understand, pretty distinctly, that he wished *his* son to select a wealthy bride, and that any other one would never be received by him as his daughter.

"I think I understand, although I cannot entirely sympathize with you, my dear uncle," said Alice, in a low trembling tone. "All this has been said for my edification. That your mind may be perfectly at rest on this subject, I must say what may be deemed presumptuous: I would not, could not marry your son, either with or without your consent, or under any circumstances whatever."

"Alice! my dear Alice. How could you suppose I made any allusion to you? Oh! Alice, Alice!"

And the old man talked himself into a fit of remorse, sure enough. He believed Alice, although he could not believe his son. The old gentleman's uneasiness was not entirely dispelled; for although Alice might not now love Richard, yet time could make a great change in her sentiments.

Alice Raymond, the orphan niece of Colonel Delany, was the daughter of an officer in the British army. Mr. Raymond was the youngest son of an old, wealthy, and haughty family, in Dorsetshire, England. At a very early age, he married the youngest sister of Colonel Delany. Having nothing but his pay, all the miseries of an improvident marriage fell upon the young couple. The same hour that gave existence to Alice, deprived her of her mother. The facilities to amb't'on offered by America, and the hope of distracting his grief, induced

Mr. Raymond to dispose of his commission, and embark for the Western World. Another object which, though the last named, was the first in deciding him to cross the Atlantic. This object was to place his little Alice in the arms of her maternal grandmother, the elder. Mrs. Delany, then a widow, and a resident under the roof of her son, Colonel Delany. A few weeks after the sailing of the ship in which, with his infant daughter, Mr. Raymond took passage, the small-pox broke out on board, and he was one of its earliest victims.

With his dying breath, he consigned Alice to the care of the captain of the ship, a kind-hearted man, who undertook to convey the poor babe to her grandmother. On the arrival of the infant at the mansion of Colonel Delany, a new bereavement awaited her. Mrs. Delany, whose health had been declining ever since her settlement in her new home, was fast sinking to the grave. Colonel Delany, however, received the orphan infant with the greatest tenderness. Sixteen years of affectionate care had given him a father's place in the heart of Alice, and a father's influence over her. Within the last year, the sunshine of Alice's life had been clouded.

Richard Delany, the only son and heir of Colonel Delany, had been sent to England at the age of fifteen, to receive a college education. After remaining eight years abroad, the last year of his absence being spent in making the grand tour, he returned to his adopted country, and his father's house He was soon attracted by the beauty and grace of Alice. I say by her beauty and grace, because the moral and intellectual worth of the young girl he had not the taste to admire; even had he had, at this early period of his acquaintance with her, an opportunity to judge. The attentions of Richard Delany to his cousin were not only extremely distressing to her, but highly displeasing to his father, who had formed, as we have seen, the most ambitious projects for his son. Richard Delany was not far wrong in his conjecture concerning the young usher, who was no other than our old friend William Dulan, little

Willie, who had now grown to man's estate, the circumstances of whose introduction to the Delany family, I must now proceed to explain.

To pass briefly over the events of William Dulan's childhood and youth. At the age of ten years he entered, as a pupil, the collegiate school over which Dr. Dulan presided, where he remained until his nineteenth year. It had been the wish of William Dulan and his mother, that he should take holy orders, and he was about to enter a course of theological study, under the direction of his uncle, when an event occurred which totally altered the plan of his life. This event was the death of Dr. Dulan, his kind uncle and benefactor. All thoughts of the church had now to be relinquished, and present employment, by which to support his mother, to be sought.

* * It was twelve o'clock at night, about three months after the death of Dr Dulan. The mother of William, by her hearth, still plied her needle, now the only means of their support. Her son sat by her side, as of old. He had been engaged some hours in reading to her. At length, throwing down the book, he exclaimed—

"Dearest, dearest mother, lay by that work. It shames my manhood, it breaks my heart, to see you thus coining your very health and life into pence for our support; while I! oh, mother, I feel like a human vampire, preying upon your slender strength!"

The widow looked into the face of her son, saw the distress, the almost agony of his countenance, and quickly folding up her work, said gently:

"I am not sewing so much from necessity, now, dear William, as because I was not sleepy, being so much interested in your book."

The morning succeeding this little scene, William, as was his wont, arose early, and going into the parlour, made up the fire, hung the kettle on, and was engaged in setting the room in order, when his mother entered, who, observing his occupation, said :

"Ever since your return from school, William, you have anticipated me in this morning labour. You must now give it up, my son—I do not like to see you perform these menial offices."

"No service performed for my mother can be menial," said Willie, giving her a fond smile.

"My darling son !"

After breakfast William took up his hat and went out. It was three hours before he returned. His face was beaming with happiness, as he held an open letter in his hand.

"See, mother, dear, kind Providence has opened a way for us at last."

"What is it, my son?" said the widow anxiously.

"Mr. Keene, you know, who left this neighbourhood about three years ago, went to ———— county and established a school, which has succeeded admirably. He is in want of an assistant, and has written to me, offering four hundred dollars a year for my services in his institution."

"And you will have to leave me, William !"

These words escaped the widow, with a deep sigh, and without reflection. She added in an instant, with assumed cheerfulness :

"Yes, of course—so I would have you do."

A month from this conversation, William Dulan was established in his new home, in the family of Mr. Keene, the Principal of Bay Grove Academy, near Richmond.

The first meeting of William Dulan and Alice Raymond, took place under the following circumstances. On the arrival of Richard Delany at home, his father, who kept up the good old customs of his English ancestors, gave a dinner and ball in honour of his son's coming of age. All the gentry of his own and the adjoining counties accepted invitations to attend Among the guests was William Dulan He was presented to

Miss Raymond, the young hostess of the evening, by Mr Keeue. Young Dulan was at first dazzled by the transcendent beauty of her face, and the airy elegance of her form; then won by the gentleness of her manners, the elevation of her mind, and the purity of her heart. One ball in a country neighbourhood, generally puts people in the humour of the thing, and is frequently followed by many others. It was so in this instance, and William Dulan and Alice Raymond met frequently in scenes of gayety, where neither took an active part in the festivities. A more intimate acquaintance produced a mutual and just estimation of each other's character, and preference soon warmed into love.

From the moment in which the jealous fears of Richard Delany were aroused, he resolved to throw so much coldness *and hauteur* in his manner, toward that young gentleman, as should banish him from the house. This, however, did not effect the purpose for which it was designed, and he finally determined to broach the subject to his father. Old Colonel Delany, whose "optics" were so very "keen" to spy out the danger of his son's forming a misalliance, was stone blind when such a misfortune threatened Alice, liked the young man very much, and could see nothing out of the way in his attentions to his niece, and finally refused to close his doors against him, at his son's instance. While this conversation was going on, the summer vacation approached, and William made arrangements to spend them with his mother.

One morning, William Dulan sat at his desk. His face was pale, his spirits depressed. He loved Alice, Oh! how madly. He could not forego the pleasure of her society—yet how was all this to end?—Long years must elapse before, if ever, he could be in a situation to ask the hand of Alice. With his head bowed upon his hand, he remained lost in thought.

"Mr. Dulan, may our class come up? We know our lessons," said a youthful voice at his elbow.

"Go to your seats, boys," said a rich, melodious, kind voice; "I wish to have a few moments' conversation with Mr. Dulan;" and Dr. Keene, the Principal, stood by his side.

"My dear Dulan," said he, "you are depressed, but I bring you that which will cheer your spirits. I have decided to give up my school here, into your sole charge, if you will accept it. I have received, through the influence of some of my political friends, a lucrative and permanent appointment under the government, the nature of which I will explain to you, by and by. I think of closing my connexion with this school about the end of the next term. What say you? Will you be my successor?"

Dulan started to his feet, seized both the hands of his friend, pressed them fervently, and would have thanked him, but utterance failed. Dr. Keene insisted on his resuming his seat, and then added:

"The income of the school amounts to twelve hundred dollars a year. The school-house, dwelling-house, with its out-buildings, and numerous improvements upon the premises, go into the bargain. Yes, Dulan, I have known your secret long," said he, smiling good-humouredly, "and sincerely though silently commiserated the difficulties of your position; and I assure you, Dulan, that the greatest pleasure I felt in receiving my appointment, was in the opportunity it gave me, of making you and Alice happy. Stop, stop, Dulan, let me talk," laughed Keene, as William opened a battery of gratitude upon him. "It is now near the end of July. I should like to see you installed here on the first of September. The August vacation will give you an opportunity of making all your arrangements. I must now leave you to your labours."

Every boy that asked to go out, went out that day. Every boy that said his task got praised, and every boy that missed his lesson, got blamed. The day was awfully tedious for all that, but evening came at last, and the school was dismissed William, after spending an unusually long time in the "out

vard a'lorning," hastened with a joy beaming countenance to
the home of his Alice. In the full flow of his joy, he was
met by a sudden disappointment. The servant who met him
at the door, informed him that Col. Delany, Miss Raymond,
and Mr. Delany had set off for Richmond, with the intention
of staying a couple of weeks. Crest-fallen William turned
from the door. This was only a momentary disappointment,
however, and soon his spirits rose, and he joyfully anticipated
the time of the Delanys' return. They were to be back in
time for the approaching examination and exhibition at Bay
Grove Academy; and in preparing his pupils for this event,
William Dulan found ample employment for his time and
thoughts. I will not weary you with a description of the exhibition. It passed off in that school, pretty much as it does
in others. The Delanys however had not returned in time to
be present, nay, the very last day of William's stay had
dawned, yet they had not arrived. William had written to
his mother that he would be home on a stated day, and not
even for the delight of meeting the mistress of his heart, the
period of whose return was now uncertain, would he disappoint
her. William was engaged in packing his trunk, when Dr.
Keene, again the harbinger of good tidings, entered his room.

"My dear Dulan," said he, "I have come to tell you that
the Delanys have arrived. You will have an opportunity of
spending your last evening with Alice."

William shuffled his things into his trunk, pressed down the
lid, locked it, and hastily bidding his friend good evening, took
his hat and hurried from the house. Being arrived at Colonel Delany's, he was shown into the drawing-room, and was
delighted to find Alice its sole occupant. The undisguised
joy with which she received him, left scarcely a doubt upon
his mind, as to the reception of his intended proposals. After
a few mutual inquiries respecting health, friends, and so forth,
William took her white hand in his, and said, or attempted to
say—I know not what—it stuck in his throat—and he re

mained merely silent, holding the hand of Alice. There is
something so extremely difficult about making a premeditated
declaration of love. It is much easier when it can be surprised from a man. William knew the moments were very
precious. He knew that Colonel Delany or his son might be
expected to enter at any moment, and there would be an end
of opportunity for a month, or six weeks to come; yet there
he sat, holding her hand, the difficulty becoming greater every
minute, while the crimson cheek of Alice burned with a deeper
blush. At length footsteps approached. William heard them,
and becoming alarmed, hastily, hurriedly, but fervently, and
passionately, exclaimed :

"Alice, I love you with my whole heart, mind, and strength.
I love you as we are commanded only to love God. Dearest
Alice, will you become my wife ?"

"Miss Raymond," said Richard Delany, entering at this
moment, "my father desires your presence instantly, in his
study, on business of the utmost moment to yourself. Mr.
Dulan I hope will excuse me, as we have but just arrived, and
many matters crave my attention. Good evening, sir;" and,
bowing haughtily, he attended his cousin from the room.
William Dulan arose, and took his hat, to go.

"Farewell, Mr. Dulan," said Alice kindly, "if we should
not meet again, before your departure."

"Farewell, sweet Alice," murmured William Dulan, as he
left the house.

_____

It was a glorious Sabbath morning early in August. The
widow's cottage gleamed in the dark bosom of the wood, like a
gem in the tresses of beauty. Everything wore its brightest
aspect. The windows of the little parlour were open, and the
songs of birds and the perfume of flowers were wafted through
them. But the little breakfast table with its snowy cloth, and
its one plate, cup, and saucer, looked almost piteous from its
solitude. Upon the clean white coverlet of the bed sat the

widow's little black bonnet and shawl, prayer-book, and clean
pocket-handkerchief, folded with its sprig of lavender. It was
Communion Sunday, and the widow would not miss going to
church on any account. She despatched her breakfast quickly—poor thing, she had not much appetite. She had sat up
half the night previous, awaiting the arrival of William, but
he had not come; and a man from the village, that had called
at her cottage early on this morning, had informed her that the
mail-stage had arrived on the night previous, without any
passengers. As the stage would not pass again for a week, the
widow could not expect to see or hear from her son for that
length of time. After putting away her breakfast things, she
donned her bonnet and shawl, and taking her prayer-book,
opened the door, to go out. What a pleasant sight met her
eyes. A neat one horse carriage, or rather cart, stood at the
door—her son was just alighting from it. In another instant
he had clasped his mother in his arms.

"Oh! my William, my William, I am so glad to see you,"
exclaimed the delighted mother, bursting into tears. "Oh!
but this is so joyful, so unexpected, dear William! I looked
for you, indeed, last night; but, as you did not come, I gave
you up, unwillingly enough, for a week. But come in, darling,
you've not breakfasted, I know."

"No, dear mother, because I wished to breakfast with you;
but let me give something to the horse, first, and you sit in
the door, dear mother—I do not want to lose sight of you a
moment, while waiting on Rosinante."

"Never mind, William, old Jake can do that. Here, Jake,"
said she, as the old servant approached, "take charge of Master William's horse." Then turning to William, she said—
"John sends old Jake over every morning to help me."

"Ah! How are Cousins John and Elizabeth?"

"Oh, very hearty—we shall see them this morning at
church."

"I did not come in the stage, yesterday, mother," said

William, as they took their seats at the breakfast table, "because I had purchased this light wagon and horse for you to ride to church in, and I came down in it. I reached the river last night, but could not get across. The old ferryman had gone to bed, and would not rise. Well! after breakfast, dear mother, I shall have the pleasure of driving you to church in your own carriage!" added William, smiling.

"Ah! William, what a blessing you are to me, my dear son; but it must have taken the whole of your quarter's salary, to buy this for me?" And she glanced, with pain, at his rusty and thread-bare suit of black, and at his napless hat.

"Ah! mother, I was selfish after all, and deserve no credit, for I laid the money out in the way which would give myself the most pleasure. But, see, here is old Jake to tell us the carriage is ready. Come, mother, I will hand you in, and as we go along, I will unfold to you some excellent news, which I am dying to deliver." So saying, he placed his mother carefully in the little carriage, and seating himself beside her, drove off, leaving old Jake in charge of the house.

"There is plenty of time, dear mother; so we will drive slowly, that we may talk with more comfort."

William then proceeded to relate, at large, all that had taken place during his residence at Bay Grove—not omitting his love for Alice, of whom he gave a glowing description; nor the bright prospects, which the kindness of Dr. Keene opened before him. Then he described the beautiful dwelling, which would become vacant on the removal of Dr. Keene's family, which was expected to take place some time during the coming autumn. To this dwelling, he intended to remove his mother, and hoped to bear his bride.

To all this the mother listened with grateful joy. At the church, William Dulan met again his cousins, John and Elizabeth, who expressed their delight at the meeting, and insisted that William and his mother should return with them to dinner. This however, both mother and son declined, as they wished to spend the day at home together.

William Dulan spent a month with his mother, and when the moment arrived that was to terminate his visit, he said to her—

"Now, dear mother, cheer up! This parting is so much better than our last parting. Now I am going to prepare a beautiful home for you, and when I come at Christmas, it will be for the purpose of carrying you back with me."

The widow gave her son a beaming look of love.

With a "Heaven be with you, my dearest mother," and "God bless you, my best son," they parted. They parted to meet no more on earth.

Let us now return to the mansion of Colonel Delany, and learn the nature of that "matter of the utmost moment to herself," that had summoned Alice so inopportunely from the side of her lover.

———

On reaching the study of her uncle, Miss Raymond found him in deep consultation with an elderly gentleman in black. Various packets of papers were before him,—an open letter was held in his hand. He arose to meet Alice, as she advanced into the room, and taking her hand with grave respect, said—

"Lady Hilden, permit me to congratulate you on your accession to your title and estates."

"Sir! uncle!" exclaimed Alice, gazing at him with the utmost astonishment, scarcely conscious whether she was waking or dreaming.

"Yes, my dear, it is true. Your grandfather—old Lord Hilden—departed this life, on the 6th of last March. His only living son survived him but a few weeks, and died without issue, and the title and estates, with a rent-roll of £8000 per annum, has descended, in right of your father, to yourself!"

"I shall have so much to give to William!" involuntarily exclaimed Alice.

"Madam!" exclaimed Colonel Delany in surprise.

Alice blushed violently, at having thought aloud. "Dear sir," said she, "I did not know what I was saying."

"Ah, well, I suppose you are a little startled with this sudden news," said the Colonel, smiling; "but now it is necessary for you to examine, with us, some of these papers. "Ah I crave your pardon, Mr. Reynard—Lady Hilden, this is Mr. Reynard, late solicitor to your deceased grandfather, the Baron"——

Great was the excitement in the neighbourhood, when it was noised abroad that Alice Raymond had become a baroness, in her own right, and the possessor of a large estate in England. And when, for the first time since her accession to her new dignities, she appeared at church, in deep mourning, every eye was turned upon her, and she almost sunk beneath the gaze of so many people.

In the height of the "nine day's wonder," William Dulan returned, and was greeted by the news, from every quarter.

"Oh! Alice—lost! lost! lost to me for ever!" exclaimed he, in agony, as he paced, with hurried strides, up and down the floor of his little room. "Oh, my mother, if it were not for thee, I should pray that this wretched heart of mine would soon be stilled in death."

If any human being will look candidly upon the events of his own life, and the history of his own heart, with a view to examine the causes of suffering, he will be constrained to admit, that by far the greater portion of his miseries have originated in misapprehension, and might have been easily prevented or cured by a little calm investigation. It was so with William Dulan, who was at this moment suffering the most acute agony of mind he ever felt in his life, from a misconception, a doubt, which a ten minutes' walk to the house of Colonel Delany, and a ten minutes' talk with Alice, would have dissipated for ever.

If Richard Delany was anxious before, to wed his cousin for love, he was now half crazy to take that step by which both love and ambition would be gratified to the utmost.

He actually loved her ten times as much as formerly. The "beggar" was beautiful, but the baroness was bewitching! Spurred on, then, he determined to move heaven, earth, and the other place, if necessary, to accomplish his object. He beset Lady Hilden with the most earnest prayers, and protestations, and entreaties, reminding her that he loved and wooed her before the dawn of her prosperity, and appealed to her for the disinterestedness of his passion. But all in vain. He even besought his father to use his influence with Alice, in his favour. Colonel Delany, his objections being all now removed, urged his niece, by her affection, by her compassion, and, finally, after some delicate hesitation, by her gratitude, to accept the proffered hand of his son. But Alice was steadfast in her rejection.

"A change had come o'er the spirit of her dream!"

Alas, alas! that a change of fortune should work such a change of spirit! Alice Raymond was now Lady Hilden. Her once holy, loving, meek blue eyes, were now splendid with light and joy. Upon cheek and lip, once so delicately blooming, now glanced and glowed a rich, bright crimson. Her once softly falling step, had become firm, elastic, and stately. "A peeress in my own right," was the thought that sent a spasmodic joy to the heart of Alice. I am sorry she was not more philosophical, more exalted, but I cannot help it, so it was; and if Alice "put on airs," it must not be charged upon her biographer.

Time sped on. A rumour of an approaching marriage between Mr. Richard Delany and Lady Hilden was industriously circulated, and became the general topic of conversation in the

11

neighbourhood. To avoid hearing it talked of, William Dulan
sedulously kept out of company. He had never seen Alice
since she became Lady Hilden. Dr. Keene had removed
with his family from Bay Grove, and the principal government and emolument of the school had devolved upon young
Dulan. The Christmas holidays were at hand, and he resolved
to take advantage of the opportunity offered by them, to remove his mother to Bay Grove. On the last evening of his
stay, something in the circumstance brought back forcibly to
his mind his last conversation with Alice—that conversation
had also taken place on the eve of a journey; and the associa-
tion of ideas awakened, together with the belief that he would
never again have an opportunity of beholding her, irresistibly
impelled him to seek an interview with Alice.

Twilight was fast fading into night. Lady Hilden stood
alone, gazing out from the window of her uncle's drawing-
room. She had changed again, since we saw her last. There
was something of sorrow, or bitterness, in the compressed or
quivering lip. Her eye was bright as ever, but it was the
brightness of the icicle glancing in the winter sun—it was
soon quenched in tears, and, as she gazed out upon the gloomy
mountain, naked forest, and frozen lake, she murmured, "I
used to love summer and day so much; now—" [A servant
entered with lights. "Take them away," said Alice. She
was obeyed.]—"the dark soul in the dark scene: there is
almost repose in that harmony."

"Mr. Dulan?" said the servant, reappearing at the door,
and William Dulan followed the announcement.

"You may bring in the light, now," said Alice.

"Will Lady Hilden accept congratulations, offered at so
late a period?" said William Dulan, with a respectful bow.

Alice, who had been startled out of her self-possession,
replied only by a bow.

"I was about to leave this neighbourhood for a short time;
but could not do so without calling to bid you farewell, fearing

you might be gone to England before I return" William Dunlap's voice was beginning to quiver !

"I have no present intention of going to England."

"Not? Such a report is rife in the neighbourhood."

"One is not chargeable with the reports of the neighbourhood."

Alice said this in a peculiar tone, as she glanced at the sorrow-stricken visage of the young man.

A desultory conversation ensued, after which William Dulan arose to take his leave, which he did in a choking, inaudible voice. As he turned to leave the room, his ghastly face and unsteady step attested, in language not to be misunderstood, the acuteness and intensity of his suffering. Alice did not misunderstand it. She uttered one word, in a low and trembling tone :

"William !"

He was at her side in an instant. A warm blush glowing over bosom, cheek, and brow, her eyes were full of tears, as she raised them to his face, eloquent with all a maiden may not speak.

"Angel! I love! I adore thee !"—exclaimed the youth, sinking at her feet.

"Love me, William, only love me, and let us both adore the Being who hath given us to each other."

It was a cold night on the shores of the ice-bound Rappahannock. A storm of wind and snow that had been fiercely raging all day long, at length subsided. At a low cabin, which served the three-fold purposes of post-office, ferry-house, and tavern, an old gray-headed man was nodding over a smouldering fire. His slumbers were disturbed by the blast of the stage horn and wheels of the coach, which soon stopped before the door.

Two travellers alighted and entered the cabin. The old ferryman arose to receive them.

" Any chance of crossing, to-night, Uncle Ben?" inquired the younger traveller.

" He-he! hardly, Mr. William; the river has been closed for a week," chuckling at the thought that he should be saved the trouble of taking the coach across.

" Oh! of course, I did not expect to go on the boat, I was thinking of crossing on the ice."

" I think that would scarcely be safe, Mr. William; the weather has moderated a great deal since nightfall, and I rather think the ice may be weak."

" Pooh! nonsense! fiddle-de-dee!" exclaimed the other traveller, testily; " do you think, old driveller, that a few hours of moderate weather could weaken, effectually, the ice of a river that has been hard frozen for a week? Why, at this moment a *coach* might be driven across with perfect safety!"

" I shouldn't like to try it, though, sir," said the driver, who entered at this moment.

" The gentleman can try it, if he likes," continued the old man, with a grin, " but I do hopes Mr. Dulan won't."

" Why, the ice will certainly bear a foot-passenger safely across," smiled William Dulan.

" I dare say it *may;* but, at any rate, I wouldn't try it, Master William—'specially as it's a long, dark, slushy road between here and the widow's."

" Why, Uncle Ben, do you think I am a young chicken, to be killed by wetting my feet?" asked William, laughing " Besides, at this very moment, my good mother is waiting for me, and has a blazing fire, a pot of strong coffee, and a bowl of oysters, in readiness. I would not disappoint her, or myself, for a good deal."

" If i were not for this confounded lameness in my feet, I would not stop at this vile hole, to-night," said the elder traveller, who was no other than Richard Delany, whom imperative business had called to this part of the country, and

who had thus become, very reluctantly, the travelling com
panion of William Dulan.

"Nobody asked you, sir," exclaimed the old man, who
did not seek popularity.

William Dulan, who, by this time, had resumed his cloak,
and received a lighted lantern from the old ferryman, took
his way to the river, accompanied by the latter. Arrived at
its edge, he turned, shook hands with the old man, and stepped
upon the ice. Old Ben remained, with his eyes anxiously
strained after the light of the lantern, as it was borne across
the river. It was already half-way across—suddenly a break
ing sound, a fearful shriek, a quenched light, and all was dark
and still upon the surface of the ice; but beneath, a young
strong life was battling fiercely with death. Ah! who can tell
the horrors of that frightful struggle in the dark, cold, ice-
bound prison of the waters?

The old man turned away, aghast with horror, and his eyes
fell upon the countenance of Richard Delany, which was now
lit up with demoniac joy, as he muttered between his teeth :

"Good, good, good! Alice shall be mine now!"

It was night in the peaceful cottage of the widow. All the
little *agremens* her son had pictured, were there. A little
round table, covered with a snowy cloth, stood in readiness.
An easy chair was turned with its back to the fire, and on it
a dressing-gown, and before it lay a pair of soft, warm slippers.
The restless, joyous, anxious mother was reading over, for the
twentieth time, her son's last letter, in which he promised to
be home, punctually, on that very evening. Hours flew on,
but he did not come. At length, one o'clock struck, and
startled the widow from her meditative posture. "I must go
to bed—I must not look pale with watching, to-morrow, and
alarm my good son. It is just as it was before—he cannot
get across the river, to-night. I shall see him early to-mor-

row." Removing the things from about the fire, and setting
the room in the nicest order, the widow retired to bed.

She rose early in the morning, to prepare a good breakfast
for her son. "He shall have buckwheat cakes, this morning ·
he is so fond of them," said she, as she busied herself in
preparation.

Everything was in readiness, yet William came not. The
morning passed on. The mother grew impatient.

"It is, certainly, high time he was here now," said she;
"I will go through the woods, towards the high-road, and see
if he is coming," and putting on her bonnet and shawl, she
set out. She had just entered the wood, when two advancing
figures caught her attention. The path was so narrow that
they were walking one behind the other.

"Ah! there he is—and John Dulan is with him," exclaimed
the mother as they drew near.

The foremost man was, indeed, John Dulan, who held out
his hand, as they met.

"Ah! how do you do, John? How do you do? This is
so kind of you! But, stand aside—excuse me—I want to see
that youth behind you!" and the widow brushed passed him,
and caught to her bosom—old Ben, the ferryman.

"My gracious! I thought you were my son! Dear me,
how absurd!" exclaimed the widow, releasing him.

"Let us go on to the cottage, aunt," said John Dulan,
sadly.

"Yes, *do*. I am looking every minute for William. Oh,
you can tell me, Uncle Ben—did he reach the ferry last
night?"

"Yes, madam," groaned the old man.

"Why, you alarm me! Why didn't he come home, ther?"

"He *did* try—he *did* try! I begged him not to—but he
would! Oh! dear, oh! dear!"

"Why, what in Heaven's name; is the matter? What has
happened? Is my son ill?"

"Tell her, Mr. Dulan—tell her! I could not, to save my life!"

The widow turned very pale.

"Where is William? Where is my son? Is he ill? Is he ill?"

"My dearest aunt—do try to compose yourself!" said John Dulan, in a trembling voice.

"Where is my son? Where is he?"

"You cannot see him to-day—"

"Yet he was at the ferry-house, last night! Great God! it cannot be!" cried the mother, suddenly growing very pale and faint. "Oh, no! Merciful Providence—such sorrow cannot be in store for me? He is not—"

She could not finish the sentence, but turned a look of agonizing inquiry on John Dulan. He did not speak.

"Answer! answer! answer!" almost screamed the mother John Dulan turned away.

"Is my son—is my son——DEAD?"

"He is in Heaven, I trust," sobbed John.

A shriek, the most wild, shrill, and unearthly, that ever came from the death-throe of a breaking heart, arose upon the air, and echoed through the woods, and the widow sunk, fainting, to the ground. They raised her up—the blood was flowing in torrents from her mouth. They bore her to the house, and laid her on the bed. John Dulan watched beside her, while the old man hastened to procure assistance.

The life of the widow was despaired of for many weeks. She recovered from one fit of insensibility, only to relapse into another. At length, however, she was pronounced out of danger. But the white hair, silvered within the last few weeks, the strained eyes, contracted brow, and shuddering form, marked the presence of a scathing sorrow.

One day, while lying in this state, a travelling carriage drew up before the door, and a young, fair girl, clad in deep

mourning, alighted and entered. Elizabeth, who was watch
ing beside her, stooped down and whispered very low—
"The betrothed bride of your son."

The young girl approached the bed, and taking the hand of
the sufferer, exclaimed—"Mother, mother, you are not alone
in your sorrow! I have come to live or die by you, as my
strength may serve!"

The widow opened her arms and received her in an embrace.
They wept. The first blessed tears that had relieved the
burdened heart of either, were shed together.

Alice never left her. When the widow was sufficiently recovered, they went to England. The best years of the life of
Alice, were spent in soothing the declining days of William
Dulan's mother. The face of Alice was the last object her
eyes rested on, in life; and the hands of Alice closed them in
death.

Alice never married; but spent the remainder of her life in
ministering to the suffering poor around her.

I neglected to mention that, during the illness of Mrs.
Dulan, the body of her son was found, and interred in this
spot, by the request of his mother.

"What becomes of the moral?" you will say.

I have told you a true story. Had I created these beings
from imagination, I should also have judged them—punished
the bad and rewarded the good. But these people actually
lived, moved, and had their being in the real world, and have
now gone to render in their account to their Divine Creator
and Judge. The case of Good *versus* Evil, comes on in another
world, at another tribunal, and, no doubt, will be equitably ad-
judged.

———

As I fear my readers may be dying to know what farther
became of our cheery set of travellers, I may, on some future
occasion, gratify their laudable desire after knowledge; only

informing them at present, that we *did* reach our destination at ten o'clock that night, in safety, although it *was* very dark when we passed down the dreaded Gibbet Hill and forded the dismal Bloody Run Swamp. That Aunt Peggy's cap was *not* mashed by Uncle Clive's hat, and that Miss Christine did *not* put her feet into Cousin Kitty's bandbox, to the demolition of her bonnet; but that both bonnet and cap survived to grace the heads of their respective proprietors. The only mishap that occurred, dear reader, befell your obsequious servitor, who went to bed with a sick-headache, caused *really* by her acute sympathy with the misfortunes of the hero and heroine of our aunt's story, but which Miss Christine grossly attributed to a hearty supper of oysters and soft-crabs, eaten at twelve o'clock at night, which, of course, you and I know, had nothing at all to do with it.

EVELINE MURRAY:

OR,

THE FINE FIGURE.

DAGUERREOTYPED FROM LIFE.

———◆———

The body is more than raiment.—Luke xii. 22.

"They laced her *up*, and starved her *down*,
To make her small and thin."—Holmes.

'Oh! Oh dear! I shall *die*—indeed I shall; I never can
stand this boddice all the evening!" gasped a young girl, with
the tears squeezed to her eyes. She was being inducted into
her first ball dress.

"Oh, yes! my love, you can," persisted her mother, as she
laboured to draw the hooks and eyes of the corsage together.
"you have too stout a waist entirely; you must bear this!"

"But, Oh! dear Oh! I can't, indeed I can't. I can't get
my breath," gasped the girl.

"Oh, well! you must do as well as you can. Bear this
pressure a while, and then it will cease to feel uncomfortable.
This stout waist of yours will *give in* and *go down* like, and
then you will cease to feel giddy and sick; you will breathe
easy; and then you will have a fine, round, slender waist, and a
beautiful bust and shoulders!"

"But, Oh, Oh, mother! I'm sick, *deadly* sick. My head

(173)

is swimming—I'm blind—and the room is turning round with
me!"

"There! smell this salts; you'll feel better by and by, when
your waist *gives in* and *goes down*."

How little did the mother know, or guess, that this sickness
and giddiness was the *protest* of Nature against the violence
done her, and that this *giving in* and *going down* was the
yielding and sinking of the vital organs, inflicting present discomfort, and involving, if persisted in, future loss of health
and life! How should she? She was totally ignorant of the
laws of health and life, and hugged her ignorance. She would
have been shocked at the bare mention of a "Lecture on
Physiology for Ladies." Poor mother! she loved that only
child of hers tenderly. She would not have harmed her, directly or indirectly, knowingly, for her own soul's salvation.
She would not suffer her to beat up a bed, run up or down
stairs, dip her hands in water until the chill was taken off, go
out, however well wrapped up, on a windy day, or do anything
else by which she fancied she might fatigue herself, worry herself, or give herself cold; for Eveline was consumptive, and
all her sisters had died of consumption—all her fair sisters,
beautiful girls, with such "fine figures;" but they had died,
and Eveline, the youngest, only was left; and Eveline was the
most beautiful and the least delicate of them all. And now,
poor mother, she was unknowingly commencing the course
that was to destroy the health of her fair Eveline, as it had
destroyed the lives of all her other lovely girls.

"THERE! my little queen!" said the proud and affectionate mother, as she succeeded in hooking the boddice of a
beautiful tarlton dress over white satin. "There! who would
not suffer a little pain for the sake of displaying a form like
that!" She led her daughter up before a large mirror; and
truly the face and figure reflected there might well raise the
flush of gratified vanity upon the young girl's cheek: the
stately head, with its long ringlets of flashing gold; the child

like, the infantile face, with its broad, white forehead—its large, tender, dark-blue eyes; the crimson flush on cheek and lip; the arched neck, falling shoulders, round bosom, and tapering waist, and the graceful sweep of the dress from the corsage down.

"Now, my darling, how do you feel?" said her mother, raising the candle above her head, to throw the most becoming light upon her.

"I think I feel better—I can bear it now," smiled Eveline.

"Don't you suppose Clem Dorsey will think you very much improved since he went away?"

Eveline blushed to the edges of her hair.

"Oh dear, mother! I was only fifteen years old when he went away; that was two years ago. Do you really think—that he remembers me?"

"Remembers you, Eveline?" said Mrs. Murray, with a fond, quizzing smile upon her face—"just as well as you remember *him*, little darling. Eveline! I don't intend to let you finally come out this winter; it is only because I know that you would like to see Clem Dorsey before he goes to Florida, that I sent for you from school, and permit you to go to this ball."

"Has he—has he—has he———?"

"Has he called here since his return? Is that what you mean, my dear? Yes, once. He arrived Tuesday—he came here Wednesday—he passed on to Washington Thursday—and to-night he is expected here, to be present at this ball given in his honour."

"Will he attend it, mother?"

"Don't say 'attend,' my love, or 'mother;' both are vulgar. People 'go to' or 'assist at' balls, concerts, &c., and *I* am mamma.'"

"Then, mamma, will he '*go to*' this ball?"

"Oh! without doubt, my dear. Now, love, sit down, and let me put on your slippers."

Here was another operation!

Mamma squeezed, and pressed, and grew red in the face; Eveline winced, and shrunk, and fretted, until at last, with much pain and trouble, the small foot was encased in the smaller slipper.

And then the mother pressed the little feet together, and kissed them.

"How these little white birdies will flash and twinkle over the chalked floor to-night, Evay?"

And then she hugged up the satin-slippered feet under her chin, arose, put a few finishing touches to Eveline's toilet, and contemplated her child. Her child! She was a child herself —that simple-minded, single-hearted mother. Her whole life lay in her children. In their infancy she had played with them, frolicked with them, revelled in their infantile innocence and vivacity; in their childhood, she had shared their sports and their studies; in their girlhood, whether they liked it or not, she had entered heart and soul into all their fancies, flirtations, rivalries, loves, hopes, and fears—not always judiciously, however, though always disinterestedly

Mrs. Murray was the widow of an army officer, and living on his half-pay. She had been the mother of four beautiful girls, three of whom had died between the ages of eighteen and twenty. Though but forty years of age, she was a pale, emaciated, withered, and faded woman, herself a victim to the present atrocious mode of dress. She had imparted to her children, from their very birth, an unhealthy and imperfect organization, an aptitude for disease, and in her blind ignorance, following up the same destructive course with them that had destroyed her own health and beauty, she had hurried them off, one by one, into a premature grave, and religiously bowed before what she in her self-delusion termed the "will of God." "The will of God" is the happiness of his children; and they doubly err who wantonly or blindly bring calamity upon themselves, and then charge their misery upon Divine Providence

Eveline Murray was a beauty. Her person was slight, but well covered with soft, round, elastic muscles, that turned the curved line of beauty in every graceful limb and motion. Her complexion was of that fair, clear, semi-transparent hue, that told at once of perfect health and extreme delicacy of organization—a constitution sound but fragile—one which judicious care might cultivate into robust health, or which neglect or mal-treatment might quickly and easily undermine and break down.

Now, young ladies, before I go on with my story, I have a few words to say to you; and you must read it, and not skip it, for it is the real *pill*, and the story, though every word true, is only the *sugar coat*. There, *now*, do not scrape off the sugar, and throw away the pill. It is about your dress, of course, that I am going to speak. Presuming that gentlemen will take my warning at the head of this sketch, and not read it, I will speak plainly. It is true that some improvement has been effected in dress. Corsets and stays are no longer in vogue; the lungs, at least the upper portions of them, have something like fair play; but *below* the lungs are vital organs, that you may not compress with impunity; and these long-waisted, tight, *very* tight, whaleboned corsages are quite as destructive to health, beauty, and life, through the injury they inflict upon *these* organs, as ever old-fashioned stays were, through fatal mischief done to the lungs. To tell you that by persisting in this ultra-fashionable style of dress, these horrid, long, tight waists, and heavy skirts, you will destroy your health and risk your life, would be no argument at all to you. You are *willing* to lose health and risk life for the sake of a fine figure. But suppose I tell you that you will lose not only health, but what you value infinitely more, *beauty*, and ultimately the rotundity and graceful contour of that same "fine figure" for which you are willing to risk so much health and life? Why is it that your mothers and aunts, who at thirty-seven and forty *ought* to be as much handsomer than you girls

of eighteen and twenty, as noon is brighter than morning, as
summer is more glorious than spring (for there is an analogy
running through all nature), because *they* are in the glorious
noon of their day, the summer of their year—now, why is it
not so? Why are they

"Old in youth, and withered in their prime?"

I will tell you. There are *many* reasons—such as neglect of
regular exercise, bathing, fresh air, &c.; the use of drying
and astringent drinks, such as strong tea and coffee, and stimulating meats, &c. But more ruinous than any other of these
sins of *omission* or *commission* is the barbarous style of dress
now in vogue. I do not wonder that so many of us go off
annually in consumption; but I do wonder how it is that we,
with the same suicidal habits, escape death. You do not wish
to grow old and ugly, do you, girls? You who are past twenty
dread your thirtieth birthday worse than "plague, pestilence,
or famine," don't you, girls? There is no need for this.
Abandon or considerably modify your present style of dress;
that, and not *years*, destroys your youth, and health, and
beauty. It is that abuse of yourselves that will make your
cheeks grow pale, your muscles fall, your features become
angular. On the other hand, if you will only use yourselves
well, your freshness of complexion and elasticity of muscle
will last half a century. The freshness of complexion cannot
be present without a free circulation of blood; the blood cannot circulate freely through a compressed waist, compressed
feet, or compressed arms—hence pale and sallow complexions.
The roundness, the elasticity, the spring of your muscles, depend upon the free, regular, and healthful action of the heart,
lungs, liver, &c. These vital organs cannot act healthfully
while habitually compressed together—hence falling muscles,
hollow cheeks, emaciated limbs, &c.; hence disease, loss of
beauty, premature old age, or death. Girls, do not wear these
long, tight waists, and heavy skirts; they are destructive, fatal

This is not the place for physiological detail, else I might tell you precisely how it acts; but "for your own good," as my grandmother used to say when she read me a lecture—for your own good, I will refer you to my source of information. Read Dr. Fitch's "Lectures on the Heart and Lungs," or even "Calvin Cutter's First Book of Physiology for Common Schools"—read *both*, and mind the rules laid out there for the preservation of health, and I will guaranty that your fortieth birthday finds you in high beauty. Fifty is called the "grand climacteric" of life; and so it really *should* be. A century, a hundred years, is a round sum; I always fancied that ten or twenty years lopped off at the last end of it was an unnecessary loss of so much life. Let any young person of good constitution—(yes, or of bad constitution; I will not modify it, for a bad constitution can be made a good one by proper means in youth)—let *any* young person set out with the determination that, with God's blessing, they will "live out their century" in full health, and preserve their beauty unimpaired up to the grand climacteric, and I believe they will be most likely to do it. The object is a much better one than the attainment of wealth or fame, which so many resolve and so many achieve; and the means are much more within your reach; and these means will not, as in the two other objects of wealth or fame, destroy, but increase your *present* comfort and cheerfulness.

To return from this long digression: Mrs. Murray had just finished Eveline's toilet, when a servant entering the room handed a card to her.

"Lieut. Clement Dorsey, U. S. A." read the lady. "There, now, Eveline, darling! has he forgotten you? Come, Eveline, let us go down;" and, taking her daughter's hand, she lovingly conducted her from the room.

They entered the parlour. A young man in the full uniform of a lieutenant in the United States Army arose from the sofa and advanced to meet them.

12

"Ah! how do you do, Mr. Dorsey?" said the lady, smilingly offering her hand; "this is Eveline"

"Ah! my old schoolmate, Eveline!" exclaimed the youth, gayly shaking hands with her.

After a little preliminary conversation, he blushingly tendered his services to escort Eveline to the ball; and the mother, who expected no less, smilingly consented.

When Eveline entered the ball-room on the arm of the handsome young officer, a buzz of admiration ran through the crowd. "Who is she?" "Who is she?" was whispered by some. "Miss Murray." "Miss Eveline Murray," was the reply of those who knew her by sight. "What a magnificent girl!" "Splendid girl!" "What a form!" "What a fine figure!" "Yes! what a fine figure!" were the comments of several, murmured in a low voice, as she passed; and, though her sides were aching, and her stomach sick, from compression, and though her head was dizzy and her eyes dim, Eveline bore up, and stepped more stately as she heard "fine figure," "fine figure," whispered, echoed, and re-echoed, through the room.

So Eveline was led to her seat, and soon led thence to the head of the quadrille that was forming, by the young officer. Of course the fine figure had to be displayed in motion. She expected to hear her dancing admired—for at school she was Monsieur Pace-a-way's most graceful pupil—but in this she was disappointed; no one remarked her dancing. Indeed, there were several girls in the room who had not fine figures, yet whose dancing was much more graceful than her own, and much more generally admired. In fact, she felt that the tightness of her corsage, armholes, shoes, &c., constrained the full freedom of her motions to a degree that precluded the possibility of dancing well. What she thus gained in the reputation of possessing a fine, or rather a fashionable figure, she lost in estimation as a graceful dancer. She felt this. But there was another drawback upon her claim to general admiration that she did *not* feel—it was this: notice it, young ladies, for I have observed it frequently among girls. The tightness of her dress, slightly affecting the stomach and head, spread a pallor and a languor over her features that detracted very much from the beauty of her countenance; while, as the evening progressed, her increasing sense of discomfort manifested itself in a fretfulness of expression upon her face that rendered it almost repulsive. The evening was at last over, and Mr. Dorsey prepared to conduct her home. When they were in the carriage—

"You looked very weary, Eveline; I am afraid that you stayed too long?"

"No;" said the fair girl, "I was not tired."

"You looked so."

"I am not much accustomed to these things," said Eveline; for of course she was not going to tell him that her dress was too tight.

"Ah!" exclaimed Mr. Dorsey, and the subject was dropped.

The carriage stopped before Mrs. Murray's door. It was nearly twelve o'clock at night. Mr. Dorsey handed Eveline in, and took his leave.

"And how did my darling like her first ball?" inquired the loving mother, as she set a glass of hot negus before Eveline, "to keep her from catching cold."

"Oh! mother, it was delightful!"

"And Mr. Murray?"

Eveline blushed and became silent.

"Well! Never mind, darling; but the ball?"

"Oh! it was splendid, mother!" exclaimed Eveline, who, having loosened her dress, and breathing freely, forgot her miseries. "It was very splendid; and, mother, everybody admired my figure so much!"

"I said so, my dear! I knew every one must."

"Oh! yes, mother, you should have heard them; it would have done your heart good; they all said—every one said—that I had the finest figure in the room."

" And you did not find your dress too tight ?"

" Oh ! yes, mother, it *felt* tight, but I supposed that that would wear off; and mother, don't you think that you could take in this dress a *little more* under the arms, and make it *still smaller ?* I think I could bear it *still tighter !*"

" Ah ?" smiled the deluded mother, "I thought you would be willing to bear a little inconvenience for the sake of having the finest figure in the room !"

" And will you do it, mother ?"

" Yes, love."

" And will you take in *all* my dresses, so that they may *all* fit like *this*—only *smaller ?*"

" Yes, my dear !"

" This gives such a beautiful and graceful inward sweep, from the armpits to the hips."

" Yes, love; and you must wear heavy skirts, for they will help to pull your waist down."

How much mischief that first ball-dress *had* done—was *still* to do ! Eveline naturally exclaimed against it, when first encased in it, but she had been persuaded ; had been screwed tightly up into it; had worn it to the ball; had heard her figure praised as the finest in the room, by the perverted taste of the crowd; had had her vanity stimulated by the flattery; and henceforth the fine figure, or rather the fashionable figure, was to be kept peerless in its proportions, at any cost of comfort, beauty, or health; and Eveline's doom was sealed.

" I do not know what can be the *matter* with Eveline, Dr. Drugem. She has no appetite—no spirits; she is pale, weak, and losing flesh every day," said Mrs. Murray to the family physician, whom she had called in to prescribe for her daughter.

The doctor felt her pulse, looked at her tongue, inquired more particularly into her symptoms, and announcing that her liver was affected (no wonder, when it had been compressed so much), prescribed a compound pill of blue mass, quinine,

&c. It is strange that doctors never prescribe loose dresses
in such cases.

As might have been expected, blue mass, &c., only produced
a temporary relief. The disease could not be cured until the
cause was removed; and, as long as Eveline screwed her waist
up to a span's circumference, so long continued the sick headaches, nervousness, and languor. Perhaps the health and
strength of a girl of stronger organization might have held out
longer, but Eveline was naturally frail. Soon the figure, the
very "fine figure," began to lose its beautiful lines of beauty,
its contour became thin and angular, and its want of roundness had to be supplied by padding. This was worse. The
weight of thickly padded corsages on the chest impeded her
breathing, as the tightly screwed waist impeded the circulation; and everything in health depends upon free breathing
and free circulation.

A year passed. Eveline was no longer beautiful in form
or feature. She was thin and sallow; and both these defi-
ciencies were very badly remedied by art. The medicines she
took only did harm, for the reason, as I said, that the *cause*
of her illness was not removed. At last Eveline was unable
to go out of an evening. Then in a few months she was confined to her room during the greater part of the time. Still,
with the fatuity of vanity and ignorance, she continued, whenever well enough to go into the parlour, to screw herself up
in her whaleboned dresses. It was strange that no one seemed
to suspect the cause of Eveline's ill health—no, not even the
doctor—or, if he did, he certainly never mentioned it to her,
or to her mother—just as now, there are hundreds of young
ladies in ill health, who are physicked to death nearly, and
whose parents and physicians never think of removing the
cause of the illness—their tight dressing.

Eveline was confined to her bed, and every one said that
she must die. She was emaciated until she looked like a
skeleton, and had scarcely strength to raise her poor bird-claw

looking fingers to her head. Her mother was in deep distress. She was about to lose her only child. Clem Dorsey also, who loved Eveline tenderly, and was hoping after a few years to make her his wife—Clem Dorsey grieved sincerely. He came every day, and spent many hours by the side of Eveline's couch. He seemed to love to sit in her gloomy sick-room better than to go to all the parties and balls. What were balls and parties to him, while his dearly-loved Eveline was sick? Every day he brought her flowers, or fruit, or, when she was able to be amused, a pleasant book. And he would sit by her so patiently, so lovingly, all day long—and sometimes catch himself looking so earnestly, so sadly, in her poor thin face—her face no longer pretty to any one but him. He thought it beautiful because he loved it. And how Eveline loved him! Surely, there never was a heart won under such circumstances.

"I shall pass away soon, dear Clem," she said one day, "but I shall never leave you *quite*. Oh! often when you are alone in the deep midnight watch, I will be with you; and I tell you beforehand, dear, good Clem, because I want you to have *faith;* and when you *feel* my presence, do not say to yourself that it is *fancy*, for it will be *Evy*. And when *you* are summoned hence, Clem, *I* will be the first to welcome you to the spirit world. Do not feel afraid to die, Clem; for the eyes that close on the sick-room will instantly open on the better world—on me." And at such times Clem Dorsey would walk away to the window to conceal his agitation.

"Love my mother, Clem," she would say; "love my poor childless mother."

One day, Clem Dorsey came to her with a book in his hand, looking cheerful. She raised her eyes, inquiringly—

"What is the matter, Clem?"

"I have found what I think will restore you to health, if you will follow the directions."

"Oh! some quack medicine!" said Eveline, with a faint, incredulous smile.

"Nothing of the kind, dear Evy, but an *honest, good* book, written, I think, by one who had the interest of his fellow creatures at heart. It is ' Dr. Fitch's Lectures on the Heart and Lungs.' Here are cases described, in which persons have been ill for years as you are—reduced to the point of death—some with one-half their lungs gone, who have been restored to health by reforming their habits and following the directions contained in this book. Here are authentic letters to prove it."

"Oh! that is like *all* quacks; they all work miracles—raise the dead, you know."

"Yes; but, my dearest Evy, *this* is to recommend no pills, potion, or lotion—only a *manner of life*, that will do the author of the book no kind of good if you follow it, and no harm if you don't, that I know of. The means are all in your own power, in your own room, one might say."

Then Clem turned to some of the lectures, and read them, with all their directions. These threw a flood of light into Eveline's mind, and revealed to her the whole cause and history of her complaint, as she had never understood it before—and hope sprung up in her heart. Clem Dorsey then, with his beautifully simple candour, said, "Now, Evy, there are other chapters you must read alone"—and he left the book with her.

From that day, Eveline made up her mind, with God's help, to get well. She cultivated free circulation of the blood, not having a single tight string or belt anywhere about her; and she cultivated free breathing—every day drawing as much pure air into her lungs and inflating every part of them as much as possible She grew to understand that the restoration of her health depended upon the *expansion* of that very chest and waist that had been *compressed* so long; and just in proportion as her chest and waist *expanded*, her health *returned—slowly*, because a disease *long coming on*, is apt to be *long going off.* Eveline had been a year getting ill, and it took her a year to get entirely well. And, oh! it was delightful to observe the continued joy of her mother and of Clem Dorsey, in watching her recovery.

Eveline is now in high health. She was married last month to Lieutenant Clement Dorsey, U. S. A. The Rev. J. C. S. performed the ceremony, and Dr. B. gave away the bride. Eveline looked beautifully in her white satin and pearls. To be sure, she could not have spanned her waist with her ten fingers, *now;* but then her blooming complexion, bright eyes, and the animation of her spirits, were bewitching. Clem Dorsey looked very handsome in his blue suit, with white satin vest and stock, and white kid gloves. They live with Mrs. Murray yet, because Clem Dorsey expects soon to be ordered to go on distant service, and Evy is to remain with her mother until his return. They are very happy, and they have *reason* to be. Theirs was a true-hearted affection, nurtured in sickness and sorrow, and is likely to last to the end of time— perhaps to the end of eternity.

Now, if there be one girl in ill health who reads this, I would entreat her to restore her strength by a reform in dress, diet, and habits. Instead of putting *on* strengthening plasters, put *off* tight-waisted dresses and tight shoes. Instead of taking *medicine*, take *exercise;* and above all, instead of *compressing* the waist, *expand* it, by drawing in deep inspirations—giving the lungs free play, and plenty of good fresh air. The lungs require pure cool *air*, as the stomach requires pure cool *water;* and if you wish for full and particular directions for restoring and preserving health and beauty, get and study *Dr. Fitch's Lectures on the Heart and Lungs.*

THE THREE SISTERS;

OR,

NEW YEAR IN THE LITTLE ROUGH-CAST HOUSE.

Who hath woe? Who hath sorrow? Who hath contentions? Who
hath babblings?
Who hath wounds without cause? Who hath redness of eyes?
They that tarry long at the wine: they that go to seek mixed wine.
Look not thou upon the wine when it is red, when it giveth his
colour in the cup, when it moveth itself aright.
At the last it biteth like a serpent, and stingeth like an adder.

PROVERBS xxiii. 29–32.

CHAPTER I.

INTRODUCTION.

BEAR with me, dear reader, for saying one serious word in
the gay holidays. Bear with me, that I pause a moment to
listen, amid the grand diapason of joy, for the under tone, the
low, unheard murmur, the half-suppressed wail of suffering,
of poverty, sickness, and sorrow. It is that you may, amid
your rejoicing, remember to relieve this. Christmas, while it
comes to bring joy to *all* the earth, and really does augment
the happiness of the prosperous—Christmas, the religious, the
joyous festival, absolutely increases the sufferings of the poor.
It comes at the season when want is most severely felt by them ;
it brings out into the foreground the strongest points of con-
trast between their condition and yours. This contrast is felt

(207)

in proportion to the ratio of descent in circumstances, from
your state to that of the poorest street mendicant. We all
know the force of contrast. That between the prosperous
and the suffering is brought out in greatest strength just at
this time. It augments the trials of the latter—they cannot
escape it—the rich and the poor are too closely jumbled together in locality. Have you ever seen a poor woman walking through the crowded, lighted, and merry market-house on
Christmas or New Year's Eve? Drawn by a singular fasci-
nation to torture herself by the sight of luxuries that taunt
her penury, of merriment that mocks her sorrows—ay, even
of necessaries, of common good bread and butter—that assails
her sense of smell, stimulating and tantalizing the appetite she
cannot satisfy—have you seen her haggard cheeks, her hungry
eye? If you have not, you have gone through the market
with eyes so dazzled by the light, ears so deafened by the
merry noises, mind so intent upon the purchase of your turkey,
that you have brushed and hustled past her at every turn,
treading on her toes, and crowding her into corners unconsciously. If you *had* seen her, you would have put a "loaf
of bread and pound of butter" in her empty hands—she had no
basket there, and for that matter, no *business* there. The contrast was brought out into strong relief. How do you think
it felt to her? *You* did not feel it; if you had, you would
have given her a chicken for her New Year's dinner, or lost
your appetite for your own. Have you ever seen, on Christmas or New Year's Eve, a poor little child looking wistfully,
wishfully into the windows of a toy or pastry cook shop,
knowing that none of all these fine things are for him? You
will say, nonchalantly, that "toys and confectioneries are not
the necessaries of life—children can do very well without
them,"—and so they can, if they *never* saw them, if they never
saw *other* children have them; as it is, it is a privation—not
the less keenly felt, because it is a mental and not a physical
privation. It is the reality of the suffering by contrast that I

wish to show. I do not wish to make *you* gloomy, but to be
the means of making others glad. I do not wish to cast a
cloud over your sunshine, but to send a ray of your sunshine
to gild another's cloud. I want you to "remember the poor,"
emphatically in New Year's times, to "remember the poor you
have always with you." I want you, just for the season, to
forget the mooted question as to whether almsgiving is expedient. "Assuredly" it is expedient at New Year's times. It
looks like a great expense to make all the poor neighbourhood
comfortable, as a whole—but divided, it is a mere trifle—for
—listen! Every man and woman in good circumstances has
his own or her own particular acquaintances among the very
poor—they may not be daily companions, or very intimate
friends—but you know them. A very small donation, incon-
siderable when counted with the expenses of your year, would
make the two or three needy acquaintances of each comfortable for the time, and equalize the enjoyments of New Year,
and soften the harshness, abate the friction of the temporarily
exaggerated contrast. Now that you have swallowed the pill,
you shall have the lump of sugar; now that you have dined
on solid beef, you shall have the whipped-syllabub; now that you
have listened to the little sermon, you shall have the little
story, and if any child should ask me with childish *naiveté*—
"Is it true?"—I can answer, every word is true.

CHAPTER II.

THE THREE COTTAGES.

It is a feature in our great sprawling village of Washington
City, that the ebb and flow of the tide of business is very great
The city, during the session of Congress, being busy as the

busiest thoroughfares of New York or London, and in the recess of Congress looking as desolate as Goldsmith's Deserted Village. This influence is felt from the wholesale merchant down to the plain needle-woman. All classes, from the proprietors of hotels down to the oyster horn-blowing boys, and from the printer down to the President, are overworked during the sessions of Congress, and have very little to do in the interval. But *our* business is just now with the most unobtrusive of business people—a plain seamstress.

It was in the winter of 184–, that Mrs. S———, the wife of Judge S———, Senator from Mississippi, had, like all Southern and Western ladies, come to Washington with a plenty of gold and nothing else—with the benevolent intention of patronizing our city by buying everything from our merchants, jewellers, &c., and having everything made up by our milliners, mantua-makers, and seamstresses—and—*perhaps*, as there is a leaven of unrighteousness in all things—*perhaps* to get the latest *fashions*, which our dress-makers, &c., had got from the Eastern cities, in expectation of their custom. Well! Mrs. S——— had come; had accomplished an inconceivable amount of shopping, and was now at her wits' ends to find a mantua-maker at leisure to make up her splendid satins and velvets for the season. Mrs. Polk's reception was to come on and come off on Friday evening—to be followed on Saturday evening by a ball at Madame B———o's. *This week* and *next week* were to witness a succession of brilliant parties, to be given by the ladies of the foreign embassies, and by the ladies of members of the Cabinet.

The Mississippi belle was hurried, worried, and distressed. It was absolutely necessary to have a different dress for each one of these different entertainments, and not a mantua-maker could she find at leisure, after having driven over two-thirds of Washington City. It happened to be during her tour among the mantua-makers that I left my card at her door. She called to see me the next day, and the cause of her distress broke through all the rather stately ceremony of a Mississippi morning visiter. I chanced to be able to do her and another a service. There are suburbs in Washington City that strangers *seldom*—that Senators' ladies *never* visit. On such a suburb I remembered to have seen a dress-maker's sign hung out at the neatest little two-story framed house, with the prettiest garden and yard that ever was seen. I knew from her remoteness from business localities, that the woman could have only a moderate supply of work. I volunteered to attend the lady to her house. We set off—there was no time to be lost. We arrived at the cottages.

I must describe that locality, for it was a "right pretty" place. It is the eastern slope of the Capitol Hill, as it gradually declines to the Anacostia River, reaching it at a couple of miles distance. In summer it is *very* beautiful; covered with thick, soft, green grass, and dappled over with the shade of a few scattered and hoary forest trees, and with clumps of a newer and spontaneous growth of brush-wood, and sprinkled here and there with very small white framed houses, with very large gardens. These are generally the property of day labourers in the Navy-Yird, and other poor but industrious and temperate men, who are enabled to build them by reason of the low price of lots in that section. (I have known lots sell there, at private sale, too, at a cent and a half a foot.) We, Mrs. S——— and self, had traversed nearly half the distance between the summit of the Capitol Hill and the river, going straight east, when we came to a street, or rather a lane, for in summer the middle of it was green and untrodden as the margin of a brook. We turned up this lane, and in all its distance there were but three houses. I called them the three cottages. They were all in a row, but not very close together —there was abundance of space all around each. The group stood alone, but not solitary; there were sprinklings of white houses scattered all around. These three cottages were all small, two stories high, painted white, with green blinds, and

each stood in the midst of a little garden of its own. The
house to which we were going was the first one in the row.
I had never been there before.   I had only discovered it in
passing by.   Now I noticed that though all the cottages were
neat, *this* was the neatest by far of the three.   The paint of
the house and of the fence was white as snow, and the brick
walk that led from the gate up to the door was coloured of a
lively vermillion red.   Three or four planks were laid across
the street, and a mat actually laid *outside* the front gate, to
prevent visiters from bringing the least soil upon the clean
varnished bricks of the walk.   We went in and rapped at the
door.   It was opened by a small, slender woman, whose fair
skin, flaxen hair, and blue eyes, were thrown into strong relief
by her widow's dress of black bombazine.   The inside of the
house was a miracle of brightness and cleanliness, bright
brasses, bright glasses, and bright colours in the carpet gleaming through the shade.   We passed into a back room, where
the nice home-made carpet, and neat paper blinds, spoke
volumes in praise of the little widow's industry and economy
Mrs. S·———— soon opened her business, and found a very
willing agent in the little widow, whose name we ascertained
to be Fairfield.   We soon concluded our visit, and returned
to "the city," as the neighbourhood of Pennsylvania Avenue
is called par excellence.   I went away, but did not soon forget
the Three Cottages—they attracted, interested me—with their
neatness, beauty, and isolation.   I had observed that the cen-
tral one was a little shop, with jars of candy, tumblers of slate-
pencils, stacks of clay pipes, tallow candles, apples, &c., arranged in the windows, but it appeared as yet too humble to
boast a sign-board with the name of the proprietor.   I saw no
more of the cottages, however, until the spring, when being
hurried with work, I went to seek the little widow seamstress.
I found the cottages snow-white in their green and blooming
gardens, and the little widow, neat, busy, and cheerful as ever
Very tired with the long walk, I sat an hour or two, and she

being very talkative, gave me the history of the cottages and
their inmates. The history and its denouement was rather
remarkable—I will give it to you—in my own words, for the
sake of condensation.

CHAPTER III.

THE THREE SISTERS.

MRS. ANDERSON had been left a widow with three daughters,—Mary, aged twelve, Ellen, aged ten, and Lydia, aged
two years. She supported this little family by carpet-weaving,
a trade in which there was so little competition as to afford
her an abundance of work and good prices. Mrs. Anderson
had sent her children to a public school, where they had received a good common education. More than this, she had
saved enough money to purchase three lots upon that eastern
suburb, where land was then cheap, though expected to rise
in value. These lots she designed as dowers to her daughters.
The eldest daughter, Mary, was married at seventeen, to a
young carpenter by the name of Fairfield. He built the first
cottage in the row upon the lot assigned to the bride. He
furnished it nicely, and the young couple went to housekeeping.

It was during the third year of their marriage, and when
they were the parents of two children, that the second sister,
Ellen, was wedded to a young man in the cabinet-making business This marriage was not approved by the widowed mother.
She opposed it long and determinately, and only yielded at
last to the tears and lamentations of her second daughter.
There was something in Mr. Bohrer's face, expression, and
manners, that she did not like. It impressed all observers unfavourably, at least all observers except his maiden-love, Ellen.
Yet he was a handsome, black-eyed, laughing fellow enough.

and perfectly unimpeachable in conduct. It was, perhaps, the
intangibility of the cause of her prejudice that at last silenced
the mother's opposition. Yet her instincts had not deceived
her, as the sequel of our story will show. She gave him her
daughter, Ellen, and her dower, the lot adjoining that of the
Fairfields. He contracted with his brother-in-law to build him
a cottage upon it. When it was finished, and soon after he
had moved into it, the difficulty of procuring the thousand-and-
one trifles in daily demand in housekeeping, suggested to
Bohrer the idea of opening a little shop in that humble suburb.
He fitted up the front room with shelves, counter, &c., and
laid in a small stock of family groceries, trimmings, and, in
short, of all things that go to fill up a small country or suburban
shop. He prospered in the little business, getting the custom
of all the day-labourers around. It had been very well if he
had only stopped *there*. But often, on a cold Saturday night,
when a labouring man would come in shuddering and blowing,
and meet there one or two of his neighbours and fellow-
labourers on the same errand with himself, namely, with his
week's wages in his pocket to lay in his week's supply of family
groceries, one or another would say,

"Bother it, Bohrer, why don't you keep something to
drink?"

Bohrer had no scruples of his own. It was his wife's and
his mother-in-law's prejudices against the selling of alcohol
that influenced him, but he had not the moral courage to say
so.

"Oh-h-h!" he would reply, in his musical drawl, "we are
not fixed up yet—we have no conveniences—wait a bit."

At last Christmas approached. On Christmas Eve, every
one of the day-labourers who lived in the neighbourhood, assembled in the shop of Bohrer. All were merry—merry as
they could be. They needed not the stimulus of alcohol.
Yet they fancied that something was wanting.

"Set fire to you, Bohrer! why don't you keep something

to *drink?*" inquired one of the men, with a sort of gay impatience. "Haven't you got anything to *drink?*"

Bohrer shook his head, laughingly, but soon became thoughtful—seemed calculating.

"Just think of it," said another man, "if *you* had the needful on the spot, my family could have some egg-nog tomorrow; but *now* we shall have to do without it, because we cannot get the brandy; for I do not care enough about it to trudge all the way up to Pennsylvania Avenue for it—do you, Smith? Say!—perhaps if I can get company, I will go up to Simms's—will you go, Smith—will you, Adams?"

"No! oh, no!" replied both the men, "it is too far—it is too cold."

"Well, so it is, and we are very comfortable here," said the first speaker.

But Bohrer was leaning across the counter, with his elbow resting upon it, with the tip of his forefinger pressed upon his brow, in an attitude, and with an expression of astute calculation. There were from twelve to fifteen men in the shop, and others constantly coming in and going out, all willing to take a dram, all willing to buy liquor to take home to their families, but none caring enough for it *yet* to go a mile up in the city for it. These were his weekly customers. Many of them were now taking up their baskets to go home.

"See here, friends," said Bohrer, rousing himself, "I mean to have some first-rate spirits here in the holidays—all for your convenience—for the convenience of customers, you know."

"Very well!" "That's you!" "So do!" were the various exclamations with which this announcement was received by the merry set as they hurried away from the shop.

Bohrer was as bad as his word. The second day after Christmas he had a cask of brandy and one of whiskey brought down—and as a part of the same policy, took out a license to sell it by the "dram." On New-Year's Eve, when the

13

labourers came to his shop, there was no lack of "Something to drink."

They remained until nearly twelve o'clock, converting, or rather perverting, not only the shop but the little back parlour, hitherto sacred to Ellen's privacy, into a scene of roystering festivity—they would shout the Old Year out and halloo the New Year in, in glorious style.

Ellen sat there by the side of her baby's cradle, feeling, but too gentle to *look*, far less to *speak*, disapproval of the scene. To Ellen, there was something infinitely solemn and sweet in the last hours of the old year,—the dying year. They were the last moments of an old man who had been a kind benefactor to her, and she could not be ungrateful or insensible at his death. That year, as its first donation, at its commencement, had given her her husband—that dear Wilhelm, or Willie, as she preferred to call him—and now remembering and tenderly sensible of the gift, she could not rejoice that the giver was near his end. That year, near its close, had laid upon her bosom her first babe—the little Elly, now an infant of six weeks old, and slumbering in the cradle by her side. How could she sympathize with the mad revellers whose orgies made terrible the lingering moments of the old benefactor? She sat apart, alone, and rendered the grateful homage of a thoughtful and serious vigil. Ellen was not ascetic—no one could look in her earnest, tender, gentle face, and accuse her of asceticism, yet to her the last moments of the Old Year seemed a time suggestive of devotion rather than of revelry. It was ten o'clock when the opening of the shop door and the ringing of the bell attached to it, announced a customer. Bohrer went forward, exclaiming,

"It is Frank Miller," and soon Ellen heard a cheerful, youthful voice sing out—

"Just come this evening—yes! just come—been to see Lydia, and found mother in a desperate fix for a pound of candles—it was too late for her or Lydia to venture out. par t'cularly when the streets are in such an uproar as they are in to-night, and so I volunteered to do their errand."

"Well! come in—come in," replied Bohrer, "we are keeping the season, you see! walk forward."

"Oh! no, I thank you, I must hurry immediately back."

"Ay! but step into the back room a moment! We have some prime egg-nog—come, come!"

"Well—*indeed* I am pressed for time."

"Nonsense! pressed for time with a new instalment of time within a few hours of arriving. Come in, and see Ellen and the baby."

"Well, I should like to see that baby and to speak to Ellen a minute. I do not care if I do step in for *just* a moment," and the young man came forward into the little back room, where he was greeted by a half score of acquaintances. Shaking hands and passing laughingly through them all, he made his way to Ellen's side and sat down by her. She received him smilingly. Well she might! he was handsome, frank, affectionate, and the betrothed of her youngest and favourite sister Lydia. A little too impulsive Ellen though' --a little too forgetful of past experiences, and too reckless of future consequences when tempted by the enjoyment of the moment—a little too ready to enter into any fun, or take part in any frolic that might be going forward, but so gay, so good-humoured, so disinterested with it all, that it seemed impossible to blame him. He was at this time employed at a small salary as clerk on board of one of the steamboats that run from Washington City to Norfolk. The boat had just got up, and he had just arrived, as he announced.

"Come! take a drink, Frank! it will do you good!" exclaimed Bohrer, bailing out a large glass of egg-nog and handing it to him.

He received it, and passing it untouched to Ellen, said, with a charming blending of affection and gallantry,

"Ellen! come—place your lips to the brim—consecrate
the draught for me."

"No, Frank; I cannot,"

"What! don't you like it?'

"I do not know whether I like it or not—I never tasted
it."

"Well, then try—come!"

"*No.*"

"Why not, Ellen? are you a total abstinence woman?"

"Yes."

"Taken the pledge and all that?"

"No, I have taken no pledge, because I have not fallen in
the way of taking pledges; but mother never was accustomed
to use any kind of spirits in her family, and so we all rather
dislike the taste and smell, or rather we dislike the smell, and
we think we should dislike the taste."

"*Lydia* doesn't—begging your pardon—Lydia has more
sense than any of you girls—*she* knows what's good. Why,
the other night when our boat was out—*you* know when I
took Lydia to hear the Ethiopian serenaders. When we came
out it was so cold. It was so cold and we had so far to walk,
that as it was but ten o'clock, I took her into Jones's confec-
tionery, and into the back parlour where it was warm and comfortable; and I ordered a couple of glasses of noyau and some
cakes. The whole thing was perfectly new to the little creature, and she enjoyed it, *I* tell you. We spent an hour there.
Oh, it was nice, cozy! the bright coal-fire glowing through the
polished steel bars of the grate, and the soft cushionery carpet,
and the spring elastic chairs covered with red cut velvet, and
the pictures and the mirrors. Little Lydia felt herself in a
palace. She examined all the pictures—looked at herself in
all the mirrors—sat down in all the chairs in succession to
try them, and found each one more comfortable or luxurious
than all the rest. Her verdant pleasure was perfectly refreshing to us, who am quite accustomed to those things," said the

youth, with the self-satisfied air of a man who had seen and been satiated with life, and who was inclined to patronize young people.

Ellen was looking at him and listening to his words with an air of grave rebuke. But he did not perceive her disapproval. Ellen's serious disapprobation was so gently, so delicately manifested, that none but a very close observer could see it, none but a very sensitive person feel it.

"And how," she gently inquired, "did Lydia look back upon this evening, after the excitement—for it seems to me that her pleasure was excitement—was over?"

"*De*-lightedly!" laughed the young man, with great glee. "It was fun alive to see the little one. *Every* time I have taken her out of an evening since, whether to meetings, or lectures, or exhibitions or what not—in coming home Lydia has surely become hungry or thirsty, or cold or tired! *always!* And I have laughed in my sleeve and taken her into a confectioner's—and, by the way, I wish we had her here to-night, *she* would help me drink this," said Frank, as he sipped his egg-nog.

"But, Frank," said Ellen, speaking very gently, in a low tone—speaking evidently with reluctance—"does not the idea of a young girl loving wine and cordial strike you unpleasantly?—does it not revolt you, as something—" she hesitated for a softer, kinder word, but finding none went on to say— "does it not revolt you as something coarse and sensual?"

"Now, Ellen, see here—now don't—I can't listen to 'coarse,' and that other worse word, put in the same sentence with Lydia, much less applied as adjectives to anything she says, does, or thinks! Lydia is *my* business; I do all I can for her now, but when we are married, please God, I will do *everything* for her—she shall have *just* exactly everything she *wants!* let it be what it will. Bless your soul, I want Lydia as a medium of happiness; the only way I can enjoy life in its highest is through her! To see Lydia's bright, bright eyes, shining down on the glass of wine at her lips —shining down on it as the sun shines down upon a clear lake—lighting it up! To see Lydia eat a *bon-bon*, as if her fresh, rosy lips had a separate consciousness! To see Lydia sink into an easy chair, with such *beautiful* abandonment! She enters into all these little treats with such *intense* relish!"

"Lydia has been unaccustomed to luxuries. Our mother brought up all her children plainly. These things are new to her, and she is very young—that is her only excuse."

"'Excuse!' I wish you would not talk so, Ellen? *She* needs no excuse! but there! it is eleven o'clock, and here have I been, forgetting that Lydia and her mother are sitting at home in darkness, waiting for the candles, while I have been dawdling my time away, and keeping you up too, I dare say."

"No, you are not keeping me up, I intend to stay up till these people are shamed into going home; I *must* do that; I cannot leave Wilhelm here to tempt others, and be tempted himself into any greater excesses. But you, Frank, you must go home, you are very thoughtless."

"Thoughtless! so I am, so I intend to be; I never saw the use of being thoughtful, except to turn the hair gray. But how have I been thoughtless, I pray?"

"Why, here you have set, keeping your sweetheart out of the necessaries of life, while very sincerely hearing yourself talk of providing her with all the luxuries—that is like you, Frank—you are a very earnest promiser, but a very uncertain performer."

In reply to this, Frank stooped down and kissed the baby in the cradle, and ran from the room, pausing in the shop to take a second and a hasty glass of egg-nog.

CHAPTER IV

GOING TO HOUSEKEEPING

EVERY one loved Frank Miller—it was impossible not to love him. Every one, that is of his own neighbourhood, took an interest in his approaching marriage. It was to come off early in the year, and the young couple were to reside with the mother of the bride for a few months, until their house, the third one in the row, could be completed and furnished for their reception. As this was the marriage of her youngest, her favourite, and her last remaining daughter, the old lady determined to go to the expense of a wedding, and invite all the neighbourhood to it. The unpretending trousseau of the bride had been ready a month before, and so the last week previous to the marriage had been devoted by the little widow to preparation for her guests. The day previous to the wedding she was *very* busy frosting cakes and shedding tears; yet with a mother's generous self-devotion, concealing, or trying to conceal from the little bride elect, the secret pain she was suffering at the thought of giving up her last and best beloved daughter, her baby, her pet, her *spoiled* child. She dodged and avoided Lydia as much as she could, and dropped her quiet tears into the baskets of fruit or plates of cake. A remorseful tenderness weighed down Lydia's eyelids also, as she busied herself in her chamber with the smaller details of her dress, and sometimes she would trip down stairs to embrace her mother, and to assure her that no change of her own relations should or ever *could* abate her love for " mother."

" But *will you* love me as well *afterwards*, mother? Won't you soon grow to look upon your child as an old married woman, absorbed in common-place family cares, who does not need your care and your petting?"

'Ah! but my baby, *Frank* will love and pet you, and then you will not care for my petting."

This was said in a voice of assumed playfulness, but the under tone of sadness moaned up through it.

"Mother! sit down and take me in your lap. Dear mother! no one can supply your place to me—no one can fill your chamber in my heart, or crowd you out of it, or come near it, mother! it is *so* sacred! It is the chapel of my heart—my mother! Stroke my face, mother—play with my hair—kiss me—mother, kiss me! never mind the cakes to-day, mother—*do*, never mind the cakes, mother, for once. Love me, mother—my heart is nearly breaking just now! I wish I were not a woman, with a woman's wants and responsibilities. I wish I could always have been your baby, mother." And the fair bride burst into tears. Her mother rocked and soothed her, just as though she had been a little child, and spoke to her cheerfully.

"Frank is a good, a *very* good young man, and he loves you, darling."

"Ah, mother, I do not find fault with Frank—he is *good* —*of course* he is—but, mother, there is a something, a nursing tenderness in your affection that I do not find in any other. Frank loves me as a boy loves a girl, with more fun and frolic than tenderness, and you, mother! oh, won't you be *so* lonesome when I am gone?"

"My darling!" said the mother, gently, "this is morbid in both of us—this is very weak, and we must not give way to it—no, I did not say our *love* was weak, our caresses were weak, my nursing you was weak," murmured she, as Lydia made a movement to leave her arms; "I said, my dear, this crying is wrong, ungrateful to Providence—we must not indulge in sentimentality—mother must try to remember that she gains another son, not loses her last daughter."

"Oh! mother, but why cannot we both, Frank, and I, live with you, or you with us? Why should a daughter, when she is married, have the cloud of separation from her mother thrown over the sunshine of her bridehood? Sons don't mind it, but daughters do—oh! so much! and it is such a useless shadow! Why cannot people live in great houses big enough for two or three families, and when their daughters are married keep them still at home—and when their sons are married let them go live with the parents of their brides; it seems to me, it would be so much better than to have these cruel partings. There is seldom on earth more than three generations at a time, and it does seem to me that one large house should be big enough to hold them. It would be so nice, the grand-parents, and the children and grandchildren, all united together in a band of household love. So beautiful! Oh! would it not be?"

"My baby, you talk like a young girl."

"But would it *not* be, now?"

"Perhaps so—sometimes I think so, but maybe I am only selfish when I think I am right."

"Here are you, poor, dear, lonely mother, who have toiled through all your best days, labouring hard to raise your chil-dren, to see them go, one after another, and to be left alone in your age. Mother, listen! Frank is young, and I am young; it will not break our hearts, either, if we are *not* married; if now you repent your consent to part with me, you may now recall it! Mother, indeed I am in earnest. You ought to have *one* daughter left to you. I never *felt* it before, but you *ought—ought*. It is only justice—bare justice! Tell me, mother, if you don't want me to leave you, *I won't* leave you. I won't get married; *poor Frank*—indeed I won't, poor, dear mother!"

"My little one, you would cut your heart in two, and give me and Frank each a half, if you thought it would make us happy, I have no doubt in the world!"

"Shall I, mother?"

"Cut your heart in two?" asked the widow, playfully, to make her cheerful.

"La, no, mother!" smiled Lydia, through her tears; "I mean shall I not leave you—shall I not get married?"

"My dear, you make me a proposition that both of us would regret next week if I accepted it to-night—no, love, you must be married—never mind mother's loneliness. She will come over and take many a sociable cup of tea with you, and you and Frank shall come to her often."

"Oh! yes, mother," exclaimed the childish bride, her thoughts springing off into gleeful anticipation, "and you shall have such a nice little bed-room when you want to stay all night—it shall be called 'mother's room.'"

"There! now go, my darling, and finish trimming your dress, while I frost these cakes, and mind, come down to tea with a pleasant smile. Frank will be here to tea, you know!"

"Oh! yes, so he will!" exclaimed Lydia, kissing her mother, and tripping away up stairs. The widow dropped her head upon her hands a moment, in silent prayer, and rising, went about her work.

The next evening the wedding came off. The widow's little sitting-room and parlour were filled to overflowing with guests.

The bride was beautiful, as all brides are stereotyped (not daguerreotyped—*that* is another matter) to be. The bride-groom was happy, and awkward to the last possible degree, so that Frank was in danger of losing his character for gay indifference. The company were cheerful, and enjoyed themselves as only working people *can* enjoy a festival. The refreshments were abundant. The old lady had provided tea and coffee, but no wine or cordial. This deficiency was, however, supplied in the course of the evening by Bohrer, who, judging his mother-in-law by himself, fancied that the only reason of its absence must arise from her parsimony. Exhilarated by the occasion, the company, lights, and good cheer, he caught a generous fit, and manifested it in his own peculiar manner—by running "over to the shop" for a demi-john of cordial. In the course of the evening Mrs. Anderson had an opportunity of perceiving for the first time, a weak tendency in her new son-in-law—a somewhat alarming love of alcoholic stimulus.

—————

CHAPTER V.

THE LITTLE HOME.

THE young couple passed the winter months with the mother of the bride. As soon as the spring opened, Frank engaged his brother-in law, Mr. Fairfield, to build for them a small, two-storied framed cottage, upon the third and last lot in the row. This cottage was upon the same simple plan of the other two, with its neatly laid out garden behind, and its flower yard in front. All the leisure time of the young bride and bridegroom were now bestowed in laying out and planting beds of kitchen vegetables or parterres of flowers, so that about the time at which the house was completed, the flowers and the table vegetables were beginning to grow.

Mrs. Anderson had announced to Frank her intention to furnish their house; and when it was finished she set out with Lydia to choose the furniture. The mother's devotion, and the daughter's thoughtlessness, were made manifest that day. They went first to "Griggs's," and inquiring first for chamber furniture, were shown complete sets of all prices, from common, plain stained pine, to the most highly finished rose-wood. But one set struck Lydia's fancy. Very beautiful it was indeed, and certainly very cheap, yet too costly for their circumstances. The set consisted of a French bedstead, bureau with swinging mirror, wardrobe, wash-stand, cabinet and chairs, all pine, but painted pure white, and so highly varnished as to resemble porcelain.

"Oh, mother, look! this is beautiful! this is lovely! *do* get this! What is the price of this, Mr. Griggs?"

"Eighty dollars for the whole set, madam—very low—we make next to nothing by them."

"That seems a great deal of money, but indeed they are worth it—mother!"

"Well, my dear?"

"I like this white set—come," said she, drawing her mother away into a corner, "I *do* want that set so *much*, mother—they will look so beautiful, all pure white as they are, arranged in my chamber, with a straw matting on the floor, and with white dimity curtains at the windows, and a white Marseilles counterpane on the bed by this, mother!"

"My dear, it will cost very much more than ι had calculated to spend upon chamber furniture."

"Oh! well, dear mother, just *you* buy this and no more; let Frank purchase the rest of the things needful."

"But, my love, Frank has already contracted debt for lumber to build your home, and he owes, also, for the work. Frank must not be called upon to spend much!"

"Oh, but, mother, I will economize, indeed I will."

"My dear, I have tried all that, and I know by bitter experience how it works. You can never make up by *after* economy for past extravagant expenditure. My dear, take this along with you as a safe rule. Always, if possible, economize *before* an unusual expenditure—attempts at retrenchment afterward, are usually failures"

"But, mother, to come back to the subject of this chamber furniture—I shall never be contented with dull, red pine bedsteads and bureaus, now that I have seen this beautiful set, looking like the finest white porcelain! Mother, I have the picture of a pure, clean, sweet chamber, to the realization of which, this white furniture is needful—is positively necessary; and I cannot do without it!"

"You shall have it, my love."

"Dear mother, how I thank you—I know and feel that I am selfish in this, and that you are self-devoted—are magnanimous! Yes, mother, I know how naughty I am, without being able to be anything else *but* naughty."

The mother sighed. The daughter looked up with interest—with an expression of pain crossing her features.

"Dear mother, do you think me *very* selfish?"

"*Lydia*," was all she said, in a tone of perplexed sadness. She saw the tendency to selfish indulgence in the young woman, and while too conscientious to disclaim her knowledge of the fault, she lacked the moral courage to rebuke it in the daughter whom she was so soon about to lose.

The purchase was made, and the furniture sent home. It was Mrs. Anderson's disposition to do everything she undertook *thoroughly*. Lydia's house was furnished with everything needful to comfort, even down to the minutest details. And then the bridegroom and bride removed into it.

Very sadly felt the old lady when left in utter solitude. She had gone home with the young couple, had remained to tea, and returned home immediately after. Very lonely it it was to go to bed in the silent house; very lonely to rise and get breakfast for *one;* very sorrowful to eat that meal in solitude, and to feel that this was the first day of many years of loneliness, unless—as a secret hope whispered her—unless one of her three sons-in-law should invite her to take up her residence in his family. It was a dreary prospect to grow old alone in that house, in that house where her toil had been sweetened by the society of her children, in that house whose walls had echoed the glad shouts of their infancy, and the music-laughter of their girlhood, when they loved only "mother"—that vacant, silent, cold house! This was the first painful feeling consequent upon the marriage of her last, remaining daughter.

but this in time wore off, as she grew accustomed to her solitude.

A want of reflection and of frankness is frequently the most
fertile cause of misapprehension and misconstruction among
relatives and friends. This was the case with Mrs. Anderson
and her family. She was loved as one of her gentle and
unselfish nature was sure to be loved; yet, engaged as her
sons-in-law were in hard work every day, and coming home
fatigued as they did every night, thinking only of business
in the morning, only of fireside enjoyments in the evening,
they did not reflect upon, or sympathize with the peculiar
griefs of the forsaken mother. They barely *knew* that she
was alone, they did not *feel* it; if they *had*, there would probably have been a rivalry as to who should have received and
monopolized the company of the mother. On the part of her
daughters a fastidious—perhaps you will think a *morbid* delicacy inherited from their mother—kept them from making
known their secret wishes upon the subject. Affairs went on
in this way for a year succeeding the marriage of Lydia, and
I do not know how long they would have continued to misunderstand each other, had not one of those providences of
domestic life adjusted their difficulties. Lydia was expecting
to become a mother, and the little self-indulgent creature grew
every day more unwilling, and therefore incompetent to do
her little house-work. Frank proposed to hire a girl, but
Lydia, with what Frank, in his indulgent love, called her
"pretty petulance," could not bear the idea of a stranger in
the house. Frank, whose greater affection gave him more
acuteness upon the subject of his young wife's wishes, than
either of his brothers-in-law possessed—Frank knew that she
wanted her mother, and heroically set himself to what he
honestly supposed would be a herculean labour, namely, the
task of persuading "mother" to leave her own comfortable
little rough-cast house where she had lived for thirty years,
and to take up her abode with them. It was beautiful to

observe how Frank went about it, with his modest and graceful embarrassment; and it was charming to see the quiet joy of the mother when she perceived that so far from being selfishness, it was humility that prevented her favourite son-in-law from making this proposition, until impelled by the new force of his little wife's wishes. Mrs. Anderson made Frank happy by at once acceding to his proposal, and the young husband returned to surprise his wife with the joyful intelligence that her mother was coming to live with them. That was a happy evening at "Rose Cottage." "Mother" came over to take tea, and settle the preliminaries of her removal. The house was very small, containing only two rooms, a parlour and kitchen, on the ground-floor, two bed-chambers above, and an attic; but it was large enough for them. The front room up stairs was Lydia's pure white chamber; the back room was to be fitted up for "mother," because it overlooked the garden and poultry yard, that mother would always feel interested in; because the stair-case led from this room to the attic, where mother could bestow the accumulated domestic treasure of years, treasures in the shape of patch-work, carpet-balls, &c., and, finally, because it contained numerous closets and cupboards for mother's bottles of oils and essences, and jars of jelly, &c., &c.

All these matters were discussed and arranged at the tea-table. It was now the first of December. It was settled that Mrs. Anderson should receive all her children under her roof once more upon Christmas Day, and should then remove to Rose Cottage in time for a New Year's family party to be given by Lydia. Having concluded all these preliminaries, the old lady returned home late at night, attended by Frank.

In a few days it was rumoured among the sisters that "mother" was going to live with Lydia, and a generous rivalry was excited. Fairfield, the husband of Mary, and the senior son-in-law, waited on the old lady, and said, in his open way, that if he had had any suspicion that Mrs. Anderson intended

to break up housekeeping, he and Mary should have hastened
to put in their claim to her company at their own house.

"And indeed, you know, mother," he argued, "it is our
right—we are the eldest—you slight us—you neglect us, to
pass us by and settle with little Lydia."

"But for the very reason you advance as an objection, for
her youth, Lydia needs me more than either of her sisters."

Fairfield used both argument and persuasion, but without
effect. He reported his failure to his wife and to Ellen, who
took supper with them that evening. The next day found
Ellen at her mother's house upon the same errand.

"I cannot, like Fairfield and Mary, by the rights of primo-
geniture, claim your *justice*, mother; nor can I, like little
Lydia, through helplessness, appeal to your *mercy*—but I do
desire a share of your society, mother, and I have come to ask
you if it would not be well to divide your time between us,
living four months of the year with each of your children in
rotation."

"My dear Ellen, an old woman like I am, needs a settled
home—not *alone*—that is too dreary, but a settled home with
one of her children. This moving about will not do for me.
I have decided to abide with Lydia, because she needs me
I will see you and Mary as frequently as I can besides, and
you must all of you come to me at Christmas, that I may
have all my children once more beneath my own roof."

The Christmas party came off, and after it was over, Mrs.
Anderson began her preparations for removal. The greater
part of her household furniture, together with her garden im-
plements and her poultry, were divided equally among her
daughters. The cow, the favourite white bantam chickens,
and the old tortoise-shell cat were sent in advance of herself
to "Lydia's." The rough-cast house, which was very small
and very old, was let out at a small rent, and by New Year's
Eve the old lady was at home with her favourite daughter.

CHAPTER VI.

NEW YEAR AT ROSE COTTAGE.

FRANK and Lydia had invited all their sisters and brothers with all their children. There were John and Mary Fairfield, with their three boys, Sam, Willie, and little Harry, and Wilhelm and Ellen Bohrer, with their two beautiful little girls, Susie and Bessie, and a merry New Year's party they made, now that their little excitement of rivalry had subsided—a merrier, happier party than they were ever destined to form again—no presentiment of that fact, however, shadowed the brightness of their spirits, or dampened their mirth. As soon as supper was over, the old lady, fatigued with the unusual exertions of the day, was comfortably ensconced in a large arm-chair by the side of the glowing grate, and her grandchildren crowded round her for caresses. Her attention was thereby abstracted from the general company, and it was not until the hour for breaking up arrived, and the party had dispersed, that a terrible fact was made known to her, in this manner. She had observed that Frank had kept his seat through all the bustle of the departure, and ascribed his inertness to indisposition. After seeing the last guest depart, she returned, and going up to Frank, inquired how he felt. He was sitting with his back against the wall, with both his feet lazily extended, with his hand idly thrust into his breeches pocket, and his head, with an expression of drivelling, idiotic complacency, bowed sideways upon his breast. He looked up with the stupid stare, and replied in the maudlin tones of intoxication,

"Jolly, old gal!"

The widow clasped her hands together, and gazed at him in

14

deep distress, and without one word of comment turned away
—turned away to see her daughter weeping bitterly. Lydia
was seated in a chair accidentally drawn up to a table, upon
which her arms and head were thrown in the abandonment of
grief, and sobs, such as only burst from an almost broken heart,
were convulsing her bosom. The widow approached her—
took her hand. At this touch of affection, of sympathy,
Lydia only sobbed with greater violence. Her mother drew
her softly away into the next room, and seating herself, took
her in her arms.

"Oh, mother! mother!" gasped Lydia, "I thought to have
concealed this from you, and you have found it out! Oh,
mother! do not think too badly of Frank! poor Frank!"

"Is this the first time this has happened, child?"

"Oh, mother! do not ask me! please don't!" sobbed Lydia
anew.

The mother now understood that if this intoxication were
not habitual, it was also not unprecedented.

Lydia now arose from her mother's embrace, and returned
to the other room, where she found her husband in the heavy
insensibility of drunkenness. Lydia stood over him—spoke
to him—he did not reply. She put her arms around him and
spoke very earnestly, close to his ear, begging him to get up
and go to bed. He replied to that gentle touch and tone with
a stupid grunt. It was impracticable for that delicate young
woman in her feeble condition, even with the help of her
mother, to raise and assist him up stairs to bed; yet she could
not leave him there. It was impossible to look upon that fine,
athletic, manly figure, doubled up into shapelessness in the
beastly torpor of drunkenness;—upon those handsome youthful features, fallen into an idiotic imbecility, and to leave him
there.

"Go to bed, mother!—go to bed, dear mother. I shall
remain here until I can get him up stairs—poor Frank! Oh.
mother! what a termination to our festival! What a reception

for you! Alas! what a night this is! Your first night under
our roof!. You will be going away to-morrow, mother—
will you not, mother?"

The old lady set down the night-lamp, put the extinguisher
on it, and resumed her old seat in the arm-chair.

"Ain't you going to bed, mother?"

"No, my dear."

"But, mother, you must—you will be ill—*do* go to your
room."

"My child, don't torment me; I shall sit here as long as
you do. I could not sleep, Lydia—how could I? with the
knowledge that you were alone with this—this man down
here."

"*Poor* Frank! Mother, please don't call him a man, and
he so good to us, too. Oh, mother, you will dislike Frank
now, and you will be leaving us again. I am so much afraid
you will!"

"No, my love, I do *not* dislike Frank. I pity him, sorrow
for him and for you, and I will remain with you and do all I
can to win him from this dreadful, dangerous, fatal habit!
Have you ever spoken to him about it, Lydia?"

"Oh, mother, *no*—it has *not* very often happened, and
when it has, and when it is over, upon the next morning poor
Frank looks so down-cast, so mortified, that I could not to
save my very life say one word to him about it; on the contrary, I try all I can to make him think that I did not perceive
it. or did not think much of it, or do not remember it. I try
to make nim forget all about it, and to restore his cheerfulness.
He is so handsome and good when he is in good spirits, mother,
and it is so dismal to see him suffer, poor fellow! by his severe
self-reproach!"

"You want moral courage, Lydia. Lydia, one of the most
important, and one of the most painful offices of true affection,
is to remonstrate with our friends against their dangerous
faults and foibles. You feel that, Lydia, in the case of your

husband; but, Lydia, listen! I have known a mother, through an excess of false tenderness to her child, lack the firmness to give it the necessary bitter drug that would have saved its life. Sooner than afflict her child with a momentary inconvenience, she has run the risk, and has seen it *die.* How severe must have been the self-reproaches of that mother, Lydia! You, Lydia, from the fear of giving your husband an instant's pain, refrain from assisting his self-judgment by your sympathy in *that.* Lydia, you or I must speak to him to-morrow."

"Oh, mother! I cannot! cannot! and you, mother! please never think of it! oh, mother, please do not even look as though you noticed it, much less speak of it; *please don't! please don't!* Poor Frank! he will feel badly enough without that!"

"Again I say you lack moral courage, Lydia. Lydia! do you know, have you ever seen the ultimate effects of habitual intoxication? Have you ever seen men bloated, decrepid, ragged, reeling through the streets? Have you ever seen the families of such men?"

"Oh, mother! you can never think that Frank—oh, gracious Heaven, *no!*—you never meant that!" And Lydia exhibited such acute distress that her gentle mother immediately changed the subject. At last, however, Lydia herself resumed, by saying—"But, mother, as you wish me to set my face against this drinking, and to remonstrate upon the subject with Frank, it occurs to me to say that I have heard of some husbands who have been driven into greater excesses by the reproaches of their wives—may there not be a danger of that in this case? May not Frank, humiliated in his own estimation by my attempts to reform him, plunge into dissipation of which he is guiltless now?"

"My dear! *no!*—for this reason—you will 'speak the truth in love, —as it must be spoken, to do good. All the difference in effect lies in this—the truth—spoken in anger, scorn, reproach, or *love.* You will speak the truth, not in anger, not in scorn, not in reproach, but—*in love.* Do you mark the difference ?"

"Yes, mother, but I hate to do it; I am afraid I should not do it rightly; I am afraid I should be misunderstood; I am afraid that I should give offence, and do harm. I am very reluctant to undertake it."

"That delicate reluctance, my dear, insures that you will do it rightly, if you summon the usual force to overcome it. Now, Lydia, Frank is so sound asleep that although we may not be able to carry him up to bed, we can lay him on the sofa and cover him up." This was soon effected. "And now, Lydia, you must go to bed—you are too feeble for this great tax of anxiety and loss of sleep—come !"

Lydia yielded to her mother's persuasions and retired to rest. She with her childish elasticity of spirits soon threw off her burden of grief, and fell into a deep, refreshing sleep. Not so the mother. Other causes of uneasiness besides the newly discovered habits of her son-in-law drove sleep from her eyelids. One of these was the utter unfitness of her daughter to cope with the difficulties of her position. Affectionate and benevolent even to fatuity, Lydia could never by word, look or gesture, bear her testimony against evil in any one whom she loved. She was at once very thoughtless and very sensitive. She was evidently too unreflecting to comprehend the full degree of danger in which her husband stood, and withal so tender-hearted, so delicate in mind and body, that it seemed an ungracious, and, just in her present condition, an unsafe task to let her into the secret of his great peril. The widow's tortured brain seethed with thought all night, she arose in the morning with a severe headache. She fell upon her knees and offered up her morning prayer, beseeching God to give her strength and wisdom for her new and hard duties Calmed by this prayer, she dressed herself and went below stairs. Lydia was already there engaged in getting breakfast.

"Where is Frank, my daughter?" asked the old lady, looking around and missing him.

"He has walked out, mother—he feels so badly, mother! Say nothing to him to-day."

The widow did not reply. Soon breakfast was placed upon the table, and in a few moments Frank entered, looking very sorrow-stricken and ashamed—nodded a "good-morning" to his mother-in-law, and seated himself pensively at the foot of the table. Lydia's manner was unusually tender and attentive to him. He seemed to feel this, and in some degree to sink under it.

It happened to be the Sabbath, and too early as yet for church, so that when breakfast was over and the table cleared away, and when Lydia had gone up stairs to make up her bed, Frank, instead of going out, drew a chair to the fire, rested his elbows on his knees, dropped his head upon the open palms of his hands, and gave himself up to bitter reflections.

Mrs. Anderson stood looking at him sorrowfully for a few moments, and then going up to him, took the chair by his side, and taking his hand in hers, said, with great tenderness —"Frank, my son, I am a very old woman; I am sixty-five years old, and have suffered and lived through much. Have I not earned the privilege of speaking with affectionate freedom to the youthful of my own household?" Frank neither replied, nor looked up. "Frank, I have known you ever since you were an infant in the arms. I promised your widowed and dying mother, never to forsake you, always to regard you as my own son. Frank! have I fulfilled that promise? Answer me, Frank!"

"My dearest and best mother!" murmured the young man, with emotion, as he pressed the venerable hands that had held his own.

"May I speak to you, Frank, very freely—as if you were indeed my own son? nay! as if you were my *daughter?*"

"Speak on, mother! do not spare me! I am not irritable! believe me, I am not! Speak on, mother! I shall not get angry, or even impatient! I have no dignity to support. Ay, mother, begin, and the heavier you lay it on, the better you will do your duty!"

"Lay *what* on, dear Frank? I am not going to reproach you! Shall a physician foolishly reproach a patient for whom he should only prescribe? *You* are sick, Frank, and I wish to cure you—that is all. Frank, I *know* your disease! I have had a slight personal experience in it."

"*You*, mother!" exclaimed the young man, with a recoil of something approaching to horror and disgust.

"Yes, Frank, *I*,—and I know it *all*—its symptoms and its cure. Listen, Frank: When I was nursing my last baby, your wife, Lydia, partly from having nursed her too long, and partly from grief at the loss of her father, who died, as you know, when she was but two years old, I fell into a very feeble state. My chest was very much debilitated. The doctor told me to drink port wine every day, just before dinner. Well, I got the port wine, Frank, and it was such a cordial to my weak stomach—as soon as swallowed it diffused such delightful warmth and strength through my chilled and sinking frame,—it exhilarated my depressed spirits so much, that I grew to wait for the hour of taking the agreeable medicine with impatience. Still, *for a while*, I had the self-control to refrain from anticipating that hour, or taking an over-dose when it came. But at last, Frank, I seemed to need it more and more, the longer I continued its use. The seeming good effect of the wine was only momentary, while its evil effects were permanent and increasing, stimulating for awhile, and then inducing greater debility, and consequently a seemingly greater *need*, certainly a greater *desire*. Frank, it became a disease—I could not see it *then*—I was beguiled on and on—

growing weaker, more feverish, still believing it to be the
natural progress of pulmonary consumption—still fancying
the wine a positive and growing necessity. At last, Frank,
one day, when very weak, and very thirsty, I took more than
I intended to take; it got into my head, made me drowsy, I
lay down on the sofa, and fell into a stupid sleep. It was two
o'clock, or about that, when I lay down; it was after midnight
that I awoke, or some loud noise in the street awoke me. I
rose up, but could not stand up—I was dizzy, sick, but sane
—I sank down—closed my eyes. I knew then—oh, God,
Frank, with what utter humiliation, with what anguish I knew
that I had been—*drunk*. Frank, I had enjoyed, however
unworthily, the reputation of a *good* Christian—an industrious,
benevolent, self-denying woman—a devoted wife and mother—
and Frank, I had been beguiled into drunkenness—involuntarily, unconsciously! Frank, at that moment of closing my
bodily eyes, the eyes of my spirit were opened, and I saw, as
though it had been revealed by a sudden flash of lightning,
the fearful descent down which I was hastening. I, the carefully brought-up daughter of pious parents—I, the mother of
young children, who loved and venerated me—who gathered
around my knee, morning and evening, to offer up their pure
prayers and praises to God—I, their sole dependence, whose
failure would make them paupers! Oh, Frank, my spirit was
wounded to the quick!—Frank, I have, in the course of my
life, three times suffered the very extremity of *bodily pain*—
pain that at its acme resulted in insensibility, and so had a
merciful limit; but I had now to experience, most bitterly,
how much more intense, how much more insufferable than
physical agony was mental anguish,—how much more scorch-
ing, scathing, than fire and flames to the flesh and blood, were
remorse and shame to the soul! It was so sudden! so over-
whelming, this rending aside the veil that revealed me to
myself! I do not know how long I lay there in that awful
state, or how it was that I managed to get up at last, and go

into the next room to look after the children. I found a little
night taper still burning,—Ellen and little Lydia were undressed and comfortably in bed, through the care of their sister
Mary, then nearly thirteen years of age; but Mary was sitting
on the foot of their little trundle-bed, with her elbows resting
on her knees, and her head fallen upon her hands in an attitude of grief and despair I have never seen paralleled in a
child; she looked up as I entered. Oh, Frank! if another
pang were needed to consummate my suffering, it was inflicted
then, when I saw that Mary, my daughter, understood it all.
All!—no, *not* all; she saw the sin, the shame, but not the
hidden causes that would have palliated it. Not one word
bearing upon the subject was spoken by either. 'Go to rest,
Mary,' said I, as I undressed myself, and bathed my head and
face. She obeyed me, and we were both soon in bed. I
arose the next morning, and stealing quietly, for I did not
wish by any open and decided act, to impress upon the memory
of Ellen a fact that I wished her to forget—I took the bottle
of wine under my shawl, went in the yard and turned it out,
and from that time until the night of your wedding, when
Bohrer brought it in, there has been no alcohol in any shape
in our house. Do you think my victory, then, was the complete overthrow of my enemy? Far from it, Frank—it was
but the *commencement* of a warfare that for awhile seemed to
increase in strength day by day. *That* day the craving of
this diseased appetite was worse than the pangs of hunger.
I was nearly fainting from the withdrawal of the accustomed
stimulant—but I persevered—the next day it was worse—
and the suffering continued to increase—you see I disguise
nothing—towards the last the failure of my whole nervous
system, the prostration, and the intense craving for the stimulant, that would have temporarily strengthened and exhilarated
me, was worse, I think, than the pangs of famine, but I knew
that complete victory over my fascinating foe—or a fate worse
than death, awaited me and my children; and I resolved,

with God's help, to conquer. Frank! the second week my sufferings began to abate—the third week they were over. The fourth week consummated the victory. I did not feel the slightest desire for the stimulant. Remember, Frank, I had been but *once* in ignorance beguiled into excess, yet that one error, and the remorse that followed fast upon it, has given me to understand and deeply pity that powerful disease of morbid appetite to which so many are subjected. I know that many during temporary fits of bodily debility, particularly when suffering from debility of the stomach, resort to alcohol for its warming and exhilarating effects, little knowing that this temporary strength subsides in greater weakness—little knowing the whirlpool of temptation into which they have entered. The only way is to stop short at once—bear all the short suffering that follows with heroism—persevere, and you *must* conquer."

Frank had listened with deep interest to the old lady's story; he had recognised, in her case, the pathology of his own; when she had concluded, he raised her hand respectfully to his lips, and said,

"I reverence you, mother! You are my salvation. I am not yet degraded, mother; nobody calls me a drunkard; I have been caught, perhaps, half-a-dozen times in the last year, but have made no public exposure of myself; and now I will break right off. And when I suffer a great temptation, I will come to you, and you shall encourage me, and help me to bear it—for you will understand it, and your comprehending sympathy will be a perfect support."

"That will save you and yours, my son—and now it is quite time to get ready for church. Do you attend divine service on the Sabbath, Frank?"

"Yes, mother."

"That is well; 'forsake not the assembling of yourselves together,' " said the old lady, rising to go up stairs and dress for church.

CHAPTER VII.

DIFFICULTIES AND CHANGES.

SUSTAINED by the intelligent sympathy and encouragement of his "mother," as he fondly called her, Frank Miller heroically persevered in his total abstinence; and in the course of a few weeks had apparently gained the mastery over his diseased appetite: in a few more weeks that appetite had disappeared. About this time his child, a son, was born, and in the first fresh joys of young paternity, he forgot both his propensity and his sufferings in conquering it. Never was a happier young husband and father than Frank Miller, when Lydia had recovered from her confinement and was able to take her place by the side of the nice kitchen fire, with the cradle near at hand. And when the spring opened, it was a standing amusement to that humble neighbourhood, to see Frank walk his baby out every morning, while Lydia and her mother were preparing breakfast. And after breakfast, to see his fond leave-taking of the little one, before he went out to his work. And to see the queer presents of horse-cakes, spinning tops, &c., that he would bring home every evening to the babe of three months old! Towards the summer, however, Frank's spirits flagged, he became grave, or only fitfully gay. When Lydia would tenderly inquire into the subject of his gloom—he would laugh merrily and reply, "Nonsense! I'm tired, that's all, child."

Mrs Anderson saw that there was something more serious than bodily fatigue in his gravity. She refrained from inquiring for some time, because she expected that he would voluntarily make her his confidant, but at length seeing that this was not likely to happen, she took the opportunity one day while Lydia was gone to market, to ask Frank the cause

of his sadness The ice thus broken, the waters of confidence
flowed freely. Frank at once and candidly informed her that
he was burdened with debts and worried with duns, that he
saw no way of discharging the debts or escaping the duns.

"Why, how is that, Frank?" inquired the old lady.

"Why, mother, to tell the truth, when I married I only
had two hundred dollars. I paid half of it away for some
lumber to build this house with, and I got the rest on credit.
And that other hundred, mother, some how or other slipped
through my fingers. I was foolish and thoughtless; everything Lydia admired I bought for her, whether she expressed
a wish for it or not. I had a vague idea of retrenching some
time or other, and making up the extra outlay."

"The old self-deception upon which so many have ruined
themselves, and their families, Frank; it *very* seldom answers."

"It has not answered in my case, mother. I have not saved
one cent of my wages."

"No—the habit of inconsiderate expenditure may be formed
in a short time—and it is very difficult to conquer it, when
you think you are going to retrench and make up—how much
do you owe, Frank?"

"I owe Fairfield a hundred and seventy-five dollars for the
carpenter's work upon this house. I owe Ingle a hundred
dollars for the lumber, and Purdy thirty dollars balance for
painting and glazing, that is all. I owe no small debts. I
pay cash for my marketing, and settle my grocery and dry
goods bill every month."

"Frank, you have gained one victory by self-denial—now
begin another struggle—get this difficulty conquered, and you
will be a free man in every sense of the word. Resolve to
set aside one-third of your wages to pay off these debts, and
you will be clear in six months. You can do it by cutting off
unnecessaries. Buy no more pinchbeck brooches and gilt
combs for Lydia, no horse-cakes and spinning tops for the
baby, no ugly caricature prints for the walls. Come, Frank,

I will help you in this struggle also. You shall have the renting of my little rough-cast house for the year; it is but five dollars a month, but it will help you some."

"You are *so* disinterested, mother! but I could not think of taking a mean advantage of your generosity, besides it is almost your only support."

"My son, I can manage *well* without it for a year—when I can *not* get along, I will let you know."

"You are *so* good!"

"Nonsense, dear Frank, I am good to *my own*," replied the old lady, in her peculiarly cheering and affectionate tone.

The system of retrenchment was commenced, and through Mrs. Anderson's rigid adherence to its provisions, and through her constant affectionate check upon Frank's irregularity, it was persevered in, and would have been successful, but for one dreadful calamity; that shocked from their minds all thoughts of pecuniary or selfish interest. Fairfield, while at work upon the roof of a three-story house, lost his footing, and fell to the ground. He was picked up and brought home lifeless. Mrs. Anderson went at once to her daughter, and remained to console her under her terrible affliction. Quite absorbed in her sympathy with Mary and her orphans, she ceased to remember the lesser troubles of Frank and Lydia. Indeed, they themselves forgot their little difficulties in the contemplation of their sister's great sorrow. All their little rules were broken through, and this in the course of a few weeks. Frank had lost, by carelessness, every inch of ground he had gained by retrenchment. Thus the summer passed away. Mrs. Anderson still remaining with Mary, and taking in plain sewing to help her along with the little family expenses, and now almost regretting that she had made over to Frank all the proceeds of the rent of the little rough-cast house. Poor old mother! she would have given her very last cent, and exerted her very last strength in the service of her children—and she only lamented that her ability was not equal to the demands made upon it. As winter approached another cause of anxiety was added to the many that oppressed her. Frank Miller was thrown out of employment. There was certainly no danger of immediate suffering from this, for Frank's credit with the grocers and hucksters, where he had always paid his debts punctually, was above par—still it was a very serious draw-back where two or three large debts remained to be paid, and besides, there was no telling how long he might be forced to remain in idleness. To increase the embarrassment of the family, another child, a girl, was born to them, just thirteen months after the birth of their boy; and now that Mary had in some degree recovered from the first violent ravages of grief, Mrs. Anderson came once more to reside with, and assist her youngest daughter. Truly she was a devoted mother! But the earthly trials of this faithful servant of God, and lover of her kind, were very near their conclusion. Lydia had scarcely risen from her second accouchement when she was called to take her place by the sick-bed of her mother. A bilious pleurisy had seized her. The disease in its progress defied all the efforts of the physician to arrest it, and upon the night of the tenth day her acute bodily sufferings ceased, and she sank into an easy and beautiful languor, subsiding into death. So quietly had her spirit passed, that but for a smile that flitted across her face—a beautiful smile! a young smile—an infantile smile, such as lights up the countenance of a babe awakening from a dream —a divine irradiation, that in passing from her features effaced every mark that years of grief and care had traced upon it, leaving upon the inanimate clay the tender placidity of sleeping childhood.

Her children mourned her death as only children can mourn such a mother. From her peculiar temperament the grief of Lydia was most violent and ungovernable at first, but as a natural consequence soonest expended itself. She was the first to recover her cheerfulness. Time, religion, and occupa-

tion are the great cures for sorrow—the poignant anguish of
the children at the death of their beloved mother, at length
subsided into a tender memory, united to a loving Christian
hope.

———♦———

CHAPTER VIII.

THE FATAL GLASS OF BRANDY.

THE spring opened with better prospects for the denizens
of The Three Cottages. Mary Fairfield had got a run of
custom in dress-making—just enough to keep her comfortably
employed, without driving her to ruin her health by late hours
and close confinement. With her frugal habits and judicious
management, she was doing well for her three boys, providing
them with wholesome plain food and comfortable clothing,
and sending them to public school.

Bohrer was making money and growing selfish, losing the
good-humour and bonhommie of his countenance and manners,
and getting an expression of acute calculation, and contracting
habits of reserve and silence. Ellen had once or twice endeavoured to persuade him to abandon the sale of liquor, but
without success. The obstinacy that had refused to yield to
the sound reasoning and affectionate persuasion of Mrs. Anderson, could scarcely be expected to yield to the fitful pleadings
of the weak Ellen. Yes, Ellen *was* weak, and infirm of purpose. We have seen her in the first year of her married life,
bearing her honest, but gentle testimony against the use of
ardent spirits. We have seen her gradually abandon her post
of mild remonstrance, and now we might occasionally see her
taking her tumbler of toddy, after coming in from a cold or a
wet walk. But the family of Frank Miller suffered most
severely from the death of Mrs. Anderson, in the loss of her

wise counsels and vigilant guidance. As soon as the agitation occasioned by their household afflictions had in some degree subsided, Frank looked earnestly into his little affairs. After such deliberation as his unschooled and flighty mind was capable of maintaining, Frank Miller determined that he would get clear of the burden of debt, by the rigid economy advised by his mother-in-law. Frank Miller's sanguine and energetic temperament made him necessarily very industrious—he was a thoroughly *hard* worker. And now, had Frank possessed a *sensible* as well as an amiable wife in Lydia, his difficulties would have melted away before his decision. Alas! Lydia, with all her gentleness and tenderness, was weak and capricious. It was now two years since Frank had left off drinking It was again New Year's Eve. New Year's Eve seemed a fatal day to Frank and Lydia Miller. Frank had been at work all day at his place of employment. Lydia had been at work all day at home, making economical and wholesome pies and cakes for the children. Lydia could not be parsimonious on New Year's Eve. It was near sundown when Lydia completed the baking and cleared away her pastry tables, &c., and set her kitchen in perfect order. It was a cosy, comfortable kitchen, that of Lydia Miller's—the floor covered with a dark-coloured domestic carpet, the *whole* of it manufactured by her mother—the windows shaded with dark chintz curtains—the stove glowing hot, diffusing a delightful heat through the room—the pleasant, homely smell of freshly-baked cakes and pies—the prattle of the little toddling two years old boy, the crowing of the babe in the cradle—and Lydia's pretty, *petite* form and light step as she tripped about the room—now setting out the table, laying the cloth, and placing the waiter, cups and saucers upon it—now stopping to chirrup to the baby—now to answer the prattle of the boy. Alas! that one so pretty and so good should be so weak—so unreflecting! Lydia had finished setting her supper-table, adding a couple of pies and a plate of gingerbread to the common staple fare

of bread and butter and cold meat, and had set her coffee to
boil, and was now all ready to receive her darling, merry-
hearted Frank—when, growing childishly impatient of his
somewhat protracted stay, in order to kill the time and to do
a sisterly kindness, she filled a little basket with gingerbread
to take to her nephews, the little Bohrers, next door. Slipping
the handle of the basket upon her wrist, and taking the babe
in her arms, and calling the little boy to toddle after her, she
went into the next cottage. The shop was already lighted up,
and Bohrer, behind the counter, was waiting on a crowd of
customers. Lydia passed in and through the shop quickly,
drawing her little boy after her. Ellen's parlour behind the
shop was also lighted up, and several of her neighbours were
with her. Among others, her widowed sister, Mary Fairfield.
It was evident that Ellen had got through supper early, that
Bohrer might have time to wait upon the unusual number of
customers that New Year's Eve would send to his shop
Reader!—Ellen looks very differently *now* upon *this* New
Year's Eve than she did upon the New Year's Eve of six
years ago. Ellen's face and figure have lost that delicacy of
form and complexion, and that intelligence and refinement of
expression that once distinguished her—she has a coarse,
sensual, and apathetic look as she sits there gossipping with
her neighbours. Just as Lydia came tripping in with her
childish and graceful bustle, and after smiling and nodding
" Good-evening" around the circle, had placed her basket of
cakes on the mantel-piece, and fluttered down upon a seat by
the side of her sister Ellen, a voice was heard in the shop exclaiming above the hum of conversation—

" Brew some for the women, Bohrer! Come, let's brew
some immediately and take it in."

And soon there was a tap at the little back parlour door,
and to Ellen's cheerful " Come in," entered Bohrer, with a
small hand-waiter, upon which stood six glasses of brandy punch.
He took it up first to Lydia, and lifting a glass smilingly

15

offered it to her. With childish glee Lydia seized it, raised
it an instant to the light, her eyes flashing with mirth, gave
the "Happy New Year," and placed it to her lips. Alas!
for the self-indulgent spirit that could not deny itself. Alas!
for the thoughtlessness that could not profit by experience.
Bohrer then took the waiter around in succession to all the
women, until each was supplied with the New Year's glass
of punch—all, except Mary Fairfield, who steadily declined it.
I wish you to remember these facts, namely: that Lydia's
taste for ardent spirits was hereditary—had been formed by
her mother's immoderate use of alcohol during the period of
her nursing, that Ellen's appetite for spirituous liquors had
been contracted by the constant *seeing, handling, smelling* it,
and by the example of her husband—that Mary Fairfield, the
widow, having had neither the misfortune of hereditary taste,
nor of constant temptation, was a total-abstinence woman from
unperverted nature, rather than from principle, for Mary Fairfield had had none of that bitter experience which inspires
such horror of alcohol in its innocent victims—and this ex-
plains the reason why, while refusing to touch it herself, she
abstained from all attempts to influence the other women of
the company—and this shows the necessity, while for its own
sake we keep the appetite of a child unperverted by the taste
of alcohol, we should, for the sake of others, endeavour to
form in him or her that missionary spirit of total abstinence
which will influence those that are in danger, which will "seek
and save those that are lost" Soon the exhilarating effects
of the punch were felt, and exhibited in the increased gayety
of the little company—from smiling softly and conversing
quietly, they grew noisy, talked aloud, laughed out in peals
of merriment—still this was not *intoxication*, only *exhilaration*, such exhilaration as may also sometimes be produced in
fashionable drawing-rooms and saloons, by costly cordials, wines
and *liqueurs*.

In the mean time, Frank Miller had returned from work,

and entering his house, and passing on to the kitchen, found all things comfortably prepared for his reception, and sat down to wait for his wife, supposing her to be up stairs putting the children to bed, or somewhere about the house. But when half-an-hour had passed and she had not returned, Frank rightly concluded that she had gone "in to sister Ellen's,' and he determined to follow her. He took the coffee-pot off the stove when it was just going to boil over, and setting it where it would keep warm, he shut up the kitchen and went. He entered the back parlour of Bohrer's just as the company were in the height of their enjoyment. Lydia, seeing him come in, set down her glass, and springing with youthful eagerness to meet him, exclaimed in tones of affected complaint.

"There, I knew it! I never *can* step in at a neighbour's house but what Frank must follow me. Isn't it too hard?" and drew him—both laughing—away to a seat by her side.

"Frank! take something to drink?" asked Bohrer, putting his head in at the door.

"No! no, thank you," said Frank, lifting his boy upon his knee to cover a certain embarrassment he felt in being the *only* one of the circle that refused. Bohrer, not hearing his reply, or not believing his sincerity, had withdrawn his head from the door for a moment, and soon entered the room with a glass of brandy and water on a waiter.

"I believe, Frank, *this* is your drink, is it not?"

"Thank you, Bohrer, I would not choose anything, if you please."

"Nonsense, Frank! you are dull, it will wake you up—you are tired, it will restore your strength—you are cold, it will warm you."

"Thank you, Bohrer, but I must go home soon, and then our supper is ready, you know, and with the warm stove and supper I shall be recruited."

"Well! I haven't time to pay compliments. I must return

to my customers, but I shall set this down by your side, and
if you change your mind, why it is at hand, that's all;" and
doing as he said, Bohrer left the room. By this time the attention of all the little circle was drawn to Frank. Frank felt
that the "public sentiment" of *this* company was against him
Lydia took up the glass of brandy and water, and with sincere
but deplorably mistaken affection pressed it upon his acceptance, saying,

"Take it, dear Frank! Oh, *do* take it—just take a little—
a *little* won't hurt you—it was because you always took too
much that it hurt you; but a *little* won't hurt you. Now *do*,
Frank, for my sake—I cannot enjoy my punch a bit, unless
you take something."

The fine aroma of the hot brandy was arising beneath his
nose, entering his nostrils, stimulating the long-dormant but
not extinct appetite—the sweet, tender, blooming face of his
wife was smiling up into his eyes, pleading with him. Frank
took the glass of brandy, and with a light laugh turned it off.

"After *all*, I have not broken the *pledge*, for I never
happened to take *that*—I only took a *resolution*," laughed
Frank, holding out his glass to Bohrer, who, having despatched
all his customers, had returned to the little parlour.

"Some more, Frank?"

"Yes, Bohrer, if you please—a little."

"That is a good fellow!" said Bohrer, as though Frank had
conferred upon him the greatest favour in the world, and soon
returned with the glass replenished.

"Do you know, Lydia," said Frank, when, after getting
through his second drink, he became confidential upon the subject of his neighbours' faults, "do you know that I am afraid
that poor Bohrer is on the road to ruin?"

"How so, Frank?"

"*He is on the road to ruin!*" replied Frank, with a myste-
rious air.

"Dear Frank, how you scare one! What is the matter with him?"

"*He drinks too much,*" said Frank, with the oracular air of incipient intoxication. "Don't you see how bloated he is getting? Don't you see how red his nose is?"

"Why, I never thought about that—but so it is indeed."

"*Certainly,* and his breath is like the bung of a whiskey-cask."

"Yes, it is so, *always*—but I never thought of it before—he ought not to drink too *much,* he ought to be temperate."

At that time how little Lydia understood what she was talking about! Frank Miller's judgment of Bohrer was perfectly correct. He was one of those plethoric subjects who could go on for a long time imbibing and absorbing liquor until his very blood was "liquid fire," and even perish by spontaneous combustion, without ever becoming dead-drunk, or who after a long course of such life might suddenly fall into habits of beastly intoxication.

And Frank Miller! his sight that was now so clear to discern the danger of his brother, soon became so blind to his own! Alas for the self-indulgence, the thoughtlessness, the mistaken tenderness of the youthful wife! Alas! for the weakness and instability of the young husband! Alas, for the fatal glass of brandy!

CHAPTER IX.

THE LITTLE ROUGH-CAST HOUSE.

THE reader knows that a relapse is more dangerous, more rapid, and more frequently fatal in its consequence, than a first attack of disease. As every resistance of temptation

augments the moral force, so every yielding to it weakens the
power of resistance in the tempted. It were a painful and ungracious task to trace, step by step, the downward course of
poor Frank Miller—how soon after breaking his good resolution by drinking that one glass of brandy, he grew to drinking
occasionally, then frequently, then habitually, then immode-
rately—until his work was abandoned, his family neglected, and
at last, in the course of twelve months, himself a confirmed
drunkard! Too often in real life, and in fiction, has this dis-
gusting pageantry, this sickening procession of self-indulgence,
intemperance, idleness, poverty, sickness, suffering, degrada-
tion—the funeral train of domestic happiness, passed before
the reader's tortured eye. Let me spare myself the pain of
telling it, you the pain of hearing it.

It would cost us less suffering from sympathy, but far more
disgust to trace the fall of Bohrer, whose fate seemed only a
just retribution for his sins. *He* it was, who, when "The
Three Cottages" were *each* the beautiful abode of industry—
economy, and neatness—of love, peace, religion—were *all*
united in the bonds of family affection—he it was, who, for
the sake of making more money, brought the foe that should
ruin the families, the firebrand that should ignite and lay waste
their homes.

It is sufficient to say, that at the end of three years two of
'The Three Cottages" had changed owners. Bohrer still remaining as a *tenant* in the house he had been compelled to
sell—and now habitually intoxicated. Ellen carrying on the
small shop, that still decreased in stock, and that failed to
supply enough to support their family, as well as she could.
Once their furniture was taken for rent, and nothing remained
in their once comfortable cottage except the two beds, the
three chairs, and the cooking utensils, that the law could
not touch. Still Ellen, upon whom the sole care of the family
had fallen, clung to the small shop-stand as to her last hope
of support. Now that she was the sole dependence of her

family, her strong maternal love came to her aid, and enabled
her to throw off *entirely* the false appetite for alcoholic stimulus, that with *her* had never yet approached intemperance, for
Ellen was of that sound health and of that lymphatic temperament that might go on a long time in the use of alcohol
before falling into that excess to which other organizations are
more liable.

About this time the war with Mexico broke out, and
Bohrer was one of the first that volunteered in the service.
Inured as Ellen had lately become to suffering, she could not
see her husband depart upon a distant, a dangerous, and unholy service, without bitter tears and earnest remonstrances.
Even with her phlegmatic nature there was a passionate vehe-
mence, an impetuosity in her manner, as, after seeing him embark with the troops, she returned to her shop, seized and
threw away all the liquor that the stubborn will of Bohrer had
persisted in keeping in the shop. There was almost madness
in the vengeance and the energy with which she destroyed
every tumbler, wine-glass, and decanter about the shop. Then,
with the energy of one who wishes to lose regret and the consciousness of deep mental sorrow in physical weariness, Ellen
went to work and cleared her shop and house of every vestige
of the enemy. In the course of a few days Ellen had restored
something like its old *order* if not its old comfort to her home
—sooth to say the cottage was all the cleaner, quieter, and
more cheerful, for the absence of the master. Ellen's neighbours did not scruple to say among themselves, "She does a
great deal better *without* the worthless fellow than *with* him."
But they did not know half the difficulties that still surrounded
Ellen Bohrer. How many small debts she owed in every direction. How far in arrearage for rent she was. How very
small the proceeds of her little shop were. Ellen unfortunately
had no skill in needle-work, and it requires a woman of a
great deal of skill as well as of energy and perseverance to
push herself into a circle of customers where there is such great

competition. And Ellen, with many amiable traits of character, had none of these sterner qualities. So with her best
efforts, poor Ellen Bohrer still slid down and down into deeper
poverty.

Affairs had gone still worse with Frank Miller and his
family. He also, as I said, had been compelled to sell his
house to pay his debts, and to get money to buy bread and—
liquor. In the mean time, every year had brought them a
new child, an alternate boy and girl, until now Lydia was the
mother of four children—Harry, Lizzy, Tommy, and Milly
the baby. Frank was almost always intoxicated, or just recovering from it. It is horrible to contemplate this in the
generous, cheerful, noble-hearted Frank. Let us turn from
the picture, and let me tell you one thing that was beautiful
even in this picture of ruin. Frank never was unkind to his
wife or children. With all the wrong his degrading habits
inflicted upon them, he loved them still, he loved them with
more tenderness, the tenderness of remorse, of pity—as he
witnessed their privations. Frank seemed the victim of an
inevitable disease rather than of a degrading vice. Alas! that
he could not shake off the spell that enchained him : alas! that
he could not awake from the apathy that bound him, the self-
indulgence that enslaved him! There was nothing on earth
so eloquent as the penitence, the lamentations of this once
noble but now fallen nature. Forget himself even in intoxication and abuse Lydia! or ill-treat his children ! He who was
drunk one half, and penitent the other half, would have died
sooner than have spoken, or looked unkindly at the wife and
family his conduct was nevertheless reducing to pauperage.
And Lydia, much as she suffered, she never reproached him.
It is doubtful whether she had a right to-do so. The right to
do so, however, is seldom taken into consideration by those
who indulge in reproaches. But if Lydia was too gentle to
reproach him, she was also too weak to reclaim him. Lydia
could only weep when her children were hungry or cold, and

there was no money to buy wood or food. Their rent also was far in arrears—their household furniture had, in the course of the last three years, gradually disappeared. Every article of value about the house had, in succession, been sold to purchase necessaries. All the nice parlour furniture was gone—all the pure-white chamber furniture, the gift of her dead mother, had been disposed of—everything not positively necessary to their health, had vanished, except the home-made carpet on the kitchen floor. It was the work of her mother's hands, and Lydia could *not* part with it. Thus the autumn of 1846 found them. It was one day in November, that Frank had sauntered down to the Navy Yard with his hands lazily stuck into his pockets, and his hat crushed over one eye, with that undeniable look of worthlessness which habitual intoxication gives—with a vague idea of procuring work somehow, or somewhere. Frank's appearance was so much against him as to make it probable that even where workmen were in demand, *his* services would be rejected. Frank of course was unsuccessful—and upon the fact of his disappointment, he went to the nearest tavern and drank to inebriation. It was in the swaggering stage of his drunkenness that he was met by a recruiting sergeant, and under the influence of intoxication that he volunteered to go to Mexico. Not to lose his new recruit, the sergeant took him at once to the Marine Garrison, where the company in which he had enlisted, were quartered.

That night poor Lydia, for the first time in her married life, was left all night alone, with her children. She sat up, awaiting Frank's return, until long after twelve o'clock, then slowly and sadly undressing herself, she lay down, but could not sleep, but lay there wondering, fearing, and counting the dark and heavy hours as they slowly, slowly brought on the dawn. She arose early, dressed herself and her poor children, set her poor house in order, and got her miserable breakfast of weak coffee, without milk, and corn bread ready. She determined, immediately after breakfast, to take her four children in to her

sister Mary's, leave them there, and go in search of Frank,
among his usual haunts. But she scarcely had time to finish
her breakfast, and clear away the table, when she was interrupted by a rap at the door.

"Come in," said Lydia, supposing it to be one of her
sisters or one of their children, who were always running in
and out. But a young man, a friend of her husband, obeyed
her summons and entered the kitchen. He looked gravely as
he came in. By a sudden presentiment Lydia felt that evil
tidings were coming.

"Sit down," she said, in a sinking voice, as she herself
dropped into a chair. The young man took a seat, set his hat
down by his side, and said in a hesitating tone,

"I have a message for you, Mrs. Miller."

"Well?"

"A message from your husband."

"Well?" reiterated Lydia, turning pale.

"He—he has enlisted."

"Oh! my God," exclaimed the unhappy wife, clasping her
hands firmly together, and gazing vacantly into the face of her
informant.

"His company go this afternoon in the cars, and he wishes
you to meet him at the car-office with the children, that he
may take leave of you and them."

The young man spoke rapidly, thickly. A slight, half-suppressed scream burst from Lydia's lips—she arose, sank down
again, again attempted to leave her chair, and fainting. fell
forward upon her face.

The young man hastened to raise her. The children, startled
from their play in the corner, ran to their mother, and seeing
her apparently dead, set up a lamentable wail around her.
The young man laid Lydia upon an old lounge, and hurried
out into the next house to summon her sister Ellen. He explained the cause of Lydia's sudden illness, in a few hasty
words, and soon Ellen and Mary hastened to her aid. They

found Lydia already recovering from the swoon in which her weak nerves and habitual want of self-command had permitted this ill news to throw her.

"Oh, Mary!" she said, as her sisters entered, "you are strong and you are wise. Oh, Mary, tell me what I am to do —what *can* I do?"

"Cannot Frank get leave of absence for a few hours to come and see her?" inquired Mary of the young man.

"No, ma'am, by no means; the troops are to leave the city in this evening's train of cars, and the strictest watch is ever kept for fear of desertions from the ranks. The only way in which Mrs. Miller can see her husband, is to go to the car office and wait till the troops arrive there."

Here Lydia's sobs broke out again, and her children crowded around her, her eldest boy, Harry, throwing his arms around her neck, and hugging her tightly, roared out for sympathy.

"Is there no possible way of procuring his discharge?" again asked Mary of the youth.

"You *might* try the Secretary to-day, ma'am; though I candidly tell you that the chance of getting him off is a poor one."

"Oh, Mary, try, Mary; dear Mary, try!" sobbed and plead Lydia.

"I will go—I will go at once," said Mary. "Keep up your heart, my dear Lydia, something may yet be done;" and she hurried home to prepare for her affectionate mission.

To give the reader a sample of the manner in which poor women were treated, perhaps necessarily so treated, I will *very* briefly relate the interview of Mary Fairfield with the dignitaries of the Government. Arrived at the War Department, she went up the great stone stairs, and timidly entered the great marble-paved hall, flanked with mahogany doors leading into the various rooms, and labelled above in gold letters: "OFFICE OF THE ADJUTANT-GENERAL," "OFFICE OF THE SECRETARY OF WAR," etc., and terminating in a great stone

staircase, with iron balustrades leading up into the second
story. Mary felt a little awed by her loneliness in the great
reverberating halls, and a little terrified at the idea of an interview with the great men of the place; her heart beat thickly.
She had scarcely entered, however, before she was met by a
messenger, who abruptly asked her,

"Whom do you want to see?"

"His honour, the Secretary of War if you please," answered
she.

"Oh! your husband is in Mexico isn't he?"

"No, sir."

"Well, then, your father, or your brother, or your son is?"

"No, sir, none of my kin are in Mexico," replied Mary,
whose modest deportment and simple widow's dress was beginning to win upon the case-hardened official.

"Very well; the Secretary has not come in yet; but you
can see the chief clerk, and the reason of my stopping you
was, that not a day passes, but what some wife comes here to
plead for her husband's discharge—or some widow to weep for
her son's dismissal from service; and, in short, the Secretary
has been so worried by such applications, that orders have
been issued to stop all such petitioners at the door."

"Still, I think that all such petitioners should at least have
a hearing, even if their petitions are not granted—for there is
no telling what cruelty and injustice may be inflicted by refusing to receive the appeal of such an applicant."

"It can't be done, ma'am. You see, young men, and for
that matter old men, filled with what they call patriotic ardour
—a thirst for military glory—enlist in a hurry and go to
Mexico, where the enthusiasm is taken out of them by cow-
hide boots, leather stocks, short rations, long marches, and
drillings. They want to come home, write and work upon the
sympathies of the women folks, who come up here and worry
the Secretary—*that's* the reason I stopped *you*, you know. I
thought you had somebody in Mexico."

Mary did not feel called upon to explain as she followed the messenger to a door, which he opened, saying,

"The office of the chief clerk;" and as she entered, closing the door behind her he retired.

Mary dropped a respectful curtsy. A gentleman arose from his seat at a large writing table, and urbanely handed her a chair. Poor Mary tremblingly took the seat, she was so nervous, and this politeness embarrassed her as much as an opposite deportment could have done. She began in a hesitating tone and told the object of her visit. The gentleman attended with a kind and sympathizing expression of countenance. At the end of her recital he informed her that he himself could do nothing in the case, that the Secretary was ill at his house, but that she might see General ———, who might be able to serve her in this affair. Then he directed her where to find the office of the Adjutant-General, and as Mary arose to leave the room, he kindly opened the door and called a messenger to attend her. Greatly encouraged by this kindness, Mary went into General ———'s room with strong hopes of success. In an ante-room she found a youth who told her that the general was out, but would be in in the course of a few moments, and opening a second door, showed her into an inner room. Mary sat down and had ample time to benefit by the comfortable coal fire, to admire the rich carpet and tables, the easy chairs, and the stacks of flags of various sizes and colours with which the room was adorned, before the door opened, and a little old man with closely curling red hair, and a half-developed or half-suppressed strut, one could not tell which, marched into the room with a "Well! what do you want?" sort of expression upon his countenance. Mary arose, curtsied, and resumed her silence. She had lost her presence of mind again—the appearance of this little man was *so* unpromising—she felt her task an almost hopeless one. The General had thrown himself into his official chair, wheeled it around upon a pivot, crossed his little legs, placed his open palms upon his limbs, and looked at Mary with an expression of inquiry that was *intended* to be arrogant, but was only impertinent. Mary begged pardon for intrusion, and again commenced her little tale. He arrested her narrative before she had gone on two minutes by exclaiming flippantly in his high, keen, sharp, rasping tone,

"Ah! I know it! I know all about it! You needn't tell me the rest! Heard the whole story twenty times! every week for the last year! 'Sole dependence of his widowed mother!' Know all about it! know all about it!"

"Excuse me, sir," interrupted Mary, her gentle spirit rising against this natural born morris-dancer, shuffled by chance into "a little brief authority." "Excuse me, sir, he has a young wife with four children, and his wife is as incapable of taking care of herself and family, as is the babe upon her bosom."

"That is *his* business, not mine—he should have thought of that himself when he enlisted."

"But, sir, he was not master of himself when he enlisted—he was—"

Mary blushed, and became silent.

"Was what?" maliciously inquired the manikin.

"Under the influence of liquor," said Mary, in a low voice.

"Then the army—active military service, is the very place to cure him of the propensity," said the General, rising, and holding open the door for his visiter's departure.

Mary followed this rather decided hint, and left the room.

It was with a heavy heart that she returned home, and conveyed to Lydia the news of her failure. Lydia had wept all day; she was now lying exhausted upon the old lounge, and Ellen was taking care of her house and children, and making vain efforts to soothe her distress. The entrance of Mary with her evil tidings, brought on a new burst of sorrow, though Lydia persisted in saying, dismally, that she had expected nothing else. In the afternoon Lydia arose, made an effort, and dressed herself and her children, to go to the

car-office to take leave of the husband and father. Lydia was
so weak from having wept all day—so thoroughly incapable
of walking, that Mary Fairfield hired a hack, placed her and
her children in it, and entering it also herself, accompanied
her sister to the place of parting. They alighted from the
hack at the car office, and remained watching for the advance
of the troop. Several other women were there upon the same
sad errand. Lydia stood trembling, supported upon the arm
of her sister Mary. At last the music arose upon the air from
afar, down towards the Capitol, and soon the blue coats, nodding
plumes, and flashing arms of the soldiers were seen coming
up the Avenue. Lydia made two or three springs, as though
she would have run to meet the troop, and singled out Frank.
But Mary held her fast. Arrived at the depot, the soldiers
were permitted, under certain restrictions, to take leave of their
assembled friends. Unmindful of the gathered crowd, at the
first sight of him, Lydia had sprung forward and thrown herself, sobbing convulsively, upon the bosom of her husband.
Frank drew her away, behind the shelter of a stack of boxes,
held her weeping to his heart, kissed her again and again,
while his own tears fell fast upon her face—then gently releasing himself from her feeble but frantic clasp, he called
their children, raised them one by one in his arms, kissed his
farewell upon their innocent lips, blessed them, prayed for
them, wept over them, and—at the word of recall—thrusting
his bounty money hastily into the hands of Lydia, strained
her once more to his bosom, and broke away to rejoin his ranks,
leaving his wife fainting in the arms of her sister. An hour
from this, Lydia was lying, half stunned with grief, upon her
bed, at home and the troops in the cars were nearly half way
to Baltimore

It was a week before Lydia Miller, the once petted and
spoiled child of both mother, sisters, and husband, could exert
herself to do anything for her family. Lydia, enervated by
indulgence and self-indulgence, was by the first shock of this

separation rendered totally unequal to the exigencies of her position. In the second week the two older sisters held a consultation as to what was to be done with and for this youngest, this child of the family. The sisters, as the reader knows, were poor, *very* poor. Mary Fairfield, the widow, the seamstress, the *total abstinence* woman, being the only one who had held on to her dowry, the cottage and lot. And in passing, let me say that this fact is worthy of remark, that while Lydia and Ellen had the help, or ought to have had the help of their husbands, with the superior wages that men's labour receives, they yet *lost* through intemperance, the possession of their houses; while Mary, though losing her husband, and having nothing to depend upon but the scanty remuneration of her needlework, yet retained her house and all her acquired property in fact. Mary, the hard-working widow, was almost wealthy in comparison with her two sisters who had husbands, capable of making six times her wages. There was one little piece of property owned in common between the sisters; this was their little old homestead, their native cot, their mother's little rough-cast house, that stood out in the field alone, with a small, weed-grown garden all around it. But this little house was so old, small, and dilapidated, and so far out of the way, that it brought in *now* only three dollars a month, which of course, divided, gave each sister only a dollar a month. As this little rough-cast house was now vacant, and as Lydia was already in arrears for rent, it was decided between the sisters that she and her family should be removed there, and that they should not require of her their own share of the rent. To give her this house rent-free was all that the sisters could now do for her, unless—yes, Mary said that she would try to obtain needlework for her, though Lydia's want of skill threatened to be a great obstacle to her success. When Mary and Ellen proposed this plan to Lydia, and advised her to remove before her little furniture was seized for rent, she gratefully acceded to it. In a few days Lydia was settled once more in the humble home of her happy infancy. Lydia had honestly paid five dollars out of her bounty money to her landlord, and with the other five (Frank had sold his liberty for only ten dollars) she bought shoes all round for the children, as it was now growing cold and frosty under foot. The winter was now setting in, and the greater wants produced by the cold weather and the harder work, and closer economy required in order to meet them, quite absorbed the two elder sisters, so that in the care of their children, they were forced to leave Lydia very much to her own guidance. That was a hard winter on the poor. By the early closing of the river, wood rose in price to one-third more than its usual value. Because of the war with Mexico, the famine in Ireland, the partial failure of our own grain-crops, and other adverse circumstances, the price of breadstuffs were nearly doubled, flour arose to eight, nine, ten dollars a barrel, and this at a time when the support of large families was thrown upon feeble women with their limited fields of labour, and the miserable pittance of wages,—by the absence of fathers, husbands, and brothers in the Mexican War. I scarcely know how the Three Sisters contrived to exist through that dreadful winter. Mary and Ellen managed to do without the aid of public charity, but their best efforts failed in saving Lydia from that necessity. Mary had succeeded in procuring some needlework, but Lydia's deplorable want of skill, and slowness in acquiring it, was an almost insuperable obstacle to her success.

For weeks at a time, in the bitterest weather, Lydia would be without wood. The fence all around the little rough-cast house had to be pulled down and burnt, to save herself and her babes from freezing. For whole days Lydia would be without food, and in such exigencies she would, sometimes, when everything else failed, apply to the benevolent societies. Twice her crying necessities were relieved; upon the third application, assistance was necessarily denied her. The society, through the unusual demand upon its resources, had involved itself in debt, and was obliged to retrench. The long and weary winter, with its terrible sufferings, was at length
16

over. It had passed without bringing to the desolate wife any
tidings of her husband. Spring opened, and relieved from the
pressure of the severest want of the season—the want of fuel—
the sisters began to look up more cheerfully. Their faces
seemed less pale, haggard, and hungry. Lydia had now acquired
some knowledge of cutting and fitting children nice clothes,
and the spring had brought its increased run of business. The
three sisters, among them, took one copy of "The Star." It
was a penny paper, and they took it for the sake of seeing the
army news. It was usually carried to Mary, who read it, and
then sent it round to her sisters. One day, just as Lydia was
entering Mary's front gate, the newsboy passed, and threw
in the paper. Lydia caught it up, and hurried into the house
with it, greeted her sister hastily, and sat down to look over
the paper. She turned first to the columns usually devoted
to army news, and read with a curdling che and freezing
heart—in great capital letters—"GLORIOUS NEWS FROM
MEXICO. GREAT BATTLE FOUGHT. *American* TROOPS VIC-
TORIOUS." Glancing breathlessly down the column—suddenly
with a wild shriek she leaped from her seat into the air, and
fell forward upon her face, as though an arrow had pierced her
heart. The name of Francis Miller was among the killed.
For days the life of Lydia hung upon the weakest thread.
She would recover from insensibility only to fall into convulsions at the first dawn of consciousness and memory, and this
continued until her strength utterly failed under it, and it was
feared that she was sinking into death. At last youth and
nature conquered, and she began slowly to recover. She arose
from her bed of illness at first only the ghost of her former
self—so emaciated, so wan, so wild-looking through her eyes.
But soon that singular strength, that latent strength that is
the growth of trial and suffering, began to develop itself in
Lydia. She looked life steadily and firmly in the face, and
began to gather up the fragments that remained of her broken
happiness, that nothing might be wasted. Through all that

summer as her strength returned, Lydia devoted herself to the care of her children, with a mother's perfect love, and while the summer and fall lasted she managed by perseverance, if not by skill in work, to supply their necessities. With the approach of winter, however, troubles thickened around her. Work became very scarce, and wages very low, nor was it possible, in every instance, to obtain from her employers even the scanty pay for which she had contended. It was thus that December, 184–, found her.

CHAPTER X.

NEW YEAR'S EVE.

IT was once more New Year's Eve. Lydia was once more preparing for the New Year. But, oh! under what different circumstances to those in which we have before seen her making ready for the festival.

Take a look at her home—herself and her children *now* It is early, *very* early in the morning. The snow-storm has been driving against the windows all night long. Lydia has not slept a wink; how could she sleep, with the children continually waking up and crying with the cold—how could she sleep, with the knowledge that there was no wood, no, not one log left in the house to make a fire with in the morning, that there was no food except a very little handful of meal in the bottom of the barrel? Lydia arose as soon as it was light, for she had a job of work to do that was strictly required to be finished against New Year's Day. It was a dress for a little girl, whose parents lived on the Avenue, and who, in the press of work accumulating in the Christmas holidays, had employed Lydia to make it. By rising early she might finish the job

by evening, and so please her employer and get the money to
buy a few necessaries for the New Year. She had set up at
work late on the preceding evening, until the candle borrowed
from her sister Mary had burnt out in the socket and left her
in darkness—still there was a day's work to do yet, as the
dress was a merino one, to be trimmed elaborately with braid.
As soon as it was light enough to see to work, Lydia arose,
shuddering at the biting cold, and dressed herself with numb
hands. She covered the children up warm, telling them to
lie close. Then she descended the stairs into the cold, dark,
fireless kitchen. First she tried to open the kitchen door, to
see how deep the snow might be, and if there was any possibility of getting over to Mary's to borrow a log of wood. But
Lydia had to make many ineffectual efforts before she could
pull open the frost-bound door, and then an avalanche of
drifted snow that had been piled up against it fell in upon her,
and a gust of falling sleet and snow blew into her face. It
was dreadful to look out over those white fields of drifted
snow, in which the fences had disappeared, and in which ever
small houses were half sunk. It was totally impossible to get
over to The Three Cottages that morning, through the terrible
snow-storm. With freezing hands, and by hard labour Lydia
succeeded in shoveling out the snow, and closing the door.
Then she opened the ice-bound window-shutters, and let the
light in upon the desolate kitchen. What a scene it was.
The favourite carpet—"mother's home-made carpet," had
vanished before the food and fuel necessities of the impover-
ished family. The floor was bare, and the planks warped
apart with age let a tiny draught up through them. The
plastering was broken in many places, and the window-sashes
and panes were loose, so that the wind rushed in at every
quarter, making the room very cold, even when there was a
fire in the fire-place, and now there was none, and no probability of there being one. A few old rickety chairs, a pine
table, and a cupboard, with a few old cups and saucers of delf

ware were all the furniture of the desolate kitchen. As the
cold gray light of the stormy morning, fell in upon the cold
hearth, Lydia looked up in despair. Her limbs were becoming powerless from intense cold; her feet were like lifeless
clods, her hands were stiff and useless! What was to be
done? Were her children indeed to starve and freeze before
her? She rubbed her hands together vigorously, to restore
their suspended circulation; she went to the meal barrel, and
turning it up, emptied the handful of meal into a bowl—but
how to cook it without fire? Suddenly a bright thought
struck her—taking an axe from the corner under the stairs,
she rolled the barrel on to the hearth, and commenced knocking it to pieces. It was a light stave barrel, so that by the
exertion of all her little strength, she managed to split it up,
and taking a box of matches from the mantle-piece, she soon
had a blazing fire, then going to the foot of the stairs, she
called out, cheerily,

"You may get up, children, now—there is a fire now," and
setting her little griddle to heat, she thawed the ice from the
stone pitcher, and began to mix her corn-cake. It was baked
by the time the children came down stairs. And after she
had placed the corn-cake upon the pine table, and after the
children had gathered around it, she asked a blessing in a
cheerful voice, and broke the bread among them. A fire and
a meal had been effected, and that was enough to restore for
the hour the peace of one now inured to hardship. Little
clearing away did this humble meal require. It was soon
done, and setting down her children, girls and boys, to cut and
sew carpet rags, she took up her sewing and applied herself
vigorously to it, stopping now and then to clap her hands to
restore their congealing circulation, or to keep up the little
fire by the occasional addition of a stave.

"Never mind, children," she would say, gayly, "we shall
have a good fire to-night, and some loaf-bread for supper.
Mother has only got to finish and carry home this work, and

she will get some money, and buy some wood and some flour
and molasses, and she will see if she can't make her children
some cakes for New Year's."

"And mother, won't you get my shoes home from Mr.
Tucker's?" asked little Harry, whose little shoes had been at
a cobbler's to be mended for two weeks, and had remained
there because there was no money to pay for them.

"Yes, Harry, dear, mother will do that, too."

All day long she stitched and stitched. The children became hungry again, and the fire was almost out. They became
very cold. Hunger and cold react upon each other, each
augmenting the other. About noon the barrel that had
supplied the morning's fuel, stintingly as it had been used,
was quite exhausted, and only a few embers remained. Lydia
had three old chairs; one of them must be sacrificed, a little
fire must be had, or the children must perish. She arose and
broke up the chair—no hard matter, it was already rickety—
and placed it on the fire; the children crowded around the
little blaze—Milly, the baby, bringing her pet pigeon, whose
feet were also crisped up with cold—and the mother resumed
her needle. All day the mother and children had watched
the sky, waiting for, hoping for the cessation of the snow-storm
with an anxiety only to be realized by the very poor and suffering. At length, a little after noon, the storm subsided, the
sun shone out in splendour.

"See, children, it has cleared off beautifully," exclaimed
Lydia, by way of calling their attention to the brilliant flashing of the sun upon the snow without, as she plied her needle
with renewed zeal and cheerfulness; but soon as the afternoon
waned, her good spirits flagged,—a weariness, a chilliness, an
inclination to yawn, a headache, crept upon her. These slight
chills followed by hectic fevers, the effects of constant anxiety,
work, exposure, and slow starvation, she had felt at irregular
periods before, but always in the afternoon or evening. But
now, as she sat there, the symp' ms increased—an insupporta-

b:e weariness, a death-like chill; shiverings, glows, mortal sickness seized h. 'r. Still, she crept nearer the fire, and worked harder, faster, to complete her task—it *must* be finished, or the children must famish with cold and hunger. They had eaten nothing since morning—the fire was dying out a second time, and now the second chair was split up and put upon the decaying embers. It was near sunset when the dress was finished. With her cheeks burning with high fever, with her very throat and lips scorched with the flame of her breath, with a splitting headache, Lydia tottered to her feet, smoothed out the dress, and, folding it neatly, pinned it up in the carefully preserved paper in which it had been brought home. Then sinking quivering and exhausted in her chair again, she called two of her children to get ready and carry it home.

" Let *me* take it, mother," said Harry, the eldest boy.

" No, my dear, you have no shoes—Lizzy's and Tommy's shoes are good—let them go."

Then she sent Harry up stairs for two pair of his own well-darned stockings, and calling the two little ones, she drew the socks over their shoes to keep them from filling with snow, and then wrapping them up in their little linsey cloaks, and tying on Tommy's little cat-skin cap, and Lizzy's brown stuff hood, she gave Lizzy the bundle and started them. Then returning, she dropped upon the old lounge, utterly prostrated. Harry was at her side again in an instant.

" Mother, you are sick, dear mother, ain't you very sick?"

" Only a little, darling; I have had a chill, and now have a fever, that is all. Look at your little sister, Harry, lift her up and put her in the cradle," said the mother, straining her eyes anxiously to a corner of the room where the baby had cried itself to sleep for hunger, and lay coiled up with its still fat cheek doubled up under its dimpled arm, and the pet pigeon sheltered to its bosom. " Lift her up, Harry, and lay her in the cradle; cover her up warm, Harry."

The little boy raised his sister with difficulty. She half

waked, sighed, but fell asleep again as he placed her on her little bed and tucked her up. The pet pigeon cooed uneasily, hopped up on the edge of the cradle, plumed itself, and fluttering down upon the pillow, nestled lovingly against the infant's cheek.

"Mother, can I do nothing for you?" asked the child, coming back to his mother's side. "Can't I cover *you* up? Can't I hold your head?"

"Yes, Harry, darling; you can get a quilt from up stairs and lay over my feet; and close the window-blind to keep out this light—it makes mother worse, my dear."

Harry did all that was required of him, and then sat down in the dark, cold room, with his infant sister sleeping in the cradle, and his suffering mother lying upon the lounge. He sat down by her side with a saucer of cold water, in which he continually wet his little hand to cool her head.

"Never mind, dear Harry," said she, in a low, weak voice, "be patient, dear Harry; mother's fever will go off by-and-by, and brother and sister will return with the money and with your shoes, and you shall go out and buy some wood and groceries—you shall have a good fire and a good supper yet."

An hour passed, the high fever was going off in the perspiration that concludes an attack of ague and fever, and she was waiting for this also to pass off, when the baby awoke and began to cry for food. The mother got up at once and went to her child, took her up in her arms, and walked the floor with her, trying to soothe her with caresses, with soft words and gentle smiles, and promises that she should have something to eat when her sister and brother came home.

"But me *hundry*, me *so* hundry," wailed the child, incessantly, "me no b'ead so *lon'* time, mammy! div Milly b'ead, mammy!" tearfully coaxed the infant, clinging around her mother's neck, unable to understand *why* its mother could not satisfy its wants. But if the piteous complaints of her babe were torture to hear and to bear, not the less agonizing was

the sight of her poor patient boy, with his broad fair brow,
large hollow eyes, and sharp chin, sitting on a little old trunk,
with his thin hands locked together. He was her first born,
and if she did not love him best, at least they understood each
other best; he was in her confidence, and now he comprehended
that melancholy look with which she regarded him, and starting up, he ran to her, and embracing her, said,

"It is most time for them to be here, mother, and if yc.
and the baby can stand it, I can, dear mother."

It *was* time, *high* time that the children had returned; it
was getting dark, and their mother, though momentarily expecting them, was growing every moment more anxious. It was
horrible—the approaching night, that freezing room, that fireless hearth, the starving but patient boy, the wailing infant,
the growing darkness, the intense anxiety for the two little
wanderers, the desolation, the despair—oh! perhaps the death
closing all around them.

"Oh! where *can* my children be? Oh! God, have mercy
on me—they must have fire, they must have food, or die before
me." She set down the infant, and calling her son, said,
"Harry, come and try to help me split up this table, it is the
very last thing, except the baby's cradle, that will burn, about
the house." And the table soon shared the fate of the chairs;
and as the cheerful blaze once more arose on the cold hearth,
the eye of the mother fell upon the children's pet pigeon: a
bright thought like an animal instinct, suddenly lighted up
her face, and then a shadow fell upon her brow, and a tear
dimmed her eye. "No, poor thing, I can't take your life,
at least not yet, not quite yet; you have suffered hunger
and cold with the children, and you love them and they love
you," thought Lydia, and then again raising the baby—
who had exhausted itself by weeping, and was now quiet,
up in her arms, she went to the window to look out for
her wandering children. No sign of them could she see,
though she looked eagerly, far, far over the undulating drifts

of snow that stretched on towards the city. She watched
till the sky grew too dark for her to discern anything.

In the mean time, the two little children had toddled along
leg-deep in the drifts of snow, but bearing it bravely, as
children always bear such things, until they got to the pavement running around the Capitol. It was good walking there,
and on the flag-stones crossing to Pennsylvania Avenue, and
down the Avenue, and the children ran on until they got to the
line of fancy stores, toy shops, &c., and there they would pause
and gaze—not knowing how soon time would pass and night
would be on them. They saw well-dressed children of their own
age, going into toy-shops with their mammas, or coming out with
their hands or little baskets filled with dolls, tops, guns, drums
—things that to these poor children looked *so* splendid and
seemed *so* desirable—and farther they would go on and stop
and gaze with hungry eyes into the confectioners' shops, where
the very *smell* of the freshly-baked cakes stimulated anew the
appetites of the half-famishing children. They went on, and at
last came to the by-street down which they had to turn to take
the dress to the family to whom it belonged. It was a teacher's
family; and when the children got to the door, and Lizzy pulled
the bell, it was the teacher himself in his wadded dressing-gown,
who opened the door. When he saw two little bits of children
there, two tiny little human wrens, as they were, so late in the
evening, through such a deep snow, he paused a moment in
pitying amazement. Then he pulled them gently in out of
the cold, before he inquired—

"What do you want, little ones?"

"Please, sir, mother has sent home the work."

"Ah, yes! hem! Elly's dress, I suppose.—Well, come in,
little folks, and warm yourselves. Mrs. Anson is in the back
parlour," and, leading the way through a narrow passage to a
sitting-room, where there was a warm stove and a tea-table set,
the teacher made the children sit down near the stove, and
took the bundle from them and handed it to his wife, who had

just entered. She opened and looked at it, seemed well pleased, and said, turning to her husband—

"Have you a dollar-and-three-quarters in change, Mr Anson?"

"Is that the price she asked for making this dress?" inquired the schoolmaster.

"Yes. It is heavily braided, you see, it must have taken her four or five days to make it."

"Yes it *did*," chimed in both the children here.

The teacher stopped and looked at them. Saw their poverty, their hunger, their enjoyment of the stove, their eager but covert glances at the bread on the table.

"Is not supper nearly ready, wife?" he asked.

"Yes—Kitty is just going to bring it in,"—and as she spoke, Kitty entered, and placed a pot of coffee and a tureen of oysters on the table.

"Well, then, let's sit down; come, little folks," he said to the children, "come up and get some supper. Kitty, put two plates here for these children."

The schoolmaster's own sons and daughters now came in and took their seats at the table, and Miss Elly, the youngest girl, kindly removed the wet cloaks of the poor children, and showed them where to sit. It did the hearts of the kind-hearted family good to see how the famished children enjoyed this feast, until little Lizzy suddenly stopped, and burst into tears.

"Why, what is the matter, little one? Don't cry. What are you crying for?"

"Because moth—moth—mother ain't got any!" sobbed the child.

"Well, never mind, mother shall have some—we will put some in a little tin bucket, and give you, to carry to mother—you are a good girl, to think of mother."

"I thought of her, too!" chimed in Tommy, with his mouth full, "only I can't cry like Lizzy, because I'm not a gal."

As soon as supper was over, the teacher's wife put up a little pint pail of oysters, and placed it in the hands of Lizzy, saying—

"You may take the oysters to your mother, and *you* may keep the pail," and the teacher gave Lizzy a two dollar bill, telling her to tell her mother, "Never mind the quarter."

And the children, now warmed, fed, and comforted, set out upon their return. The schoolmaster and his wife knew nothing of this family; nothing at all of the extreme destitution into which they had fallen; nothing of the distance the children had to traverse, else you may be sure that they would have sent a servant to see them safely home, and a basket of provisions to farther relieve their necessity. The children hurried along, merrily enough, until they came to the Avenue again. Here they paused and sauntered—the gas-lights of the streets, the brilliantly illumined windows, the cheerful crowd, hurrying up and down the pavements, fascinated their attention, and, when some crowd of boys, firing off squibs, would sing out—"Hurra for New Year's!" Tommy—poor, thoughtless child, would clap his wings, and crow out in reply—"Hurra-a-a-a!" until the earnest little Lizzy, pressing his arm, reminded him that mother was waiting, and they hastened on. The children got on well all down the long Avenue, and round the pavement of the Capitol, until they left them, with their bright lights, behind, and struck out into the snow-clad fields beyond. Here it was dark, but for the star-light and the snow, and here the drifts of snow were very deep, and what was worse, the ground under it was very uneven, traversed with gullies and ridges, and the children plunged on through the drifts nearly up to their waists, sometimes above them, and sometimes almost lost among them. Presently, in climbing up a snow-covered ridge, poor Lizzy slipped, and rolled over down the other side, drawing heaps of snow after her, until she was buried in the deep drift at the foot. With a scream of terror, Tommy run and slid down to her rescue—

dug her out hastily with his hands, and pulling her up with all his little might, asked breathlessly—

"Are you hurt, Lizzy?—are you bumped?—is it bleeding anywhere?"

"No," sobbed the child, looking around her, "but—but I have lost the money and the oysters, and—and oh, I have lost the *sweet little pail!*" she exclaimed with a new burst of grief; "oh, help me to look for the pail, brother."

The children began to grope about among the snow, until their hands and feet were stiff with cold. Of course the money was lost beyond recovery—but at last they found the pail, and weeping bitterly with cold and disappointment, they toiled on their laborious way through the snow drifts towards their home. Arrived at the door, they saw by the flickering light on the windows that "mother" had some fire. Their hands too numb to double up for a rap, they pushed against the door, which was quickly flung wide open, and their mother received them both in her arms, exclaiming—

"Oh, children, where have you been—what kept you so long? I have been *so* uneasy about you!" and, without waiting an answer, she drew them to the small fire, and began to pull off their wet shoes and stockings. Not until she had made them as comfortable as she could with her small fire, and not until they had told her of the schoolmaster's kindness to them, did she ask,

"Where is the money, children—and did you remember to call for your brother's shoes?"

"Oh, mother, we lost the money, and so we couldn't get the shoes."

"Lost the money!" exclaimed the mother, in despair.

"Lost the money!" cried Harry, in dismay.

"Yes, lost the money! indeed we could not help it, mother! I carried it carefully in my hand, but I fell down in a snow-bank, and as I opened my hand to catch myself, I lost the money. You ain't mad with poor us, mother, are you?"

"Angry with you, Lizzy!" exclaimed the mother in a tone of utter despair, "angry with you, poor child?—no, it is not that!"

She now turned to look at the baby in the cradle. It had ceased its noisy complaints, and now was wailing with a piteously low moan, as though its strength was quite exhausted. She turned from that sight to look on Harry. His eyes, as he stood in the corner by the fire, were cavernous with famine. And then she went and caught the pet pigeon, which flew to her bosom. Harry's large, haggard eyes followed her suspiciously with their bright glare.

"What are you going to do with Pidggy, mother?" he asked.

"Kill it, my love—kill it."

"Oh! mother, no! no! no!" exclaimed Lizzy and Tommy, in a breath.

"Children, *you* have supped—your brother and sister are starving."

"Oh, mother! not for *me*," pleaded Harry, "spare poor Pidggy—see how she loves you, and tries to get in your bosom."

And now all the children except the famishing baby in the cradle, crowded around their mother pleading for "Pidggy." Tears rolled down Lydia's cheeks as she turned away from them, and pointing to the cradle, said,

"Your little sister complains no more—she is dying for food. Pidggy's life taken will save hers—go away—it will only be a moment. Pidggy will not suffer much." And she gently pushed the children off, and went to a dark corner, whence she took a hatchet, and holding the head of Pidggy down upon the hearth, raised the hatchet. A startling rap at the door arrested her hand.

"Who is there?" inquired she, turning around. The knob was turned, the door opened, and a handsome, well-dressed

man entered. A loud scream burst from Lydia's lips, a ;
dropping the living pigeon, she sprang to his bosom—

"Frank!"

"Lydia!"

"Good God! is this you? Am I dreaming, or has troubl
driven me mad?"

"I, Lydia! it is I; compose yourself, Lydia; compose
yourself, dear Lydia," said our old acquaintance, Frank Miller;
for, of course, it was he who had returned safe and sound, and
was now soothing, caressing, and—yes, weeping over his wife.
"Lydia! how are you? How are the children? Oh, God!"
he exclaimed bitterly, looking around, "you are so poor!"

"Oh! I am rich! I am rich!" replied Lydia. "You are
restored—you are restored. The grave is not inexorable, it
has restored you to my love."

"What grave, dear Lydia? You are talking very wildly,
love."

Need I tell the reader how quickly the scene was changed
in that miserable home—how soon a hot fire blazed in the
chimney, how soon a hot supper smoked on the table, how the
children gathered around it, transported between the joy of
seeing their father's return, their mother's joy, and the much
needed supper before them?

Need I tell that a mere mistake in the military report, had
occasioned Lydia's supposition of her widowhood? How the
irregularity of the mails had prevented the rectification of the
mistake? Need I tell you with what joy, as she and Frank
with the two youngest children on their laps, and the two
eldest seated between them, were seated at the fire, Lydia
heard that Frank and Bohrer had met in Mexico, had both
reformed, had both taken the pledge two years before, and had
kept it faithfully ever since—that Bohrer had returned with
him to Washington, and was now at his own home with Ellen?
The next day, New Year's Day, Mary Fairfield (from whom
I got this whole story), who had the only comfortable home

in the family, invited her two sisters and brothers-in-law to a
family dinner at her house.   And perhaps in all the rejoicing
in the city of Washington, there was none so heartfelt as theirs.
The sale of their bounty-land, and the savings from their wages,
enabled Bohrer and Frank Miller to repurchase their homes
at a considerable advance upon the price at which they had
been sold.   And *now* The Three Sisters, two of them under
happier auspices than ever, are once more settled in The Three
Cottages.

ANNIE GREY;

OR,

NEIGHBOURS' PRESCRIPTIONS.

---

and a man's foes shall be those of his own household.—MATT. x. 36.

> If thou would'st, doctor, find out her disease,
> And change it to a round and pristine health,
> I would applaud thee to the very echo,
> That should applaud again.—SHAKSPEARE.

> Sick people commonly recover,
> If only *neighbours* give them over.—BUTLER.

IT might not be considered polite "to talk to physicians of fevers," in stories, more than in drawing-rooms; yet, if I so offend, pardon me, for the sake of a good motive, as the lady said when she killed her friend by advising the wrong physic. *Besides*, I "hold these truths to be self-evident"—that it would be a wanton waste of my own leisure, and an impertinent trespass upon my readers' time, to obtrude upon their notice a pure fiction, without object or aim—such being the prerogative only of those monarchs of fancy and imagination who have divided among themselves the empire of romance and poetry. (The reader will please consider inserted here the names of his or her favourite novelists or poets.) *Therefore*, I shall only "deferentially solicit," as the office-seekers say, the company of my clement reader to a gossip about the errors and foibles of our neighbours, faithfully promising to exaggerate and embellish no more than is customary with other retailers of scandal. And the first thing we will talk about, dear reader, will be neighbours' well-meant but oft-times inju

17

dicious and fatal prescriptions for the sick. And it is a matter far too serious to be lightly treated; therefore, attention !
I have known *many* cases in which neighbours' prescriptions
have retarded the convalescence of the sick; I have known
several, in which they have rendered recovery impossible. The
first illustration in point, that occurs to me, is the case of a
relative, a man in the prime of life, who was recovering from
a severe attack of bilious pleurisy. He was so far convales-
cent as to require no farther aid from medicine or attention
from a physician. He was able to sit up, but very weak.
While in health, he had been a moderate drinker of wine and
brandy. Now that he was suffering under the debility consequent upon a severe fit of illness, he fancied that he required
his accustomed stimulant. A neighbour, tender-hearted to
the extent of weakness, mixed and presented to him a glass
of brandy toddy. From the moment in which he swallowed
it, his fever arose, and he grew rapidly and alarmingly worse.
The family physician was hastily summoned, and, upon his
arrival at the bedside of his patient, he demanded to be informed what he had been taking. The conscience-stricken
neighbour answered, in faltering tones, " Nothing in the world,
Doctor, but a little drop of brandy toddy, which you know
could not possibly hurt him—could it ?"

" He will be stiff enough in three days," was the *literal*
reply of the blunt old physician.

And *he was* " stiff enough in three days;" and to the end
of her long life, the kind-hearted but ill-judging neighbour
reproached herself with having "killed poor George G——."

Let me try to recall the circumstances of the next case.

Yes! I remember. There was poor B. He was a good
youth—"one of the excellent of the earth"—his mother's
heart—his father's right hand. While suffering under a slight
indisposition, induced by a long pedestrian journey through
the heat of an August sun, he was persuaded by a neighbour
to try somebody's pills, an infallible remedy for all diseases—

hydrophobia and whooping cough, croup and corns, mania and
measles, erysipelas and everything. He bought a box, poor
boy! and took the pills; but the more pills he took, the worse
he grew—and the worse he grew, the more pills he took—until
the box was empty, and himself past cure. The pills in his
particular case acted as a potent poison, and killed him in two
days. His medical attendant (called in when he was dying)
said it, and his parents knew it.

I wish that Congress would leave quarrelling for a few minutes, and pass a little by-law, making it murder to kill with
kindness, and felony to prescribe without a diploma. There
would be some lives and medical reputations saved, perchance,
though at the cost of depriving some worthy people of a favourite amusement.

It is rather hard that physicians not only have a downright,
aboveboard, open enemy, in a *disease*, to encounter, but that
in neighbours' prescriptions they have to contend with a secret
foe, who works in the dark, whom they do not suspect, and
cannot surprise—because, when the step of the Doctor is heard
upon the stairs, the bottle or the bowl is always thrust under
the bed or into the cupboard. These neighbours, while enter-
taining the kindest intentions, and making the most plausible
professions, contrive by their prescriptions to counteract the
Doctor's treatment, baffle his skill, and kill his patient—by
giving a stimulant where he has ordered a sedative, an astringent when he has directed a cathartic, or an opiate if he has
prescribed a febrifuge—and *vice versa*. And the physician
comes and finds that a case, the successful treatment of which
has cost him deep research, severe study, anxious thought,
constant vigilance—a case in which not only his professional
reputation is involved, but his social sympathy is enlisted (for
the family physician, though a constant attendant at the bed
of suffering, is not case-hardened; he feels the imploring glance
of his patient, who seems to think life depends upon the Doctor's skill; he sees the anxious looks of friends, who scarcely

breathe while listening to his fiat)—a case which he has brought to a certain point of convalescence, suddenly wrested from his hands, and placed beyond his reach, not by the invetcracy of disease, not by the inefficiency of medicine, but by the officious intermeddling of some well-meaning but injudicious neighbour In many such cases, the physician must be utterly at a loss to conjecture the cause of his patient's unexpected change for the worse; for, more than half the time, neighbours and friends are unconscious of having caused the mischief, or unwilling to acknowledge their agency in it—so that, notwithstanding the physician's cross-examination, the truth is seldom elicited. I have often heard people say, in such cases—

"Lord bless you, we were afraid to let the Doctor know."

And so the Doctor, seeing this failure, may lose faith in his excellent mode of treatment, and in the next case change it for a worse one.

How rational people can trust to the prescriptions of neighbours whom they know to be as ignorant of medicine as themselves, I cannot tell; for if there be *any* truth in the gibe, that "physicians are men who put drugs, of which they know little, into stomachs of which they know less," it is very certain that most neighbours and visiters of the sick know nothing at all of either drugs or stomach, pharmacy or physiology.

But I must make an end of "oratory," and, skipping at least twenty good illustrations of my caption, come to the last and most affecting instance on the list; and I must introduce it story-fashion, too, lest it should not be read. *Imprimis.*

One fine summer morning, in a neat bed-chamber, the floor covered with straw matting, the windows shaded by white muslin curt——! *Miserabili!* Here I am in the midst of another description of another room. I beg the reader's pardon, with all my heart. The subject *is* trite (so is everything else, bread and butter and sunshine included); but a bad habit is so hard to shake off. It sticks to one with the fidelity of—of a bad habit. The reader will please to imagine, for him-

self or herself, the neatest, cleanest, coolest, pleasantest, little
summer chamber that can be conceived, so that it comes within the means of a poor journeyman mechanic—for such a one
was the father of the two delicate young girls who occupy the
room. Upon a little French bedstead, covered with a white
counterpane, reposed the fair, fragile form of Annie, the elder
of the twin sisters. She was thin, even to emaciation, yet
very beautiful as she slept. Her long black eyelashes rested
upon a cheek white as marble, transparent as pearl; her long
black hair, escaped from her cap, floated over the pillow. Her
slender white arm was thrown above her head, across the black
tresses. The other sister, Clara, was moving about the room
silently, as though fearful of awakening the sleeper. This
girl was the fac simile of her twin sister, except that she had
a burning red colour on her cheeks and lips, and an unnatural
sparkle in her bright, very bright eyes. Her slender form
was arrayed in a loose white wrapper. The sleeper stirred,
murmured, opened her eyes, and said—

"Are you there, Clara?"

"Yes, love; what will you have, dear Annie?" inquired
Clara, approaching the bedside softly.

"Give me your hand, Clara. This dear little hand! how
lovingly and patiently it has tended me, through this long,
long illness. This poor little, thin hand"—said Annie, fondly
playing with her sister's fingers—"But how hot it is, Clara;
how very hot your hand is! You are feverish, sister; you have
confined yourself too closely. Raise the window a little way
to give me air, and then go and take a walk—won't you?"

Clara raised the window, and opened an opposite door, so
that a current of air could pass through and ventilate the
room, without blowing upon the sick girl. Annie drew a long,
deep breath, and smiled.

"That air is so pleasant. It breathes so sweet, and fresh
—it gives me new life."

Clara returned to the bedside, and said cheerfully—

"You are a great deal better this morning, dear Annie !"

"Yes ! a great deal better—I slept so well—and have waked up so refreshed. My fever is off, my skin is moist, the heat and tightness have left my chest, and, above all, I can draw a dear, blessed, good, *deep* breath. Oh ! Clara, you can't conceive what a blessing it is to be able to draw a free breath — you would have to be half suffocated for a month, as I have been, in order to realize it."

"You have been a great sufferer, my poor dear Annie, but thank God—*thank God*—you are better now. And you *look* so much better, too," said Clara; suddenly checking the fervour of her feelings, lest it should agitate Annie.

"Now, then, Clara, go out, and take a walk, won't you? Indeed, I'm afraid you will make yourself ill, by such close confinement. Go now—there's a dear."

"Presently, presently, Annie."

"No—*now.* I'm going to make you go; or, if you won t, I'll talk, and bring on a fever; or else, as the spoiled children say, 'I'll *cry*, and make myself ill;' " said Annie, smiling.

"Oh ! I am so glad to see you so merry, Annie."

"Will you do as I bid you?"

"After a while—when we've seen Dr. Wood; his carriage is before the door."

"And here he comes up the stairs," said Annie, listening.

The family physician now entered the room. He was an elderly man, with a tall, thin figure, blue-gray hair, and a red face. He walked up to the bedside of his patient, laid his hand upon her forehead, held her wrist, and remarked cheeringly—

"You are very much improved this morning, my child "

"Oh, yes ! Dr. Wood, that last medicine did me a great deal of good. I slept sweetly last night, and I have waked up this morning—*so* hungry. What can I have to eat ?"

"Still thinking of her stomach ! Clara ! Tell John Brown, I say, he had better go into the eating line. Set up a refectory

or something. Annie 'll be an excellent helpmate in such a
concern; she'll be able to cater for other people's palates by
the test of her own."

Clara laughed merrily; but Annie pretended not to hear,
and reiterated her complaint and question.

"I want something to eat, Doctor! What *can* I have to
eat?"

"Why, you *can* have roast beef and plum pudding, but you
shan't."

"Pshaw! Can I have a cup of coffee, and an egg, and
some toast?"

"Yes," said the Doctor, complainingly, "you can have a
cup of——rice water, and a soda cracker"——

"Oh, Doctor!" groaned Annie, making a face.

"Or some good——water-gruel."

Annie turned her head away in disgust.

"Or else some excellent——barley-water."

Annie exhibited strong symptoms of hydrophobia.

"Oh, Doctor!" exclaimed she, "can you give me nothing
but a choice among the different preparations of——*water?*
Can't I have a little chicken soup?"

"Not for a day or two to come, my child."

The Doctor then assured his patient that she was getting
well fast; and that by Sunday she should have something
savory for dinner, and took his leave.

"Clara! do you hear? The Doctor says I shall have something good to eat Sunday, and that is day after to-morrow.
And it shall be fried chicken—no!—it shall be stewed oysters.
Clara! do you hear? Tell father the Doctor says I am to
have some stewed oysters by day after to-morrow—do you
hear now?"

"Yes, yes, darling, I hear; I will tell father."

But Clara did not think that the Doctor had particularly
recommended, nor did she believe that he would particularly
approve, the dish selected. However, unwilling to vex her

beloved invalid, she refrained from opposing her now, and followed the Doctor out of the room.

"Clara! come back here!"

"Well, darling?" said Clara, returning.

"Come close—ask the doctor, when you get down stairs, if he thinks my lungs are affected—ask him *confidentially*, you know, and then come up and tell me the truth—will you?"

Clara left the room, and soon returned with a very cheerful countenance.

"Did you ask the Doctor, Clara?"

"Yes, dear Annie; and he assures me that you are not at all consumptive, at present, and will never be so, if you take care of yourself. He says that you have been suffering from an attack of neu—neu—I forget—but, any way *not* consumption."

Annie smiled.

"That is a great deal off my mind, dear Clara; I have such a dread of pulmonary consumption; I was so much afraid I had contracted it, and, indeed, I didn't want to die yet."

"And make poor John Brown a widower, before he becomes a husband—to be sure not; but there's no danger these fifty years to come, thanks to our good Doctor."

"Yes; thanks to our good Doctor, for he is good, Clara; and I feel such a glow of gratitude to him, when I think of all his kindness—his attending poor mother for two years before she died, and his 'tending me so constantly through this tedious illness"——

"Yes, indeed. And father asked him for his bill last week, and what do you think he said? Why, 'You don't owe me anything, Mr. Gray.'"

"And he with such a large family, too!"

"Yes; he is a poor man himself. But he is like all others of his profession. They do more good, and get less thanks, than any other set of men whatever; they jump up at all hours of the day or night, and in all weathers, to wait upon all sorts of people, rich or poor, paid or not paid—thanked or abused, it is all the same—and they get no credit; it seems to be expected of them, and they do it. I have known a Doctor to jump up in the middle of the night, in a severe snow storm, to visit a poor man with the rheumatism, from whom it would have been folly to have expected pay; and the man, too, seemed to consider it quite a matter of course; and I don't believe he ever even said, 'Thank you, Doctor.'"

"Oh, well! he thanked him in his heart, Clara; at least, if he feels like me, he did. I, for one, say, God bless the medical faculty in general, and our own dear old Doctor in particular. Oh! Clara, you don't know how grateful one feels towards the person who has conjured away all our bad feelings, and restored us to comfort and enjoyment. And he has raised me almost from the grave. Oh! I love the good Doctor so much. And when he laid his hand upon my forehead, just now, I wanted to take the dear, kind hand and press it to my lips and to my bosom; but that would have been very shocking, I suppose?"

"Very," said Clara, laughing.

"I'm in earnest, though," said the sick girl, as the tears swam in her eyes, "for I love the good Doctor more than either of my uncles, and next to my father, for he has 'tended me long and patiently, and saved my life; and I like life, Clara, and I don't like to die. He has taken away all my bad feelings and restored me to enjoyment—all 'without money and without price'—and so I love the Doctor, and I shall *always* love him; and the very next time he comes to see me, I am going to kiss him, and tell him so, to ease my heart; and you see if I don't; for," added the child petulantly, "I'm sick, and sick people must have their own way."

"To be sure, my pet, so you shall—kiss the Doctor or the Doctor's dog, or anybody else you please, and as much as you please"——

"Hush! Is not that father singing?" asked Annie.

" Yes, dear; he has been singing at his work all the morning; sawing wood, and singing; pumping water and singing; making a fire and singing"——

"Oh! I know," murmured Annie, as an expression of ineffable tenderness came into her face; "dear father! he's singing because I am out of danger."

"Yes; he is so glad. He says, although the Doctor won't give him his bill, as soon as he gets his month's pay he will send him a twenty-dollar bill."

"Poor father! he would 'draw the spirit from his breast, and give it' for my sake."

"Hush! here comes Mrs. Brown."

A fat, cosy, grandmotherly-looking matron, now entered the room, sat down in the rocking-chair, sighed, and inquired in a sad tone—

"How do you feel, this morning, dear?"

"Very much better, I thank you, Mrs. Brown. Clara, ove, go down now, and give father his breakfast; it must be near time for him to go to work; and get your own, Clara; you must be faint, you've been up so long. Mrs. Brown will remain with me until your return. Can't you, Mrs. Brown?"

"Yes, yes, to be sure;" said the old lady. "Go, Clara, I'll stay with Annie."

Clara left the room.

"There, honey, see what I have brought you; a nice bowl of panado, with port wine in it."

"I am very much obliged to you, indeed, Mrs. Brown, but the Doctor says I mustn't take anything stimulating."

"Fiddlestick! You mustn't mind all the Doctor says. This is very nourishing; it will strengthen you. Here, taste, and see how good it is."

"It *smells* very nice," said Annie, looking longingly at the bowl.

"Taste it. Don't be afraid of it. It is very simple."

"It looks very good," said Annie, toying with the spoon, "but I'd rather not eat anything against the Doctor's orders."

"Oh, the Doctor! You must think the Doctor is omnipotent, but I don't. Here, let me raise you up. Don't be afraid, and never mind what the Doctor says. Do you think I would give you anything to hurt you? No, I would not, for poor John's sake."

The old lady propped Annie up with pillows, and set the bowl before her. Annie took the spoon, turned about the panado, and placed a morsel to her lips, in a cautious and gingerly manner.

"There! Ain't it good? Poor John went all over town to get that port wine genuine."

"Did John get it?" asked Annie, raising her eyebrows in an inquiring manner, and poising the spoon half way between the bowl and her lips.

"Yes, he did; went to a dozen places before he could get the real stuff. There, honey, eat it *all* up."

And with renewed confidence, as if nothing hurtful could come through her lover's hands, Annie did "eat it all up."

Annie had scarcely finished her meal, when the hectic spot appeared upon her cheek, her lips grew bright, and her eyes blazed up with the fearful light of fever.

"There, now!" exclaimed the old lady, as she received the bowl from Annie, "don't you feel better? I told you so! You look like another person. You've got some colour now. Oh! If I had you, I'd get you up in no time. Dear me! here are all the windows up; this will never do. It will give you your death of cold!" and the grandmotherly old lady let them all down, and shut the door. The morning was very sultry, and the room soon became very warm.

"Dear Mrs. Brown, this is suffocating; please raise the windows again The Doctor says there must be a free circulation of fresh air in the room."

"My dear child, I shall do no such thing It might be the

death of you. You mustn't put so much dependence in what
the Doctor says. Sure, if he is such a knowing man, it is a
wonder he loses so many patients."

It is a wonder he did not lose *all*, when Mrs. Brown, who
was a regular visiter of the sick, followed, like fate, in his
footsteps.

"There, my dear, I hear them coming up stairs. I must
be going. I have got to call and see Mrs. Piper's baby; it's
got the summer complaint."

"You are very good to the sick, dear Mrs. Brown."

"It's no more than my duty, Annie," said the old lady,
with solemn self-complacency. "Good-bye, honey; make
haste and get well, and be my daughter, you know. John's
house is nearly finished. I believe I hear John's voice now,
down stairs."

Mr. Gray now entered the room, to bid Annie good-bye,
before going to his work.

"How do you do, Mrs. Brown? Won't you sit?" said he
to the old lady.

"Ah! good-morning, Mr. Gray. No, I thank you, I was
just going; good-day." And the old lady went down stairs.

"You are looking very well this morning, my pretty Annie,"
said Gray.

"I am *almost* well, dear father."

"What is that I must get for you by Sunday, darling?"

"Oh! father! yes; some oysters, some nice Nanticoke
oysters, to stew by Sunday. The Doctor says I am to have
something nice on Sunday; and so I want oysters."

"Very well, my dear Annie; father will get them," said
he, stroking her hair.

"Is John Brown down stairs, father?"

"Yes, darling, waiting to come up. Are you well enough
to see him?"

"Oh! yes, dear father, let him come."

"Well, then, my sweet Annie, I must bid you good-bye for

the present. I'll send him up; and see here, Annie," lowering his voice, "get well, and then—won't we have a fine wedding?" Annie reddened. The father was going out—she recalled him.

"See here, father, make Clara take a walk, will you? She is too much confined."

"Very well. I'll attend to it. Good-bye, darling."

"Good-bye, dear father. Don't work too hard," said Annie, as she put her arms around his neck, and received his parting kiss.

Annie's next visiter was John Brown, her betrothed, who came in, accompanied by Clara.

"Now, dear Annie," said John, "why didn't you let me come in before; I have a thousand things to tell you about, and not ten minutes to say it in. Why, Annie! my gracious! how well you are looking. Beautiful! *You* sick? Why, your checks and lips are glowing, and your eyes brighter than I ever saw," exclaimed John, in admiration, mistaking the burning fire of fever for the blooming rose of health. "Come, you mustn't be there much longer; you must get up, and come and see my little new house (*our* little new house, sweet Annie," said he, lowering his voice to a whisper); "it is so pretty—painted lead colour, with close white shutters. I have got the fence put up, and the garden laid off; and I've planted some peas (which we will have for dinner the first time Clara and the old man come to see us, dear); and I want you up, that you may go with me to select some furniture. I have got seventy-five dollars towards it."

"And I have got twenty-five," said Annie, "saved from my needlework."

"Keep it, keep it, darling; surely, if an American lad can't furnish a little house for his bride, without taxing her earnings, he must be a very worthless fellow."

Annie smiled, but in the midst of her smile an expression of pain traversed her countenance, the colour died away from her face for an instant, and then rushed back in a crimson glow. Clara approached the bed, and bent over her anxiously.

"What is the matter, dear Annie?"

"Nothing—a sharp, sudden pain; it is over now," said Annie.

"A stitch," suggested John.

Annie's face again quivered, grew pale, then flushed. She grasped her sister's hand lightly.

"Dear Annie, you are suffering; you have had too much company; you have been excited and worried. John, go home—that's a good boy; you may come again this evening."

"Good-bye, Annie," said John Brown.

"Good-bye, good-bye," replied Annie.

John Brown was gone.

"Oh! Clara, I am very ill."

"Dear, dear Annie, I am so sorry; where are you sick?"

"I am in excruciating pain," cried Annie, as her face flushed and paled rapidly.

"I will send for the Doctor."

"No, no; he could not be found now; he is on his round. Send for John's mother; she is a sort of doctress; she, perhaps, can think of something to relieve me."

Clara hurried down stairs, overtook John, and sent him for his mother—then hastened back to her sister. Annie was extremely ill. The stimulating food that she had taken had excited a violent inflammation. The old lady, Mrs. Brown, soon came in, exclaiming—

"Well, well; what's the matter now? John came running after me, as though he were crazy. Young people are so quickly frightened—and you all alone by your two selves—pity, poor things, but what you had a mother. Where's your misery, Annie?"

Annie explained.

"Ah ha! I knew it. That cold, windy water-gruel has disagreed with you. So much for following after the doctors

Here! Clara, run and fetch me some brandy and ginger, and boiling water. Quick, now! Be in a hurry! She must have some brandy-toddy, with ginger in it. Make haste!"

Mrs. Brown made Clara fly about and bring her all the things. Mrs. Brown was in her glory. Nothing pleased that dear old lady better than to see a fellow-creature writhing in an agony of pain, if the sufferings afforded a fair opportunity for the gratification of her darling propensity—doctoring. It was to her what game was to the sportsman, play to the gambler, or bull-baiting to the Spaniard. Yet Mrs. Brown was called, and believed herself to be, a very benevolent woman, very kind to the sick, and an excellent nurse. The old lady concocted the dose, and carried it to her patient. Anne drank it all, and thanked her poisoner.

"And now, honey," said she, "I must go. I promised to call in and see Mrs. Piper's baby again to-day. The little one is getting no better, although I gave it a dose of medicine of my own preparing. Indeed, I think it is getting worse. They've got that young Doctor Jones attending it. What does *he* know about babies! good-bye, Annie. That toddy will ease you. You will sleep after it."

And the old lady departed, with the comfortable conscious-ness of having performed a good action. She met John at the street door, and told him that he might go to work, as Annie was better, and John, careful not to disturb the sick one, left the house without saying good-bye. As may be readily supposed, Annie grew rapidly and alarmingly worse. She suffered excruciating torture. Clara was in despair. She sent for her father, and for the physician. Mr. Gray followed the summons immediately. The Doctor came in the afternoon. He never suspected the cause of, and was wholly unable to ac-count for, the dreadful change that had taken place in his patient. He taxed his skill to the utmost for her relief. He remained with her all the afternoon; then, promising to re turn early in the morning, he left her somewhat easier, and went to another patient.

Not far from Mr. Gray's humble dwelling stood a house of more pretensions to quality. It was occupied by Mr. Piper, a rising young lawyer, and his wife. They had one infant, upon whom they both doted with all the fondness of young parents for their first and only child. But now the babe was ill, and the father and the mother wild with alarm. Mr. Piper had called in Doctor Jones, a young physician of eminent talent, one who had already acquired a large practice, and who had effected several remarkable cures. When he arrived at Mrs. Piper's house, he found the pale young mother, with the babe in her arms, walking him about the floor. She sat down, and laid the babe across her lap for the Doctor's inspection, watching the expression of his countenance eagerly. He told her that the babe was suffering under only a very slight attack of cholera infantum, and that his recovery depended more upon *her own* careful nursing, than upon medicine. He charged her to let the child take no food whatever, except that which nature had provided; and giving a few peremptory but judicious directions for its treatment, he wrote a prescription, and left the house. The doting mother was re-assured, and smiled again. In a day or two the babe was much better, though not quite restored to health. He was recovering *slowly* but *surely* under the young Doctor's excellent method of treatment, when the evil genius of the physician sent the news of the babe's illness to Mrs. Brown, who straightway considered it her "duty" to go and see the sick baby. Upon that fatal morning, something in the appearance of the infant had aroused the very excitable fears of his mother, and she felt and looked very uneasy when Mrs. Brown entered.

"Good-morning, Mrs. Piper. How do you do? I heard that your little one was very ill, and I thought I would step in and see it."

"Indeed, I am very grateful, Mrs. Brown. Please look at him, and tell me how you think he is."

Mrs. Brown took the infant upon her lap, and looked solemnly and wistfully at him; put her hand upon his chest, and upon his head; and finally poked her great finger into his mouth, and felt his gums; then turned up the whites of her eyes, and ejaculated—

"Ah! Lord!"

"Oh! Mrs. Brown, you don't say so!" exclaimed the nervous mother, in affright. "Is he *so* bad?"

"Who is 'tending him?" inquired the old lady, without replying to the question.

"Why, Dr. Jones—Dr. Jones. Oh! *is* he very ill, Mrs. Brown?"

"Dr. Jones! *That* young man! Why, t'other day he was no taller than my knee. *He* a Doctor!"

"They say he's a very successful practitioner. But, oh! dear Mrs. Brown, please tell me—*is* the baby very sick?" said the mother, as the tears rushed to her eyes.

"Pretty sick. What has that young man (I can't call him a Doctor), ordered for it?"

"Why, this is it," replied the trembling mother, showing a little folded packet of small powders.

"Umph-humph! Calomel and prepared chalk, I suppose. That will not do it any good. If you keep on giving that to the child, you'll kill it."

"But the Doctor"——

"Oh! the Doctor! What does *he* know about babies? *He* never was a mother. I've had thirteen children—and raised two, and buried eleven; and I should think I ought to understand nursing children."

The infant here became very fretful, and the mother very uneasy, and Mrs. Brown very loquacious and didactic.

"Oh! dear Mrs. Brown, what had I better do?"

"Stop. Have you got any laudanum?"

18

" Yes; but"——

" Well, get it, girl, and bring me a spoonful of water in a cup."

This direction was given to a maid servant who was standing in the room, and who forthwith brought the required articles.

" What are you going to do, Mrs. Brown?" inquired the mother, who was pacing the floor, with the babe in her arms.

" Give the child a few drops of laudanum."

" Oh! Mrs. Brown, I'm afraid"——

" Never mind what you're afraid of. This is the shortest way to stop the child's complaints. I'm a better judge than you are," persisted the old lady, holding the cup in one hand, and dropping the laudadum slowly with the other. The timid young mother suffered herself to be out-talked and overruled. The laudanum was dropped and poured down the babe's throat. The child dropped into a deep sleep.

" There, now! Didn't I tell you so? See how nice he' sleeping. Don't tell me about Doctors; one old woman is worth twenty Doctors, for curing babies."

" Yes, indeed," assented Mrs. Piper. " He is sleeping now more quietly than he has been for a long time."

" Well, good-morning, my dear child. Whenever you want me, send for me. I am always ready to visit the sick."

" Thank you, dear Mrs. Brown! Indeed, I am very, very grateful to you. You've given my poor baby relief, and you couldn't have done me a greater favour. I shall never forget your kindness," said the poor woman, earnestly.

" I have only done my duty," said the old lady, meekly; and she went off, enjoying the reward of " an approving conscience."

" What an excellent woman!" murmured the mother, as she returned to her infant's cradle, after seeing Mrs. Brown out. But an exclamation of horror broke from her lips, as her glance fell upon the child. The infant had waked up in a spasm. A little fretfulness, a slight fever, in the babe, was euough at any time to arouse all the mother's worst fears, but *now —now* that she saw her child's features convulsed and limbs quivering, in a frightful spasm, her alarm and grief exceeded all description.

At that moment, Dr. Jones entered the room, and, seeing the state of the child, he demanded rather peremptorily, as was his custom, what had been given to the babe. And the pale and trembling mother told him, informing him at the same time who had prescribed the dose. "Out of his grief and his vexation," the young physician exclaimed—

"By Heaven, madam, she has *killed* your child!"

"Oh! don't say so, Doctor! Don't! don't! I should go mad! Oh, no! It can't be! God would not take my baby away from me, that I love so dearly!",

Losing all self-control, she sank down by the side of the cradle. Her grief became so poignant as to render her incapable of discharging her duties. Seeing the state of affairs, and being ignorant of their family resources, Dr. Jones sent off for Mr. Piper. It was near night when the babe's spasms went off, and he sunk into a coma.

———

It was the night of the same day upon which Annie Gray had received her death-draught from Mrs. Brown. The Doctor had left her comparatively easy a few hours previous. Mr. Gray, poor man, suspecting no danger, had retired to rest. Clara had lighted the night taper, and, setting it upon the hearth, took her seat by her sister. Clara, also, was free from apprehension now; but she could not, she knew not why, make up her mind to go bed. Annie was lying quite still She was easy, but with the fatal ease induced by mortification She was dying, and she knew it.

"Clara!"

"Well, Annie?"

"Won't you lie down, love?"

'Presently, dear Annie; I am not sleepy yet. How do you feel, Annie?"

"Quite easy. Perfectly free from pain of any sort."

"I am so glad," said poor, unsuspicious Clara.

The silence continued unbroken in the room, except by the ticking of the clock, for many minutes. Then Annie called, in a low voice—

"Clara!"

"Well, sister?"

"Look in my little Bible, and bring me that folded paper —and a lead pencil."

"Dear Annie, what is it you want to do? You must go to sleep, darling."

"So I will, *very soon*, and take a *long* nap; but give me them first."

"Here they are, then, Annie."

"Raise me up."

"Why, what are you going to do, darling?"

"Just to add four words to that paper."

"Let me do it."

"No."

Annie feebly scratched four words to the end of some writing, and fell back exhausted upon her pillow, retaining the paper in her hand. She lay still a long time, and again the ticking of the clock became awfully distinct. At last, again she called—

"Clara!"

"Well, darling?"

"What day is this?"

"Friday, you know, dear. Day after to-morrow you are to have the oysters."

"Friday, Saturday, Sunday. Clara! take this paper, and put it away safely; and do not read it until Monday, and then go by it, will you?"

"Why, what in the world do you mean, dear Annie?"

"Never mind what I mean. Promise me, will you?"

"Yes, love, certainly. Now try to sleep, dear Annie."

"Yes, I will."

Why was the silence in that peaceful room so awful? Why ticked the clock so loud and fast, and why fell its strokes so heavily upon the heart of the watcher? *She* did not know it was counting away the last seconds of a dying girl. At length, the dread silence was relieved by the low, sweet music of Annie's voice—

"Clara!"

"Darling?"

"Where is father?"

"Gone to bed."

"Give my love to him."

"Annie! Annie! What do you mean?"

"Nothing, only he forgot to kiss me."

She lay again silent for a few moments; then for the last time called lowly—

"Clara!"

(She seemed to love the iteration of her sister's name.)

"What now, love?"

"Tell dear John Brown, I say, God bless him."

"Annie! Annie! Oh! dear me, what *is* the matter with you? I am—I'm *so* uneasy. I—I'll call up father," cried Clara, as in her fright she seized the taper, and flashed its light upon her sister's face.

Annie's face was white as marble, but a sweet smile hovered over it. Clara's countenance was blanched to a "violet paleness," and she shook in every limb.

"Don't look so frightened, dearest sister; I'm going to sleep now."

"Are you at ease?"

"Perfectly. Kiss me."

Clara pressed her warm lips to the cold brow of the dying girl. Re-assured, she resumed her seat. Clara was nervous

Oh! why did that clock tick so loud and fast, and why jarred its strokes so heavily upon the excited nerves of Clara? It counted away, fast and faster, the fleeting seconds of the parting seraph.

"Father! Clara! John!" whispered Annie.

Clara bent over her sister, and looked silently on her face. Her eyes were closed, her countenance was still, save for the smile that still hovered upon her lips.

"She is talking in her sleep," thought Clara.

"Mother! mother!" murmured the dying girl.

Again Clara looked upon her sister's face, but it was perfectly still; even the smile had fled. Annie Gray's gentle spirit had passed away.

"She has gone sound asleep at last, thank God," said Clara.

Morning dawned. Mr. Gray rapped at his daughter's chamber door, to inquire how Annie had slept. Clara opened the door.

"What! been up all night, poor Clara? Could you get no one to sit up but yourself?"

"I could not have left Annie, father."

"How does she seem?"

"Better. Still sleeping."

"Thank Heaven!"

The father hurried away from the door, to finish dressing. After having raised the window and opened the blinds, Clara returned to her beloved sleeper, and looked upon her face. The face was cold and stiff—the eyes half open, and stony—the blue lips were apart, and the white teeth glistening between them. The hand that Clara had taken fell heavily from her grasp. With a heart-rending cry, Clara cast herself upon the body of her sister, and fainted. That cry brought the father back into the room. The father was a strong man. He suffered, as he gazed upon his dead Annie, as deeply as Clara had; yet no tear sprung to his eye—no groan broke from his lips. The muscles of his iron face worked convulsively—his broad

chest heaved, as he stood some moments looking upon the
sisters. Then, gently lifting the insensible Clara from the
body, he bore her to the next room, laid her upon the bed,
and calmly walked down stairs to send for Mrs. Brown. That
benevolent lady was not at home. She was occupied with
laying out Mrs. Piper's baby, which had just expired. Some
other neighbours, however, tendered their services to see to
things.

———

Sunday came—the Sunday of poor Annie Gray's funeral.
Clara had exhausted her strength by giving way to the wildest
expressions of grief and despair, and now lay prostrate upon
the very same bed on which Annie had yielded up her gentle
spirit. Clara lay quivering, gasping, fainting, under the weakness induced by a violent outbreak of sorrow. Low moans
and sighs were all that escaped her now. The rooms below
stairs were filling with funeral guests. Mrs. Brown, who had
taken the direction of affairs, was in a high state of excitement
and business. Poor Mr. Gray was standing about in everybody's way, having nothing to do, looking heart-broken, gazing
into vacancy. Mrs. Brown, in her flying hither and thither,
ran against him, and nearly overturned him; started, begged
his pardon, and asked him for his hat, "to pin a piece of crape
'round it." Poor Gray put his hand to his head, and looked
around in perplexity.

"Your hat, Mr. Gray—your hat, if you please, to pin a
piece of crape on it."

His face worked convulsively. He gave her the hat, and
turned away. The old lady looked at him, and said, while she
fixed his hat—

"Dear! dear! Mr. Gray, don't take on so—don't. Bear this
like a man—a Christian man. Annie's gone to heaven She
was a sweet, good"—

"Don't, don't," whimpered poor Gray.

"But I must—I must talk to you. It's for your own good. You know I'm your best friend, don't you?"

"I know you have been very kind to me and mine, Mrs. Brown. You were like a mother to the poor girl that's— that's——

"That's gone. Yes; and if she had taken my advice, instead of following after Doctors, from the first, she would have been living now."

"God bless you, Mrs. Brown—God bless you. I shall never forget your kindness to the poor motherless girl. May God reward you."

Should not that blessing have "heaped coals of fire upon her head?"

"I've tried to do my duty, Mr. Gray," said the self-sufficient old lady, as she moved off with a bundle of white cambric for the hack-driver's hats.

In the mean time, Clara lay upon the bed in the upper room. The guests continued to arrive. She heard their slow steps, their murmuring tones, and their whispered condolements. At last, all was still. Then the tones of the clergyman's voice were heard, as he read the sublime funeral service of the Episcopal church. At length, his voice ceased. Then, by the moving of many feet, and the slow rolling of carriage wheels, Clara knew that the corpse was being borne out, and that the funeral procession was in the act of being formed.

"Farewell, Annie! Farewell, playmate! Farewell, sister!"

These words burst from her lips in heart-breaking sobs, many, many times; and as long as the retreating sound of the wheels was heard, she gasped, from time to time—

"Farewell, Annie! Farewell, *dear* Annie!"

"How often," says a celebrated divine, "is the excitement of thought and feeling so great, that but for the interruptions of humble cares and trifles—the interpositions of a wise Providence—the mind and frame would sink under them entirely?"

The mechanic's daughter could not indulge her sorrow in

inaction. Her father would be coming back, bringing his
brothers to supper. So, after a while, she was compelled to
arise. She bathed her eyes, and went into the kitchen to prepare the meal.

On Monday morning, Clara thought of her sister's paper
She went to seek it. It merely contained some common but
too much neglected rules for the preservation of health. It
was evidently written for Clara. It was dated a month back,
at a time at which, as Clara recollected, Annie had despaired
of recovery. The four concluding words were written upon
the last night of her existence, and in very unsteady charac-
ters. It was headed—

Annie's Legacy to the Consumptive.

You are, or you believe yourself to be, consumptive. You
wish, above all things, for health and strength. You are poor,
and wish that you were able to buy some of the patent, all-
curing, all-promising specifics advertised in the newspapers.
Thank God, rather, for the poverty that prevents your pur-
chasing. Taking patent medicines is like drinking in the
dark, where some of the vessels are filled with wholesome
drink, and some with deadly poisons. You may chance upon
the right draught, or you may not. It is a great risk. But
the medicines for *your* debility are *cheap*—cheap as sunshine ;
and safe—safe as nature. They are—*air, water, exercise,
diet*. There is nothing original in the rules I am about to
transcribe. They are as old as common sense. You may
read them in many books and newspapers, and hear them at
lectures ; but yet you may not heed them more than I did,
before it was too late. Perhaps, though, when they come as
a legacy from your sister, who has lost health and life by the
neglect of them, why, then they may exercise all the moral
influence of "the last dying speech and confession" of a man
about to be hanged.

1. Bathe in tepid water every day. The "benefit of bathing

can only be justly estimated by those that practise it." Wear flannel winter (and summer, too, if you can bear it) next your skin. It will keep the skin in a healthful condition.

2. Take a walk every fine day. But that will not be exercise enough, or of the kind, for a consumptive. Make beds, rub tables, sweep, or do something else that will exercise the arms and chest. Sing or read aloud.

3. Ventilate your rooms, air your bedding, clothing, &c., every day. The lungs require pure air, as well as the palate requires pure water. *Item.* Do not keep a stove in your common sitting room; what it saves in fuel, it costs in health. I have found from experience that the burnt air from hot stoves, and the thick vapour from anything that may be cooking upon it, is very unpleasant, and very injurious to weak lungs. Use a fireplace or a Franklin stove in preference; for then everything injurious is carried up the chimney.

4. If you can, leave off gradually the use of strong tea and coffee. They keep up a slow, consuming fever in your system (it has been so with me); drink milk instead. When you are feverish, do not use pepper, mustard, spice, &c., in your food. Try this way of living for a month; and if you are not stronger, take the advice of a regular practitioner. *Never take Neighbours' Prescriptions.*

Reader! Poor Annie's rules were *not* neighbours' prescriptions; they were mostly taken from a work recently published by an undeniable M. D.

After Clara had in some measure got rid of her grief, she sat about getting rid of her consumption. I am happy to say that she has succeeded. She certainly looks much heartier, and I think she will be a robust woman yet. I do not think John Brown's little new house will want a mistress long. John Brown commenced by grieving with Clara, continued by loving her for Annie's sake, and ended by loving her for her own sake.

But, reader, a word in your ear: Mrs Brown is at large yet, and busy as ever—so, take care

ACROSS THE STREET.

A NEW YEAR'S STORY

The poor ye have always with you.—John xii. 8.

Ah! little think the gay and laughing crowd
Whom pleasure, power, and affluence surround,
Ah! little think they, as they dance along,
How many pine in want or drink the cup
Of misery! Sore pierced by wintry winds,
How many shrink into the sordid hut
Of cheerless poverty!—Thomson.

How gay seemed the city on New Year's Eve! How crowded the markets, and how crowded the shops; how full the pantries, and how busy the kitchens! Every heart seemed full to overflowing, with life, and hope, and hilarity—yet *no*, not *every* heart. Away, in obscure streets, in filthy alleys, and in dark and dismal dwellings, in forgotten neighbourhoods, cowered and shivered many a cold and hungry body, to whom Christmas brought no joy, but rather an aggravation of misery, by bringing out into stronger relief the contrast between the comfortable position of their happier neighbours, and their own sordid wretchedness.

Such a contrast might be seen on —— street, running from the avenue south down to the canal. There stands on the east side of the street a row of low-roofed one-story framed

(305)

houses. They are of a dirty white colour, and lean forward as if about to fall. They each have one door and window below, and two little square windows above, facing the street; but the doors are off the hinges, and the glass broken out of the windows, and its place filled with old hats, clothes, &c. It would be curious, doubtless, to pry into the history of each wretched family in this miserable row.

Doubtless, drunkenness has had much to do with it. I think so, because drunkenness seems to be the only vice upon which one *never* thrives. But that corner house at the northern end seems almost a redeeming feature in the row. For see, the door has two hinges, though the bottom one is of leather; and the want of glass is supplied with clean paper, pasted on. It is that northeastern corner house, in that front room so exposed to the blast, that you and I will peep to see what the inmates are doing. But before we go in, just look across the street, and see—there is but one house on the whole square, and that is a very handsome one with a large court-yard on each side and back of it. Now we will go in and observe. The room is very bare, floor uncarpeted, and the planks full of chinks, through which the wind blows, freezing the feet. That searching wind! it comes in everywhere. It shakes the unsheltered north end of the house (and the room), and it rattles the windows on the west. Whew, this cold room! it would take so much fire to warm it; yet there is not a spark on that cold hearth. True, there is an old charcoal furnace in the room, containing a few coals, in which a couple of flat-irons are heating. A poor, jaded, sickly woman is ironing at a table; the door opens now, and a little boy enters with a small basket of coal, which it seems he has picked up about the streets.

"This is all that I could find, mother."

"Never mind; put them on, Willie; they will serve to keep the irons hot till I finish these clothes," answered the mother, as the boy threw a basket of chips on the fire. "And then, Willie, you and I will go and carry them home; and then, when I get the money—it's a dollar and a 'levenpence that Mrs. Patton owes me—we will go through market, and see if we can find a nice rabbit, or something for to-morrow's dinner; we must keep Christmas, Willie, if we suffer the rest of the week, for it was the day our dear Saviour was born, you know, Willie."

"Yes, I know. Will you buy some molasses, and flour, and ginger, and make a few cakes? And oh, mother, will you buy some peppermint drops for poor little Lizzy, poor little thing; she's got no father."

"Bring me an iron, Willie, and hush," said the woman, as she turned away and rubbed her check apron across her eyes. "You bother me. My gracious alive, child, can't you see that money's hard to come at? One must stop somewhere's; it *won't do* to be so extravagant." The little one handed the iron, and sighed as he sat down. "There," said she, "mother's not mad with you, child, poor little fellow! but she is *not able* to get so *many* things. She's got wood to buy."

"I can fetch chips."

"What, with snow on the ground, Willie?"

"Oh, I forgot."

"Now, then, Willie, wipe your nose and tie your shoes, and get ready to go with me. Stay, your hat won't stay together any longer, I see. Crawl under the bed, and get your poor father's fur cap out of the box."

"Too big."

"Never mind, it will come down over your ears, and keep the back of your neck warm. There! ain't that nice?"

"Yes, indeed, it's as warm as any *thing*."

Then the poor woman sat down, and took a pair of thin slip-shod shoes, and sewed strings to the back to keep them up at the heel, and brushed and straightened her crumpled bonnet, put on her shawl, and giving one basket of clothes to her son, an' taking another herself, went into the street.

After trudging through the snow for four squares, they turned the corner and came upon the avenue. How lively and beautiful it looked! The western sunlight streamed down the street, as down a vista, lighting up the gay windows of the toy-shops and the confectioneries. The pavements and shops were thronged with people, making purchases for New Year's.

"Oh! mother, look! look! *Do* stop and look at this beautiful window; such beautiful monkeys, and drums, and guns, and great dolls and things. Oh! mother, how much money *would* it take to buy that dear *little* doll for baby?"

The child pulled his mother's hand so hard, and looked so eager, that she was fain to stop; and she, too, became interested in the scene. There was a portly, motherly-looking woman coming out of the shop, with a basket on her arm, followed by a gang of children, their hands full of gingerbread, nuts, &c.; and peeping out from under the basket-cover were to be seen the feet of dolls, ends of drums, &c. This woman was good-natured, and smiled on the child as she passed.

"There, mother, that woman has bought ever so many things for *her* children. Why can't you buy something for me and baby?"

"I keep telling you, Willie, that I'm *poor*, *very* poor, and *not able*, and you keep forgetting. Willie, *I've* got something to show *you* now." And she took him half a square on, where a milliner's and a dry goods merchant's shops were side by side. "There, Willie, ain't they nice bonnets?"

"Yes, indeed, mother."

"And ain't that a nice warm shawl?"

"'Taint nothing else!"

"Don't say that, Willie; it's wicked, that is; not *wicked*, but *not genteel*. Well, then, you see that nice bonnet and shawl; now look at mother's. Isn't it thin, and isn't her bonnet old and ugly?"

"Yes, indeed."

"Well, ᵀ tell you, Willie, that mother looks with as much

longing on *this* window, as you looked on *that.* So you are not the only one. Mother wants things she can't get as well as you do."

"Well, mother, don't fret; when I get to be a man, I'll work hard, and give you all the money, and only keep a half-dollar myself to show to the boys."

"God bless you, my poor dear child. I know you will be a blessing to me. Yes, Willie, mother will *try* this evening to get you something pretty, that she will; because you've been a good boy, and will be a blessing to me."

"Yes, that's what I will; and not go away and leave you, like my father!"

"You bad boy! Oh, that is very wicked. Who put that into your head?"

"Mrs. Ryley told me."

"Told you what?"

"Told me how I was the image of my father, but hoped I wouldn't be such a good-for"——

"There, hush! You mustn't say such things. It's *very* wicked. Your poor, dear father, too, who was killed in Mexico, defending his country."

They crossed the busy avenue now, and turned down D street, where they went in at the side gate of a comfortable-looking framed house, the residence of a substantial mechanic, for whose family Mrs. Jones washed. They knocked at the back door, and were admitted into a large, well-warmed kitchen. Yes, it *was so,* so comfortable. There stood the large Union cooking-stove, glowing and roaring with fire; and there stood a great, fat, greasy-looking coloured woman, in the act of taking a pan of cakes from the oven; and all along upon the lower dressers were ranged mince pies, waiting to be put away; and before a table stood the mistress of the house, with her sleeves rolled up above her elbows, cutting out cakes; and at the end of the table stood her daughter, beating up eggs. She turned as Mrs. Jones came in, and said:

"Oh, have you brought the things, Sally? Here, Rebecca, you take them. Are they well aired?"

"No, ma'am; I was short of wood."

"You ought *always* to bring them home well aired! Well, Rebecca, hang them to the fire up stairs in my room. Won't you go to the stove and warm yourself?"

Mrs. Jones led her son to the stove, and stood waiting, to see if her employer would offer her payment.

"Take a chair," said the coloured woman, setting one.

She took it, and there they sat, the mother and son, who had eaten nothing since breakfast; there they sat, inhaling the provoking savour of freshly-baked mince pies and cakes. And as the coloured woman wiped cake after cake with a clean napkin, and laid them one by one in a basket, the hungry child followed her eagerly with his eyes, until his mother twitched his arm and rose to depart, for the sun was getting low. She went to the table where the "lady" was busy, and said, modestly, "You know how much that little bill of mine is now, ma'am."

"Yes; seventy-five cents."

"No, ma'am; if you please to count up you will see."

This was an expensive time with Mrs. Patton; so she must *screw* for the thirty-seven cents difference.

Here followed an altercation, in which, as usual, the weaker party had to yield; and Mrs. Jones finally said:

"Well, ma'am, let it be seventy-five cents; and if you could make change, I should be very much obliged to you to let me have it now."

"I always pay all my bills the third of the month, when Patton gets paid off. Come the third of January; I'll pay you then."

"Yes, madam, but I'm very much in want of it."

"Well, you shall *have* it, I tell you. It's *good*, you know. Come next week."

"But indeed I am very much"——

"Dear me! Was ever any one so worried? I tell you my money's *good*; and I *really* can't pay you till next week."

"Come, Willie, we must go home."

"Oh, my dear Willie," said the mother, as she left the house, "what shall we do now? It's night, almost, and clouding up as if there was going to be more snow, and we with not even a chip to light a fire with when we get back."

"Oh, mother, the smell of the nice cakes has made me *so* hungry. Let's go through market, *any how*, mother; I want to buy three cakes for us and baby."

"What with, Willie?"

"Oh, with my cent the coloured woman gave me. I know *she'd* given me a cake if they'd been hers."

So they went into market, poor things, strangely but naturally impelled to aggravate their sense of privation by looking on the good things that they couldn't buy. Some of my readers know what the market on Christmas eve at night is, with the stalls all lighted up, and the light shining down on abundance of all sorts of good things.

"Oh, mother, ain't here *a sight* of meat?" said Willie, as they walked between the butchers' heaped-up stalls.

The widow sighed a reply.

How lost they seemed in that jolly scene! Every one was buying and selling, bargaining, laughing, and chatting. The spirit of frugality seemed banished from the market that night, and money, the vital fluid of the world, flowed as briskly through the market, as blood through a young man's veins.

Willie bought with his cent three very small cakes; "one for mother, and one for me, and one for baby," he said; and then they went home, not starving and freezing exactly, but with an appetite whetted to the keenest edge by the fresh and frosty air. Oh, reader, would it not have been comfortable for them, if they could have gone home with a full basket to a warm room, a glowing fire, and a good supper? It was snowing very fast now, and the wind was driving

19

it fiercely in their faces. The flakes of snow, sharp with frost, seemed to cut into the pores of their skin, and find its way over the folds of their clothes, wetting them through, and over the tops of their old shoes, soaking their feet. The poor woman struggled on through the driving and whirling snow-storm, holding on her bonnet with one hand, and dragging Willie with the other. Oh, reader, if *you* had known this, would you not have hastened to kindle a fire on that cold hearth, and spread with food that bare board? Oh! if you would, it is not too late yet. "The poor shall never cease from the earth." And just over the way, per-chance, or around the corner, in the next street or alley may, nay, *must*, be suffering equal or greater than I here depict. Dear reader, *the poor in thine own immediate neighbourhood* are *thy poor*—the legacy of Christ *to thee.* "The poor ye have always with you." And if Providence has, as it were, dropped them immediately in your way, for the purpose, it may be, of eliciting from you a spirit of Christian love, do not shut your eyes, and close your heart, and pass them by. Do not try to shift the responsibility on to public charities; they can do but little. Do not withhold from "thy poor" the food and raiment for which they are suffering—the *work* with which they might supply their own wants—the advice and the sympathy that would encourage them to effort.

The mother and son reached home. The snow was banked up against the door. They pushed the door open, and the snow fell in upon the floor.

"Oh, dear, mother, I believe my sock is frozen to the bot-tom of my foot; I can't get it off," cried the child, as he tried to divest his feet of their cold, wet covering; and so it was.

"Stop, Willie," said his mother, "I must put your feet in cold water, or else they'll be frost bitten;" but when she went to the bucket, the water was frozen. At this moment, too, the baby awoke, and began to cry piteously.

"Here, mother, give babe this cake; never mind, mother, I can get my stockings off now. I held my warm hands to them; my hands were warm, because I kept them in my pockets."

His mother handed him a pair of dry socks out of "the box under the bed."

"Mother, what have we got for supper, anyhow?"

"Hurrah! for New Year's!" shouted a voice in the street

The woman went to a basket in the corner, and looked into it, saying, "We have got about a dozen potatoes, Willie, if we only had a little fire to boil them with; but, dear me, they are all frozen hard—frozen hard, like my heart; for now, though I see my poor things suffering, I cannot even have a good cry;" and in proof thereof the poor woman burst into a copious flood of tears. Willie ran and twined his greasy jacket-sleeves around her neck : "Don't cry, mother; there, don't cry; indeed I'll be good, and not ask for supper;" which only made "mother" cry the more.

"What *is* the bustle, then, mother? Has our Father in Heaven gone and left us too?"

"Oh, no, Willie; what makes you ask such a question?"

"Why, when father left us, and you were sick, and baby came, you said how we had a Father in Heaven, who would 'never leave' us, 'or forsake us;' and you used to repeat texts about him—I remember them yet."

The mother drew her arm around his waist and kissed him, as she said—

"Repeat them to me, Willie; they will comfort me."

"'Cast all your care upon Him, for He careth for you.'"

"Yes, I will. Go on."

"'Do not two sparrows sell for a farthing? Verily I say unto you, not one of them shall fall to the ground without your Father. Fear not, therefore; ye are of more value than many sparrows.

"'Behold the fowls of the air; they sow not, neither do they reap, nor gather into barns, yet your Heavenly Father feedeth them. Are ye not much better than they?

" 'Therefore, take no thought, saying, What shall we eat,
or what shall we drink, or wherewithal shall we be clothed,
for your Heavenly Father *knoweth* that ye have *need* of all
these things. But seek *first* the Kingdom of God and His
righteousness, and all these things shall be added to you.' "

" Oh, the gracious promises! Oh, the gracious Father!
Kneel down, Willie, and place your little hands together, and
ask our Father to remember us in our need, and ' give us our
daily bread.' "

And the little child, nothing doubting, raised his infant
voice and pure heart in supplication to his Heavenly Parent.
And when at last he arose, and met his mother's eyes, her
tears had fled, and her face beamed down on him like the face
of an angel.

" How beautiful you are, dear mother—how beautiful you
are now. You look just as you used to look when father came
home from his work, and you took the baby up to show him."

" *Woor-or-rah!* for New Year's !" shouted another voice,
rushing past the house; at the same time the snaps of torpedos
sounded on the side walk, and Willie, child-like, ran to the
window, and looked out. The boys with their rattle-traps had
gone past.

" It's done snowing, mother—that's a blessing," said he ;
and then the house across the street fixed his attention.

" It's four o'clock, mother; the gentleman has come home,
and he's got three pair of little shoes dangling on his arm :
that's for Rose, and Ella, and Johnny," said Willie, as a thin,
stooping, yellow-visaged man bent on towards the house and
entered. He was followed by a boy wheeling a hand-cart,
filled with all sorts of good things. He could afford it. He
was a clerk in the receipt of a good salary, and his wife and
daughter kept a select first-class day school.

The evening waned.

" Our Father has sent us nothing *yet*, mother," said Willie

' My dear child—my poor, silly child—listen ! God does

not always grant our prayers, but sometimes, for good and wise purposes, withholds compliance with them."

"But our Father is good—*so* good, and I asked him *so* faithful. I'm sure something will turn up, mother."

And the child climbed up and leaned his chin upon the back of a chair that was sitting against the window, and gazed out; but gusts of wind rattled the glass, and a driving snow-storm darkened the air.

Night was coming on, yet still the child, kneeling upon the chair, clasping its back with his little hands, and pressing his thin, sharp face against the panes, looked out, shivering, when the wind rushed against and through the crevices of the old window.

Night was coming on, and the handsome house across the street was lighted up. The blinds were not yet closed, and the light glowed through the crimson curtains upon the snow, making the street rosy red. And it pleased the child's little unselfish heart to see it, and to think how light and warm it must be in that room, and how happy the children *there* must feel. At length a coloured boy came out and closed the blinds, and the little one could no longer see the light from the warm room. He could no longer see anything from his cold post; so he got down, and, going up to his mother, said—

"Let me say my prayers and go to bed, mother;" and as he drew off his socks he said—

"It's no use to hang up my stockings *to-night*, mother."

About the same hour that Willie and his mother went to carry home the washing, within that comfortable house across the street, in a close back room warmed by an air-tight stove, sat a pale, dyspeptic, anxious-looking woman. Upon the bed, and over chairs, lay various articles of unfinished finery; over her lap, a handsome visite upon which she was sewing a rich, heavy fringe. She would pause occasionally to lean her head upon her hand, or place her hand upon her side, and sigh and

go on again. A ring at the street door was soon followed by
the entrance of a lady younger than the worker, who came
forward, and saluting her by the name of cousin, remarked—

"I left a woman below stairs, who came in with me. She
wants to know if you have any needlework to put out?"

"Tell her no, I have none. Go tell her, Ella." (This
was to a little girl.)

"Yet you seem to have a great deal to do, cousin."

"Yes! I have, and I'm almost worn out."

"Well, then, why in the world *don't* you put some of it
out?"

"Because *I'm not able*, Harriet."

"And *why* are you not able?"

"Why, because our income is very moderate, and our expenses are heavy; house-rent and the grocery bill—and
marketing and wood—keeping three fires—and the girls *must*
dress. Yes! and there is the doctor's and the druggist's bill
to be paid soon—they always render it the first of the year.
Now I beg of you to tell me how I can put out my sewing;
and tell me if you think it would be *right* for me to do so?"

This was said in a tone of querulous irony, but the younger
lady replied good humouredly—

"With pleasure. In the first place you are confined to
your school-room all day long except Saturday, when you are
going through the house setting things in order—and Sunday,
when you go to church—is it not so?"

"Yes."

"Very well. That leaves you only evening for healthful
relaxation, such as visiting, walking, conversation, light reading, or active domestic duties."

"Yes."

"Then a good portion of your evening should be *given up*
to such healthful relaxation. Again, you are well paid for
teaching, are you not?"

"I am paid."

"Very good. Then you should be content, and not covet-
ous—giving the poor needle-women a chance to live also; dis-
pensing to them a portion of your work. Now this is my
notion of the division of labour. Would not this be only
just?"

"Ah! I can't afford it."

"But I will *convince* you that you *can* afford it. You are
subject to indigestion, sick headaches, loss of appetite, &c.,
and you have to take pills, and sometimes you have a serious
bilious attack, and have to call in a physician, at a dollar a
visit. Is it not so?"

"Sometimes."

"Yes, oftentimes. Now I am going to assure you that, if,
when you come out of school, instead of sitting down at your
needlework from four o'clock to eleven or twelve, you would
only take a walk for an hour or two every evening, your health
would be better, and you would save more dollars in physician's visits. Those same dollars you might pay to some poor
woman for doing that portion of your needlework that would
have been done in the hours you devoted to healthful exercise."

The lady smiled ironically.

"That is a narrow view," she said. "You are benefiting
one portion of the community at the expense of another."

"What, the doctors! Don't you believe it. Be you never
so careful of your own health, there are fools enough in the
world who are ruining *theirs* with tight lacing, and heavy
clothing, thin shoes, and hot stoves, and close rooms, and other
malpractices. The doctors will live. But, come, will you not
now put out a portion of your sewing?"

"I *can't*, I tell you! The girls and myself *must* dress
genteelly."

"Ah! there it is. You don't mind if your eyes are red,
and your face pale, and your countenance dejected, so that
French flowers bloom on each side of the pale cheek, and a

costly shawl is folded over the weak chest, nor how the poor body *inwardly* suffers if it is *outwardly* adorned."

"But these things should be bought not only for our own gratification, but to encourage art and usefulness."

"True; but people in moderate circumstances should use them in moderation; and you should allow the poor work-woman an opportunity of encouraging manufactures too, albeit it may be of a coarser description," said Miss Harriet, smiling.

"Well, you ought to go and talk to Mrs. Brown; she has nine in family to sew for, and dresses them all handsomely; and she never puts out a bit of her sewing, though her hus-band gets fifteen hundred a year. And there's Mrs. Rice, and Mrs. Briggs, and Mrs. Stone, all having large families, all doing their own sewing, and all sickly, although their hus-bands are getting good salaries. You had better go and talk to them."

"I wish sincerely I had the privilege, for I believe these ladies act from a mistaken sense of duty, in endeavouring to make a little money go as far as possible. They believe that they are doing good service by sitting up half the night toil-ing to economize money, that they may spend it on rich apparel. With eyes intent upon *one* point of economy, they lose sight of *other* points, and often realize a *small* gain at *great* loss. For instance: by sewing half the night, they can save money to procure fringe of a little greater depth, and richer or more costly feathers and flowers, at a loss of health, cheerfulness, and beauty. It is not the fault of the men, for I believe they would all prefer that their wives and daughters cared more for their health and beauty, and less for the finery.

"I am sure that our women do not want benevolence or good sense, but they want time and opportunity for observing and understanding the distress that is caused by withholding their work from the poor. I wish they could see as I, who

live among them, have seen, a poor widow surrounded by her
children, whom she is obliged to keep from school on account
of their destitution of shoes and clothes, sitting over a miserable fire, or partaking of a wretched meal—a corn griddle-cake
broken up among them—and *know* that this is not an *extra
ordinary*, but an *every* day affair, and hear her say, that if
she could but get sewing enough, she would do *so* well, and
hear her complain that the '*ladies do all their own work*'
now. I know that ladies would cheerfully assist her; and
when, in addition to all her other misery, she is laid upon a
sick bed—I know that women would sacrifice their dearest
piece of finery to relieve her wants."

"Oh! dear, you are drawing a fancy picture; it is *not*
so?"

"It *is* so, very close to my own home, there are two such
cases of extreme destitution, for the want of work—come and
see for yourself. And how many more in other parts of the
city, God only knows."

The lady was engaged in deep thought for a few minutes,
and then said:

"Well, I'll tell you what, my arrangements are nearly all
complete for this year, but next year I will adopt a different
plan. I will walk out with you after school hours and see,
and carry some of my needlework to one of these poor women
you speak of."

"No, *I* will take care of my two families. I have divided
my own needlework among them, and shall take care to procure from our own neighbourhood work for our own particular
poor first; then, if we have more, we will give it to others.
Do you do likewise—*look after the poor of your own immediate neighbourhood.* To wit: there is a row of houses just
across the street—visit them; no need to go out of the ——
ward"

The younger lady soon after took her leave, and the elder
lady exclaimed, as the street door closed behind her,

"Thank God, that old quidnunc is gone. Heavens! haven't I been worried? Now I'll finish the visite."

An hour after this, the happy family group were assembled in the front parlour. The father had come home from market, and the mother and children were there, gathered around the glowing grate, telling each other what a severe change there had been in the weather, and wondering how long the cold would last, and how deep the snow would be, &c. Ella, the youngest girl, was looking out upon the storm. At last she turned her great blue eyes around, and said,

"Mother, I don't believe there has been a spark of fire in that house over the street to-day; and there's a little boy lives there, big as me, and he has not got any brothers and sisters to play with, neither."

"How do *you* know, Miss Ella?" inquired her mannish little brother, joining her.

Ella protruded her full red lips, and disdained to reply to impertinent questions.

"What makes you think that there has been no fire there, Ella?" inquired her father.

"Because, father, there has been no smoke coming out of the chimly all day."

"'*Chimly*' now, '*chimly*'—that's a pretty way to talk!" interposed Johnny.

"Yes, it is! Father, make Johnny let me alone."

"Johnny! hush. Do you know who lives there, Ella?"

"A little boy, big as me."

"Big as *me*—how do you parse that?" said Johnny, *sotto voce.*

"Father!"

"If I have to speak to you again, Master Johnny, I shall send you off to bed."

"Well, Ella! A little boy, you say, and who else?"

"Why, a tortoise-shell pussy cat, and a speckled rooster, and a woman. There used to be a man lived there, but I

reckon he's gone away. I haven't seen him for a good while.
There's tae pussy cat now, sitting in the garret window, washing her face. I wonder if her foot's got well; she used to
limp when she walked."

Mr. Wood was now looking out at the opposite house. An
expression of pain came into his face, and he said,

"My dear *soul*, wife! I do believe it is as she says. Good
Heavens! to think of being without a fire on such a night as
this!"

"I reckon pussy's foot was frost-bit. Let her and the
little boy come over *here* to live, Pa! They can sit by our
fire," interposed Ella.

"Who are the people, wife; do you know?"

"Indeed I don't, poor creatures. But I'll warrant they
are intemperate."

"No, it ain't, mother, it's *Link*," said Ella.

"What do you say, Ella?"

"I say the little boy's name is Willie Link; Susan says so."

"Wife, we must see if they are in want; call Susan up."

Susan happened to know the circumstances of the family,
and gave every needful information.

Sarah Jones, ten years before, had been a young, healthy,
happy country girl. She had married a young mechanic, and
removed to Washington. For a few years they lived comfortably, and then he "*took to drink*," and then followed the
usual train of circumstances—*the funeral train of happiness.*
Lower and lower, year by year, he sank into intemperance and
brutality. One by one the children that had been born to
them fell victims to want and misery, until none remained but
one sickly boy and a young babe. At last the war with
Mexico broke out, and Jones enlisted, and that was the last
his poor wife had heard of him. The poor woman was without
a trade and without friends; and besides, she was country
bred, bashful, and inexperienced, and so could do little for
herself and children.

"What! Jones the carpenter, who volunteered? Why, wife, I owed that poor fellow a small balance on the work he did here. I did not know his family lived so near us. We must do something for them now, and I will pay to-morrow."

Accordingly a basket was procured, which Mrs. Wood filled with a paper of tea, coffee, and sugar, a piece of cold mutton, a pie, and a piece of cheese, and sent it over by Susan, who was accompanied by a boy with a wheelbarrow of wood. Johnny's feelings came out strong under the circumstances. He sent "his all," a fip pound-cake and a cent's worth of fire-crackers. Ella sent a doll, with its head broken off. All Ella's effects were in a dilapidated condition.

It was dark and freezing in that miserable room where the poor woman was undressing her hungry boy.

"There, Willie, kiss me; God bless you. Go to bed and sleep, and forget that you are hungry!"

Just at that moment there was a rap at the door. The mother and child trembled. Who could be coming that dark, cold night?

"Come in," said the mother, faintly.

And the latch was lifted, and a sound of footsteps, and of something set heavily down upon the floor, was heard; a lucifer match was scraped on the wall, and a light was struck that revealed the scene. There stood Susan with her baskets.

"Mrs. Wood has sent you some things, ma'am," said Susan, showing them. "Come in, Jim, with the wood."

The boy brought an armful of wood in, and threw it on the hearth, while Susan lit a candle and handed him some paper to start the fire, which soon blazed up the chimney. Then Susan filled the kettle and hung it on, and pulled out the table and set out the good things upon it, saying—

"You must excuse me for taking so many liberties, Mrs. Jones, as you are poorly and tired."

"Oh! you are very good—very good indeed—too good. I shall never be able to repay you, or Mrs Wood either."

"Never mind, we may, any of us, want a good turn sometime or other," said Susan, making the tea; and then the good girl departed.

What a magic change was wrought in that cold room; how bright, and glowing, and genial, the fire was—how warm to their chilled limbs; and fragrant smelled the tea—the rare luxury.

"Oh!, mother, we are glad! ain't we glad—I say, mother, ain't we in luck?"

"Don't say that, Willie. Thank our Heavenly Father, who hath given us meat in due season."

"I do! indeed I do *so*. Oh! mother, let's wake *poor* baby up to give her some tea. She was so hungry that little cake warn't nothing."

"Hunger will wake her soon, poor little thing! Run round to Mrs. Bayley's and get a cent's worth of milk against she wakes."

Willie did his errand in a twinkling, and then returned. And now, dear reader, we will leave Willie and his mother, with the babe in her arms, sitting down to the supper, before the fire that their kind neighbour had provided, and follow Susan "Across the Street."

When Susan had stamped the snow off her feet, and presented herself in the parlour, she gave such an account of the destitution of the Jones's, as to enlist warmly all the kindly feeling of the Wood family; and when she added, "She was the same woman, ma'am, who begged so hard for work the other day," Mrs. Wood looked up from her sewing.

"And you refused it her, when you had so much on hand! Oh, wife!"

"I didn't know she was so destitute."

"Oh, I'm *sorry*. How many turkeys are there in the pantry, wife?"

"Three. My gracious alive, Mr. Wood, you're not dreaming of sending them a turkey?"

"Why not? It's a luxury they might have once a year, poor souls! Send them the small one; I gave but fifty cents for it."

"But it's extravagant; I never heard of such a thing," remonstrated the housewife.

But the children—children are always benevolent when there is no self-denial involved—took part with their father, and implored also that mother would put in the basket some jumbles and doughnuts to go in the little boy's stocking. "And tell Mrs. Jones that I'll be over shortly, and see about finding regular employment for her."

The next morning the Woods went to church, and returned to meet a party of friends at dinner, who remained all the afternoon and half the night. And I have no doubt the family enjoyed their New Year's dinner and friends all the more keenly for the consciousness that their poor neighbour across the street was comfortably provided for. And they, how did *they* spend their New Year's? Why, in the morning the mother arose and kindled her fire, and set on her kettle, and swept up the room, and dressed her children in their clean clothes, and laid the cloth for breakfast; and after breakfast was over, she put her little turkey in the oven to bake, leaving Willie to mind it, and went to church; also then returned, and dined upon her turkey, and spent the afternoon in telling stories to her children, watching the people go by, and particularly amusing herself with noticing the company go in and out of the house across the street.

The next day the snow was gone, and the winter sun shone out brightly. Just as the poor widow had finished cleaning up her house, and was getting ready to do some washing that had been sent her, there was a rap at the door, and Mrs. Wood entered.

"Take a seat, madam," said the widow, setting a chair.

"Thank you. You called at my house last week to get sewing to do—did you not?"

"Yes, madam."

"I had none ready then. I have brought you some now, however. I am in no hurry for it. You can do it at your leisure—when you have no other work for other people on hand. There are two pair of pantaloons and two jackets; how much will you charge?"

The woman looked at the garments, and then replied:

"I will do them for eighty-seven and a half cents; that is, three fips a piece for the jackets, and a quarter a pair for the trowsers."

"That is cheap," thought the lady. "It would take me every evening for a fortnight to make these four garments."

"As it is so cheap, I will pay you now," said the lady, taking out a purse. She first thought of paying the woman a round dollar, but the spirit of economy prevailed—she made the precise change.

But Mrs. Wood went away, determined to do as much as she could for the poor widow without injuring her own family, should an opportunity present itself.

Mr. Wood was more active in the service of the soldier's widow. He found out from her the name of the company to which her husband belonged, the date of his enlistment, &c., and soon discovered the fact that he had fallen at the storming of Monterey. Long inured to sorrow, the widow received the news of this bereavement very calmly. Mr. Wood interested himself further in her cause, and in a few weeks procured her the grant of a land warrant and pension. The land warrant she sold for a hundred and fifty dollars, and with this small capital, she opened a little thread and needle store. She is now doing a fair business in a small shop. But, reader, there are many others, spread all over our city, who are suffering for work. Let them have it. Our city owes all its inhabitants a living; and there is work enough, if it were only equally divided and well remunerated, to supply every one with the necessaries of life.

"What can I do for you?" inquired a lady of distinguished benevolence, when she called to see a destitute widow with a handful of children.

"Give me work," was the literal answer of the poor, but high-principled woman. Give the poor work, that they may not need alms!

CPSIA information can be obtained at www.ICGtesting.com
Printed in the USA
BVOW05s0004270215

389498BV00005B/18/P